Total Inclusivity at Work

Despite inclusivity's importance and most people's desire for it, understanding inclusivity can be tricky. This book introduces the concept of Total Inclusivity to organisations, their leaders and employees around the world. It aims to help organisations and those people who create them to become Totally Inclusive Communities, wherein diversity is valued, healthy identities are enabled, respect for difference prevails and every member counts – regardless of their identity mix.

The book provides insights into how identity works and defines Total Inclusivity as concept and practice. Whitehead suggests what organisations can do to safeguard and nurture diverse organisational identities. The book also provides easy-to-follow guidelines on how we can implement Total Inclusivity in organisation through individuals.

Written in an accessible style, while informed by contemporary research into the self, organisations and identities, this book will not only guide organisational members – owners, CEOs, leaders, managers, administrators and every staff member – along the pathway to creating a Totally Inclusive Community, it will establish a bold and provocative ethical standard for organisations to follow as they venture further into this century.

Stephen Whitehead is a British sociologist and educationalist. He is an internationally recognised expert on men and masculinities, gender identity and international education. This is his fourteenth book. Stephen lives with his wife in Chiang Mai, Thailand. Learn more at www.stephen-whitehead.com.

STEPHEN WHITEHEAD

Total Inclusivity
at Work

Routledge
Taylor & Francis Group

LONDON AND NEW YORK

Cover image: Gettys

First published 2022
by Routledge
4 Park Square, Milton Park, Abingdon, Oxon OX14 4RN

and by Routledge
605 Third Avenue, New York, NY 10158

Routledge is an imprint of the Taylor & Francis Group, an informa business

British Library Cataloguing-in-Publication Data
A catalogue record for this book is available from the British Library

Library of Congress Cataloging-in-Publication Data
Names: Whitehead, Stephen (Stephen M.), author.
Title: Total inclusivity at work / Stephen Whitehead.
Description: Milton Park, Abingdon, Oxon ; New York, NY : Routledge, 2022. |
    Includes bibliographical references.
Identifiers: LCCN 2021057892 (print) | LCCN 2021057893 (ebook) | ISBN
    9781032154206 (hardback) | ISBN 9781032154190 (paperback) | ISBN
    9781003244073 (ebook)
Subjects: LCSH: Diversity in the workplace. | Multiculturalism. |
    Communication in organizations.
Classification: LCC HF5549.5.M5 W49 2022 (print) | LCC HF5549.5.M5 (ebook) |
    DDC 658.3/008—dc23/eng/20211209
LC record available at https://lccn.loc.gov/2021057892
LC ebook record available at https://lccn.loc.gov/2021057893

ISBN: 978-1-032-15420-6 (hbk)
ISBN: 978-1-032-15419-0 (pbk)
ISBN: 978-1-003-24407-3 (ebk)

DOI: 10.4324/9781003244073

Typeset in Joanna
by Apex CoVantage, LLC

FOR MAM

Contents

This book was conceived and written during the first two years of the COVID-19 pandemic. I hope that by the time you read it COVID-19 is at least under control and you are fully vaccinated. But while this book is not about any viral pandemic it is concerned with another type of pandemic – the pandemic of prejudice, hatred and ignorance which infects large swathes of humankind and has done since time immemorial. This latter pandemic is not so easily vaccinated against, ignored or dismissed as 'nothing more dangerous than the flu'.

We live in a world of multiple violences, made more vivid by our unavoidable awareness of them through social media, 24/7 news bulletins and the rest. We are all, every single one of us caught up in this vortex whether as contributors, witnesses, perpetrators or victims.

Just scanning the daily torrent of depressing if not dreadful news pouring out from all four corners – pandemics, climate change, wars, murders, abuse, terrorism, death, famine and environmental destruction on unimaginable scales – would test the most emotionally resilient of us. And a great many of us are not emotionally resilient, we are insecure, vulnerable, frightened and angry with it.

This book offers only one solution to the growing crises facing us – unity through inclusivity: recognising that we are all in this together – in the final reckoning, society is all we have.

However, when faced with existential threats many humans may decide to ignore them, dismiss it all as fake news and media hype, decide the experts are part of some global conspiracy, not get vaccinated, not wear a face mask, not give a damn about anyone else but instead carry on regardless.

One can recognise the comfort zoning going on in these types of responses – because once you accept there is a problem there is no going back. You cannot unknow it. For a great many of us, ignoring racism, misogyny, sexism, ableism, homophobia, transphobia and deciding white privilege and unconscious bias don't exist leaves us blissfully removed from having to address these problems in our own behaviour.

Only we cannot be blissfully removed. Not anymore. We live in a world which can only survive if we each recognise, accept and embrace our interconnectedness – our mutual humanism. Those of us choosing not to join the community will be left on the outside – excluded by choice, just as those who enter infected places unvaccinated and without a face mask, determined and obstinate in refusing to cooperate, are therefore fated to suffer the consequences.

Total Inclusivity is offered as an antidote not only to violence, hatred, aggression, ignorance and prejudice but also as a counter to rampant and selfish individualism, greed and stupidity.

This book's message is: do not wait to become a victim before realising there is a problem out there. Do not wait to become a witness before seeing what is amiss in society. And do not wait to be told how to respond before knowing in your heart what response you must have.

Total Inclusivity is the term used throughout this book, but in essence it is all about empathy. Do you care enough to want to be part of the change that needs to take place, or not? Have you the emotional resilience to begin the journey?

Maybe you began your journey of awakening to the need for global diversity, equity, inclusion and justice many years or even decades ago. Perhaps you've already arrived at a place of sad enlightenment due to you having to confront these issues in your own life. In which case this book will merely confirm much of that knowledge. It will mirror what you have experienced and seen for yourself.

Or maybe you consider all the 'woke stuff' to be a load of 'politically correct nonsense', deserving only to be dumped in the dustbin of history along with face masks, climate change data and Facebook's 58 gender identities?

It is your choice. You have the right to choose your personal/political standpoint. But then with choice come responsibility and consequences. There is no escaping the consequences of our decisions, and right now humanity is facing its most testing and important decisions.

Total Inclusivity at Work is one of three books I have authored/co-authored on this concept, all first published by Routledge during 2022. I devised the concept of TI in July 2020 following race awareness training I co-delivered[1] to the senior management of one of the UK's leading private schools. It was clear to me from the training and the comments of the participants that focusing on race and racial issues in schools, while vital, was not enough. As I stress throughout this book, inclusivity cannot be partial, and any attempt to make it so only creates more problems than it solves.

I felt it was time to go further. It was time to go total. Hence Total Inclusivity.

My other two books on Total Inclusivity look at universities (co-authored with Pat O'Connor) and schools (co-authored with Angeline Aow and Sadie Hollins). All three books have much in common and follow the same principles and concepts. *Total inclusivity at Work* is, however, somewhat different in both tone and presentation, and that is deliberate because it is aimed at a much wider audience: ordinary workers, managers, owners, anyone who cares about the direction in which organisations are currently heading and who wants to help ensure that direction is beneficial for humankind.

I've chosen to present Total Inclusivity as central to the world of work and organisations because work and organisations do not just structure and support our lives; they have the capacity to structure and support our very identity, sense of self. However, if you've come to this book expecting a deep dive into intellectual and organisational analysis, loads of supporting sociological and psychological references all packaged as a balanced intellectual narrative, then you will be disappointed.

This is not an academic book; it is intended to be bold, challenging and, in places, provocative.

This book is not offering arguments for and against Total Inclusivity – it has a singular position, and it is for you to determine the veracity of that position.

Writing as a white, male, Western, straight, middle-class sociologist/educationalist (and a baby boomer to boot!), I acknowledge my own privileges. And I must accept that, inevitably, my particular identity mix will not only inform the book but subject it to some limitations. I hope not so many limitations as to diminish the book's message, but that is for you to decide. Undoubtedly, there will be issues/identities/topics I've focused on more than others. That is not intentional. I have tried to write it with a global-mindedness, recognising that Total Inclusivity should embrace all of us, whatever our identity mix.

Although I claim credit for coming up with the Total Inclusivity concept, I don't own it. And nor do I claim that this or any of my writings on Total Inclusivity cover all that can be said about the concept. Aside from the hope that this book spurs at least some readers to push for TI to be actioned in their workplaces and organisations, I hope that more gets written on TI and that it gets tested through further research and debate.

In sum, my two aims in writing this book are, first, to show how the TI concept can and should be actioned in organisations – those vitally important and influential sections of society – and second, to encourage TI to take root in the global consciousness. I feel passionate that TI should not just become a commonplace phrase but, more importantly, a human aspiration; because regardless of who you are, the concept involves you.

All very serious stuff. Not much room for humour, then, in Total Inclusivity.

Well, yes and no.

This book is written with passion and intent, but also with one eye on the bizarre, the strange, the crazy and the downright ridiculous. And there is plenty of all that in the world today. It's just a shame that it is all too often accompanied by stuff which is nasty, abusive and lethal.

So unwavering as it is, you'll find my examination of Total Inclusivity to be interspersed with a little humour, some cynical asides and a few cartoons just to keep you smiling on the journey.

Stephen Whitehead
January 2022

NOTE

1 My colleague on the training course was Viv Grant, CEO of integritycoaching.co.uk.

Acknowledgements

All those who have played a role in the development of my understanding of diversity, equity, inclusion and justice, from childhood to the present day, are a part of this book. There are too many to name, but I would highlight Prof. Sheila Scraton and Prof. Jeff Hearn. Both were especially influential during my 40s, which is when my Total Inclusivity journey really kicked off, even if I didn't recognise it at the time.

Looking back over the past three decades, one person stands out – Prof. Roy Moodley. He has been a friend, guide and mentor throughout this time and, indeed, remains my core reference point for all things related to diversity, equity, inclusion and justice (DEIJ).

And then there are all the students, from my earliest days as a fledgling further education lecturer in Leeds, UK (circa. 1990), to my decades spent teaching in higher education in both the UK and Asia. I'm not sure what you learned from me, but I surely learned a lot from you.

Regarding the concept of Total Inclusivity, as I note in the Foreword, that came into my mind in the summer of 2020, and the first people I shared it with were Patrick Lee and Denry Machin. Both are the best critical friends anyone could hope to have, and each has informed Total Inclusivity as both concept and (educational) practice.

As for the book itself, Sadie Hollins and Laura Davis made important contributions to the developing manuscript, and I am grateful to both of them for their insightful guidance and suggestions. Similarly, my thanks to the anonymous reviewers who commented on various drafts of the original manuscript.

Finally, I am pleased to acknowledge my debt to the Routledge editorial team, Katie Peace, Yong Ling Lam and Kendrick Loo. Not only did they support the whole Total Inclusivity project from the outset, they provided stable and professional guidance throughout.

Recognising that a number of people have directly or indirectly contributed to this book, indeed to the concept of Total inclusivity itself, I take total responsibility for what follows.

One

One

When I informed a friend of mine that I was planning to write a book titled *Total Inclusivity*, her reaction was amazement: "Wow, that's a massive concept!" she said. And she is correct. Indeed, anyone who doesn't recognise it as a 'massive concept', frankly, doesn't get it.

'Total' means exactly that.

Diversity, equity, inclusion and justice (DEIJ) are the buzz words of the early 21st century, at least in Western countries. Fifty years ago, the buzz words were 'equal opportunity'. Once upon a time finding any organisation with an 'equal opportunities' policy was as unlikely as finding a major organisation headed by an openly gay black person. Nowadays, most every organisation has its equal ops policy, usually occupying a small space in an HR office cabinet.

Very soon, every half-decently run organisation will be claiming to be a *Totally Inclusive Community*. At least I hope so, because that is one of the aims of this book.

However, I won't consider it social progress or success for the book if all it results in is another well-intentioned policy document gathering dust in Personnel.

Total Inclusivity is action – purposeful, reflective, informed and relentless.

But it won't happen unless you make it happen. Yes, you, the reader. Total Inclusivity is no one person's responsibility – it is every person's responsibility.[1]

However, it is unlikely you'll need convincing of this. If you've opened the book and started reading, then very likely you are at least curious, and most likely you are committed to the concept of inclusivity and diversity in organisations, in society. Maybe all you need is some guidance to take you from where you are right now to where I hope you'll be at the end of this book – an Advocate for Total Inclusivity.

Because without you, the Advocate, Total Inclusivity will remain a great idea which never caught on.

The concept of equal opportunities[2] eventually did catch on. But only through the sheer determination of individuals from every part of the globe. People like you made equal opportunities real. Well, mostly.

It may not be correctly practiced everywhere and in all organisations, but at least people now understand what equal opportunity means, what it stands for. There is no room for ambiguity.

Total Inclusivity will have the same impact, because *Total* and *Inclusivity* not only sound right together, they are self-evidently right together. Like equal opportunities, there is no room for ambiguity here, either.

In other words, inclusivity cannot be partial, and any attempt to make it partial immediately kills it – stone dead.

Just as opportunity must be undeniably equal, so must inclusivity be undeniably total. If Inclusivity is not Total then it is no more than a sound bite, a rhetorical gesture towards a fairer and more just society.

And surely, after all this time, after all those decades of equal opportunities as policy and practice, after Stonewall, MeToo, Black Lives Matter, Rodney King, Stephen Lawrence, George Floyd, Gay Pride and every other attempt to raise the bar of organisational accountability, personal accountability, social justice, we've arrived at the point of Total Inclusivity or nothing.

DEFINITION

To turn Total Inclusivity into social justice action that people can participate in, and do so without feeling they are getting trapped in some ideological minefield, we need a simple but powerful definition. And this is it:

> Total Inclusivity means recognising, valuing, protecting and nurturing diverse identities, including those of race, gender, sexual orientation, class, disability, age, religion and language.

If you recognise the inherent worthiness of that intention, if it speaks to both your heart and your head, then you are on your way to being an Advocate for Total Inclusivity.

You may ask why not include every other possible aspect of human identity within this definition. The answer is simple: it would be impossible to create such a definition without losing its impact; the list would, in theory at least, have no end. Why? Because every single one of us, each of the 7.7 billion people alive today, is unique, occupying and experiencing a different mix of identities across different cultures and communities. And there is a second, equally valid reason; anyone who can accept to 'value, protect and nurture' race, gender, sexual and class differences, together with those of age, religion and language and do so across the human spectrum, will be for inclusivity in total.

So does anyone get excluded from Total Inclusivity?

No.

Those for Total Inclusivity exclude no one.

Those against Total Inclusivity exclude themselves.

THE CASE FOR TOTAL INCLUSIVITY

At time of writing, the British royal family is under siege following accusations of racism from two of its most prominent members; global counterterrorism experts are debating whether the misogynist incel movement should be classified as a terror threat; hate crimes against Asians are spiking in the USA and UK; sexual assaults and harassment are being reported in colleges and universities around the world; a former boss of one of the world's biggest companies is forced to resign for claiming that the concept of unconscious bias is "complete and utter crap"; the Chinese government is attempting to 'mitigate male femin-isation' by teaching 'proper masculinity'; rape allegations are sweeping across Australian politics; Women's Day protests turn violent in Mexico; towns across Poland have passed anti-LGBTQ+ resolutions; the World Health Organization reports that 1 in 3 women worldwide is subject to physical or sexual assault during her lifetime; while the USA is still recovering from the recent physical and political assault on its democ-racy and Capitol by self-declared anti-Semites, neo-fascists; misogynists; racists and white supremacists.

Summarising one core aspect of the problem, the World Health Organization states:

> [male] violence against women is . . . causing harm to millions of women and their families and has been exacerbated by the Covid-19 pandemic. But unlike Covid-19, violence against women cannot be stopped by a vaccine.
>
> (UN News, 2021)

We don't need to make a case for Total Inclusivity. The case has already been well and truly made.

The question is, perhaps, not so much do we need Total Inclusivity, but are we too late to have Total Inclusivity?

See the news on any day of any week of any month and you'll see the same stories – prejudice, bias, male violence, assault, rape, harassment, injustice, discrimination, hatred, ignorance and mindless death and destruction, not just of each other but of the planet itself.

If an alien landed today and saw the state we were in no one would blame her if she immediately got back on her spaceship and hurried home to Planet Z. Of course, what the alien would have missed is the larger context. Dire as things appear right now, and despite the pushback by fringe social elements and the plainly misinformed, as I claim below, society is becoming more, not less, civilised and this includes a greater awareness, acceptance, tolerance and willingness to embrace diversity.

For this we can largely thank the massification of further and higher education over the past five or six decades. As global research is revealing, young, college-/university-educated people (Generation Z and

Credit Line: Cartoons drawn by Advanced Standard Group Co., Ltd.

millennials) are much more likely not only to embrace diversity but to demand it (Pew Research, 2019).

And it is this younger generation which will bring in Total Inclusivity, hopefully supported and encouraged by many of those over 50 years of age.

Encouraged by elders or not, Total Inclusivity will arrive sooner or later.

Just as there was and is an undeniable logic and justice to anti-slavery, universal suffrage, anti-racism, equal-opportunities legislation, gay marriage and trans rights, so there is the same undeniability to Total Inclusivity.

Which is why I believe TI is unstoppable.

Though that won't deter some from trying to stop it.

Which takes us to one of the points made in this introduction: fear of the other, the unfamiliar, the different.

No single book can remove fear of the unknown, the other, from the minds of all humanity – this trait is too deeply embedded in the human psyche. But what a single book can do is explain why a concept such as Total Inclusivity can bring benefits to individuals and, in this case, organisations also.

In other words, Total Inclusivity will be good not only for you and your identity mix but also for your organisation, your work, your whole relationship to employment.

Social change towards greater justice and less ignorance can and should be backed up by legislation, the judicial system, education and, where necessary, positive action to force an end to deeply rooted discrimination. As part of this push we can insist on 'zero tolerance' towards fascism, racism, misogyny and homophobia and back this up by laws and the full weight of judicial systems. However, in the final reckoning the individual has to accept this change, believe it to be best for themselves and society and not fear it. Such transformations in thinking and culture will only come about because the greater mass of people demand it.[3]

Globally, we are at a tipping point and have been certainly since the late 1990s. The tipping point is towards the dominance of progressive thinking regarding race, gender, sexuality and class. However, that outcome is not guaranteed. That there is a fierce backlash against social justice and fairness should not surprise us. Certain sections of society will be required to rethink their relationship to women, LGBTQ+ people, Black people, and indeed all those social and ethnic groups which have hitherto been on the receiving end of bias, discrimination and prejudice.

This book is, therefore, not creating Total Inclusivity, it is predicting it. TI is not offered as a strand of progressive thinking but the very definition of the changes which no single book or person began but which billions of us around the world now accept as necessary, proper and right for humanity.

But more than simply predicting Total Inclusivity, this book aims to convince you, the reader, to become an Advocate for change; to become confident, secure and bold enough to say, "yes, I am for Total Inclusivity and will work towards bringing it about in both my personal and professional lives".

Of course, it is very possible you are already at that point and have been working for such change for most of your life. If so, then please use this book as a support, a guide and a reference point, especially with regards to one of the key aspects of change which needs to take place if humanity is to become more just and fairer – organisations and their cultures.

RELATIONSHIP TO ORGANISATIONS

The inherent character of humanity has never been isolation but association. We start with families and build it up from there; networks, groups, villages, towns, cities and eventually the modern nation state, which many historians consider first emerged in 1648 with the Treaty of Westphalia.

The material drive behind this merging and organising is quite simple: safety and productivity.

Slowly but surely, over many millennia, humans have been organising themselves to the point that today we could not survive without organisations. They provide the essential framework for our continued safety and prosperity.

Consider this question: how many organisations have to exist just to make your life tolerable?

You cannot begin to calculate. Truth is, no one knows how many organisations there are in the world right now. Nor do you have any idea just how many organisations you have a personal stake in, directly or indirectly.

You drink, eat, wash, work, travel, communicate, learn, listen, get health care, pay taxes, open a bank account, go shopping, get a credit card, watch a movie, buy a pizza, listen to music, post on social media, switch on a light, flush the loo, phone a friend, read a book, look for a job, join the army, navy or air force, go to school, college or university, get mugged and call the police and then your lawyer, set fire to a chip pan and call the fire brigade and then a decorator followed by your insurance company.

None of these activities can happen without organisations, countless numbers of them, whose task it is to ensure your life runs smoothly enough.

No one, not even the homeless person wandering the streets of London, Paris, Mumbai or New York, can exist without organisations to offer some degree of protection, safety, possibility of survival.

But as is explained in this book, organisations are more than material providers. They are also existential providers.

You may not be tempted to invest your sense of identity in your local tax office, but you most certainly will in your work role, your professional status, your job title, your employing organisation.

For a great many of us, our relationship with paid work is more important than our relationship with our family. We may not like it to be that way, but that is the reality.

During our most productive decades (mid-20s to mid-60s) we will spend far more time at work than with our loved ones, our nearest and dearest. Over the course of a lifetime, one-third of our life will be spent working in organisations, approximately 90,000 hours. Then add in the time spent commuting, doing Zoom meetings from home, answering emails during the evening and weekend and worrying about office politics.

Yes, organisations dominate your life, and there is no escaping that fact.

In which case, it is a great shame some studies suggest 80% of us hate our jobs.

Actually, I doubt that is true. Most of us enjoy our jobs, though we may well come to despair of the organisation we work for.

We can always change our jobs, but we can never escape organisations – even if we can afford to drop out of the rat race and write that novel, organisations will pursue us.

It would be nice, therefore, if these organisations, from global media corporations to your local bus company, were loved, even liked. Unfortunately, they are not. They are, at best, tolerated and, at worst, hated. We prefer it when they just do their job and stay out of our lives.

We have a contradictory relationship to organisations; we need them to survive but we loath them at the same time.

Any organisational leader reading this should stop and think why that is the case and whether or not it bothers them.

However, please do not imagine that the primary aim of this book is to make organisations loveable!

Such an accomplishment would be far beyond my capabilities or, indeed, anyone else's.

This book is not concerned if you get frustrated and angry with your bank's online customer service, the persistent lateness of your local train service, or the fact that you cannot get a reliable plumber to fix your kitchen sink.

What is of concern is whether that organisation is contributing to society, not simply by doing the job for which we pay it but by being a Totally Inclusive Community.

RELATIONSHIP TO COMMUNITY

'Community' is one of the most powerful yet misused words in the English language, equalled if not surpassed in exploitation and emotional connection only by 'family'.

The Oxford English dictionary defines 'community' as follows:

> A body of individuals; the common people; members of a collective body; people living in the same locality; having the same religion, profession, etc.; a body of people living together and building goods in common; identity; the state of being shared or held in common; social intercourse, communion, fellowship, a sense of common identity.

Accepting that this is a necessarily eclectic summary of a highly complex if not subjectively understood word, the principles of commonality, association and shared identity are clear.

Most organisational leaders may like to imagine they are leading a community, but if that were ever the case it is much less so today, because society is changing faster than the organisations which serve it. As is explored in following chapters, work organisations are not always communities of belonging. They may hope to be, if only for enhancing employee commitment. But few organisations manage to break out of their performance-fixated straitjackets to become work cultures within which the individual feels and expresses, a positive emotional connection.

For many of us, the only time we will allow ourselves to embrace open community with our fellow citizens is during sports contests; notably football, rugby, soccer, hockey and, of course, the Olympic

Games. But even here, the ubiquitous flag waving, chanting and firecrackers merely hide the fact that certain identities are less welcome than others; Black football players, Indigenous-people hockey players, gay tennis players, trans athletes and intersex weightlifters being just some examples.

What humanity has managed to achieve over the past few millennia is amazing technological advancement, largely through the application of organisational effort combined with occasional individual genius.

What society has not been able to achieve is communality within organisations and certainly not between individuals. There was probably more sense of community back in the brutal and dirty Middle Ages than there is in today's futuristic, sterile metropolises.

People's sense of belonging has not been enhanced by modern technology and certainly not by social media. If anything, the opposite has occurred – millions of us feel lonelier, more disconnected, isolated, existentially insecure.

Little wonder, then, that there is now a burgeoning global industry in 'well-being' and feeling positive about oneself.

It is unfair to blame organisations for this situation, but they do have a responsibility to try and address it. For example, one can accept that Facebook was started with the best of intentions – 'bringing people together'. That it has all turned out rather different does tell us something about Facebook, though in truth, it tells us more about ourselves.

Globalisation is another example. Who could possibly be against globalisation? Well, it turns out a good many of us are. Globalisation has not brought everyone together; on the contrary, it has made the disadvantaged and disenfranchised feel angry and alarmed as the world they grew up in and felt comfortable with fast disappeared, usually to the other side of the world. Dismissing them as 'deplorables' isn't going to encourage such folk to embrace their fellows. There are large swathes of the UK and USA, for example, that are, today, 'broken heartlands' (Payne, 2021) and not unreasonably 'full of fury' (Osnos, 2021).

Total Inclusivity is not intended to burden organisations with the responsibility of remaking the world into a happier, less conflictual place. Sure, that would be nice, but let's be realistic here.

The aim of Total Inclusivity is to bring community into organisations, thereby improving workplace culture and climate. This won't happen by organisations marketing themselves as communities or 'families' in their social media. It will only happen by organisations fully embracing the diversity manifest across society; by becoming communities of belonging for all their stakeholders. In short . . .

> by recognising, valuing, protecting and nurturing diverse identities, including race, gender, sexual orientation, class, age, religion and language.

There is an urgency to this agenda because people are increasingly likely to define themselves, self-categorise, through aspects of race, gender and sexuality – not solely by place, nationhood or professional status. Identity is becoming politicised but also more complex and contested, intersectional and dynamic.

This urgency is compounded not least because the nature of work is changing fast; it is becoming increasingly automated, remote, temporary, flexible and hybrid. This leaves the employee more likely to feel remote and temporary, engendering in them a lack of loyalty and association with their organisation. Indeed, employee loyalty is rapidly becoming the exception rather than the expectation (Kreacic et al., 2022).

And then there is the endemic of toxic work cultures, examples of which are given in this book. In the past year, 1 in 5 American workers have quit their job because of toxic behaviour at work (e.g. racism, sexual violence, bullying), while 64% of UK employees report that a toxic workplace culture negatively impacted their mental health (Bishop, 2021). Research suggests that in Germany, the number of those planning to leave their jobs is 20%; France 17%, Spain and China 14%. And that doesn't include a further 18% of employees globally wanting to quit (Kreacic et al., 2022).

Employees are not happy. Clearly, the need for Total Inclusivity in organisations is overwhelming.

If bosses still don't immediately see the need for TI, then perhaps they'll recognise that societal expectations are changing, heightened in respect of organisational and corporate responsibility and made urgent, not least through the effects of the COVID-19 pandemic and enforced lockdowns. Leaders are being held to a greater accountability regarding social justice and in their public and private lives. As I explain in the book, only if an organisation can become a Totally Inclusive Community can it survive the changes which are fast arriving in the workplace. However, such a transformation in workplace culture cannot come about simply through periodic workshops in anti-racism and anti-sexism. It can only come about through change – deeper understanding and appreciation of Total Inclusivity – within every member of the organisation/community.

Organisations are not only locations where people might earn a living, they are sites of identification where individual employees at all levels can achieve a sense of belonging. But belonging to an organisation is risky and it is tenuous, especially in this increasingly transient world and its workplaces. Organisations can appear impersonal, ruthless, uncaring and insincere. Organisations may be profitable, but they can also be seen as heartless. And yet we spend most of our working lives within them, often in a fraught relationship. Even those of us who love our work rarely love the organisation we work for.

Around the world, organisations, big and not so big, are grappling with the complexities and challenges of not only generating a feeling of community and loyalty within their work culture but attempting to implement anti-racist, anti-sexist, pro-LGBTQ+, gender-equitable, non-discriminatory and individual-safeguarding policies and practices. In other words, many of them are striving for inclusivity.

However, I recognise that the concept of inclusivity, at least for complex organisations, can be tricky to grasp and harder to implement. Language, media, stereotyping, history, culture and the sheer politics of it all conspire to create confusion, and out of confusion often arises resistance. People don't understand the terms; they fear saying or doing the 'wrong thing'; they baulk at notions of 'political correctness'; they reject 'unconscious bias' and the idea of 'white privilege'. Yet they may well also recognise the vitality and importance of the MeToo Movement and Black Lives Matter and accept the concept of equality and safety for all.

We are living through highly sensitive times. But maybe that is how it must be if we, as a society, are to move forward.

This book is designed to help individuals embrace Total Inclusivity and the organisations they are connected with to become Totally Inclusive Communities, wherein diversity is valued, healthy identities enabled, respect for difference prevails, and every member counts – regardless of their identity mix.

In short, a Totally Inclusive organisation is first and foremost a community. Whether for-profit or non-profit, if an organisation is not a community, then it is failing its employees, clients, stakeholders. In which case, one is entitled to ask what is its purpose, what is its true value?

RELATIONSHIP TO YOU

Every book tells a story of some description, and this book is no exception. But where is the hero of this book's narrative? Is it Total Inclusivity? Is it Organisations? Is it community? No, it is You. You are the protagonist, the lead character, the champion.

Without you, this book is just more noise to add to the already deafening cacophony arising from 'culture wars', 'identity politics' and the rest.

The aim is not to read the book and think, 'okay, I get it, that makes sense' but then carry on with your life as before. This book is not intended as a deeply theoretical academic thesis on the merits of inclusivity and diversity – to be read and then shelved.

It is written as nothing more or less than a call to change the world around us, and that can only start with the individual – you.

At this stage, one could insert any number of profound quotes from famous individuals to emphasise the point. And this quote by French author Anais Nin (1961) serves the purpose well:

"We don't see things as they are, we see them as we are".

And that is the challenge we all face: to see beyond our own identity boundaries; to be bold and brave enough to step outside our subjective cultural comfort zone and empathise with others, strangers. Immediately we begin to empathise with others so we stop seeing them as 'the Other' (de Beauvoir, 1953). That is the best start anyone can make on the road to Total Inclusivity.

Of course, if it were that simple then why hasn't humanity already achieved this goal? After all, it is not as if we haven't had time – homo sapiens has been around more than 300,000 years.

Why are we still grasping for Total Inclusivity? Is it because of the negative traits which continue to infest the human psyche: fear, envy, greed, insecurity, ignorance?

Certainly, it is troubling to reflect that artificial intelligence will soon likely dominate the world of work. AI won't be hindered by fear of the Other, but nor will it have our capacity for love, understanding, compassion and belief in the innate goodness of people.

Organisations are under economic pressure to adopt ways of working which result in a dehumanising process. At the same time they are under societal pressure to respond to the growing demand to become more human; cultivating well-being and connection within their stakeholders.

I hope this book helps push organisations and their members in the latter direction. Because if the trend of organisations to become less humanistic accelerates, then we have a major threat to humanity. Given the dominance of organisations in our lives, it would seem to make good sense to turn them into Totally Inclusive Communities – environments which embrace not just diversity but the best of human character. Better to have Totally Inclusive Communities supporting the human race than AI-controlled organisations. Once we have the latter, then our future will not be ours to decide.

The reality is that humanity has some catching up to do. Technology is jumping ahead far faster than humans are evolving. Humanity does risk being left behind. Already we can see pockets of global society regressing to ideas, practices and beliefs which should have disappeared around the time of Charlemagne and certainly the time of Churchill.

Despite these warnings and provisos, the concept of Total Inclusivity is offered with hope and optimism. For one thing, during my 70-plus years I have personally witnessed the human capacity for tolerance and empathy and the human desire for knowledge – not least as an educationalist working well away from my own cultural comfort zone. I and countless millions like me are direct beneficiaries of the massification of education which occurred in the UK and the West from the 1950s and subsequently spread around the world, informing eventually the globalisation impulse. Globalisation may have its downsides, but it is not possible to spread one's wings and travel without realising a single truth: people around the world desire the same thing – to be valued as individuals, respected and accepted for who they are.

We all want Total Inclusivity because we all want to be included.

The only question is, when will we have it?

CHANGING VALUE SYSTEMS

It is a steaming summer's evening in downtown Detroit – not only is the weather simmering but so are racial tensions. Riotous violence involving thousands of young males, Black and white, has erupted across the city. The KKK is out in force, and mobs of white men are hunting down Black people. Detroit police have imposed an unofficial curfew but are mostly enforcing it in Black neighbourhoods. Any young Black men they catch outdoors 'after hours' are being summarily executed. Eventually, the dead number 34, the injured 433 (Detroit Historical Society, 2021).

That event occurred in June 1943 while Americans, Black and white, were fighting against fascist Germany, Italy and Japan.

Have our value systems improved since then, bearing in mind events such as this were repeated in the USA throughout the remainder of the 20th century and into the 21st? It is difficult to say categorically, though what has changed is that contemporary society is much more likely to challenge police violence against ethnic minorities and to condemn the social and institutional conditions which feed racism and racial violence. This 1943 act of official murder against Black people went largely unnoticed at the time, at least outside of Detroit, and even today one can speculate that few Americans have heard of this incident.

But in 2020, the filmed killing of one Black man, George Floyd, by American police exploded into the largest social movement in American history and the largest global social movement against racial injustice and discrimination so far seen. That signals a changing value system, and it signals social progress.[4]

However, one can reflect that after hundreds of years of individual and institutionalised racism against Black people, white people still need reminding that 'Black Lives Matter'.

Although Total Inclusivity is offered as a humanistic value system, which is as it should be, we should also recognise that humans have been struggling with value systems throughout history. Over 2,500 years ago, Buddha came up with a simple value system for humanity: treat all as equal, do no harm and be compassionate. Most every religious and spiritual value system ever since has tried to keep to the same principles – at least in rhetoric. In practice the principles too often fall prey to that most human of traits: fear of the other.

Of course, there are times when it makes perfectly good sense to fear the other – a cursory look at human behaviour down the millennia will convince you that others can be dangerous and sometimes a threat to one's own survival.

But we don't live in the ancient past, a world described by Thomas Hobbes as 'solitary, poor, nasty, brutish and short' (2017, p. 1651). We live in the 21st century: the age of globalisation; international travel; conspicuous consumption; a global middle class; 24/7 shopping, social media and entertainment; advanced technology; health, safety and longevity. Hobbes would be spurred to write a rather different book to

Leviathan if he were alive today – even if he did need to vaccinate against COVID-19 in order to do it.

The key difference between the Hobbesian past and the present is, of course, education. Today, even the poorest countries attempt to offer some level of formal education to their children. Since the end of World War II, formal education, from pre-school through to university, has developed dramatically, thereby changing our world and our prospects for the better. And while the quality of and opportunity for education can differ enormously not just between countries but within countries, the principle of education for all is firmly established as both a human right and a human expectation (UNESCO, 2009).

Sure, the reality is very different to the rhetoric. Equality of educational opportunity is not equally spread around the world; race, gender, sexuality and class all play a major role in determining your life chances, and that is true whether you are a female born in Afghanistan, a gay person born in Uganda or a male born into poverty in a European city.

Yet despite the unacceptable and ongoing differences between us in terms of opportunity, wealth and education, in my mind there is no question that an Elias-type 'civilising process' (Elias, 2000) is taking place and that it is a global phenomenon. What people in, say, the 14th century accepted as normal societal behaviour (e.g. witch burning; public torture and executions; genocide; massacre of religious minorities; slavery; absolute monarchical rule – and let's not talk about their health, safety, justice and welfare 'systems') is no longer tolerated by the mass of people and indeed is proscribed in international law – even if examples of the above remain present in sections of 21st-century global society.

It is self-evident, therefore, that our value systems are slowly improving, even while they still have a long way to go.

Which is why we now need to accept Total Inclusivity.

As members of a global society which prioritises and seeks to protect and ensure human rights, social justice, safety and equal opportunity, inclusivity can never be partial; it can only ever be total. In other words, Total Inclusivity is not just for the few; it is for each and every one of us, now and for generations to come.

HOW TO USE THE BOOK

Each chapter has its own composite character and theme, leading to the final discussion regarding Total Inclusive Advocacy. We recommend, therefore, that you read the chapters in sequence thereby ensuring you follow the reasoning and discussion but also so you are able to incrementally develop your own understanding of and relationship to Total Inclusivity.

It may be that you find some chapters more persuasive than others, some of my arguments more compelling than others. That is perfectly understandable. No book can say all there is to say on a concept such as Total Inclusivity, and I fully recognise there is a lot more to be said and written on this concept. But this book is at least the start.

At the end of each chapter is a section for reflections. Reflecting is a big part of the Total Inclusivity journey! What I have designed, therefore, are Reflection points, Guidance on how to draw Total Inclusivity into both your personal and work lives and, finally, at the conclusion of each chapter, a Commitment. I've written up such commitments to align with the appropriate chapter, but don't feel obliged to follow them. You may well decide that, given your unique life circumstances, a different commitment would work better for you.

BEING REFLECTIVE

Recognising that reflectiveness is important, it is a skill which benefits from some conscious development. If we wish to change in a self-aware, positive way (not simply as a negative emotional reaction to events) then we need to develop a little critical, constructive and creative thinking, and that entails being reflective.

This book is not intended to teach you how to be reflective, only to recognise this skill to be a central aspect in becoming a Total Inclusive Advocate.

So here is my recommended (and short) learning process towards developing reflectivity in your approach to life; the Nine Rs' of Reflectivity:

1 Recall a powerful situation, experience, event, encounter you had, or simply something you read or saw, which really stirred up your emotions. Perhaps a relationship breakup, family fall-out, a toxic encounter at work.

2 Remember the feelings you had, the types of emotions you experienced.

3 Recollect how long it took you to get over those emotions and how they dominated your thoughts and life at the time.

4 Re-examine why the emotions took so long to let go of you and how you now think of that particular situation.

5 Recognise what you learned from that situation and what you've since learned from it – not least about yourself.

6 React to that recognition with the intent to next time have more control over your reactions and behaviour – decide to see deeper into situations than emotive responses allow.

7 Reason with yourself that there is a better way to be in the world, one which is not immediately and emotionally reactive but which is secure, mindful, positive and stable.

8 Reflect on how you would now hope to behave should a similar situation or event occur in your life. Would you react the same way or hope not to? The choice is yours to make, but it starts with looking back at yourself and your reactions in a more critical, less emotional, more constructive and creative way.

9 Realise that to be the person you can be you must first see the person you are.

CHAPTER 1: REFLECTIONS, GUIDANCE AND COMMITMENT

Reflection Exercise: What does Total Inclusivity mean to you? Would you define it differently? If so, how?

Guidance for Implementation: Consider where Total Inclusivity operates in your life, where it is completely absent and where you'd like to see it operating. A good place to start is to consider when you have felt excluded from organisations (or any networks) on account of your race, gender, sexuality or class, or indeed any other aspect of your identity. How did this exclusion, discrimination, make you feel? Who, if anyone, stepped up to help you understand this experience? The first step towards Total Inclusivity is this recognition that you too have value, and you too should be respected for who you are.

And if you've never felt excluded from organisations or networks on account of your identity (e.g. race, gender, sexuality or class) then reflect on why that has been the case for you but not for so many other people. Can you move from your own privileged position to a position of recognising how and why other people are less privileged on account of their identity mix?

Commitment: Start to think about your motivations, expectations and assumptions regarding Inclusivity and diversity. How big a step is it for you to embrace Total Inclusivity – without waiting for someone else to do so first? And if it is a massive step, why is that?

NOTES

1 The South African concept of Ubuntu, meaning "I am because we are", defines it neatly.
2 Defined as the absence of discrimination based on race, colour, age, gender, national origin, religion or mental or physical disability and the right to equivalent opportunities for employment regardless of race, colour, sex or national origin.
3 The 'zero tolerance' concept with TI arose from discussion with Jeff Franz-Lien on Quora (see www.quora.com/Since-morals-change-over-time-what-are-some-things-we-do-now-as-a-society-that-will-be-deemed-unacceptable-100-years-from-now/answer/Stephen-Whitehead-)16?__nsrc__=4&__snid3__=30984515423&comment_id=240648010&comment_type=2.
4 The Black Lives Matter movement began in 2013 following the murder of Trayvon Martin. There had been multiple instances of police brutality against Black Americans prior to 2020; see https//blacklivesmatter.com/about.

Two

What age were you when you fully and finally matured as a human being? 18? 30? 45? 65?

Apologies, that is a trick question, because you cannot answer it.

If maturity means learning about the world, our place in it and our self, then it can never stop. There is no definitive age of maturity because maturity is a process not an end point. In any one life there are a great many maturity moments: experiences which push us further ahead in terms of our understanding and self-awareness. And as we move further ahead, we leave something behind: illusion.

It is not easy leaving illusion behind. Holding on to that which gives us comfort is, of course, comforting, no matter how fantastical it might be. It is no coincidence that older people tend to be slower, more thoughtful, less impulsive, more reflective than the young. Unfortunately, older people can also be less visionary and more conservative, even more cynical. But then the elderly are survivors, and one can expect survivors to be rather cautious, having seen and experienced life in all its messy emotional and physical reality.

Any young person reading the above paragraphs can be forgiven for thinking 'So what? How is that relevant to me today?'

Well the relevance is the warning contained in those two paragraphs. And that warning is to not invest too much assumption in who you think you are today, because you're going to be a somewhat different person in the not-too-distant future. The second warning is to let go of illusion. Sure, if you wish to hold on to a belief system, fine. We all need them in some form or another. But maturing is about awakening, and one of the most important awakenings any of us can have concerns our very selves.

One of the aims of this book is to wake people up. I want to encourage readers to let go of any illusions of self which, not unreasonably, they may have previously invested a lot of faith, hope and trust in.

DOI: 10.4324/9781003244073-2

Why? Because you cannot embrace Total Inclusivity if, for example, you hold on to the idea that humans are biologically programmed to think and act in ways which are based on their genitalia, skin colour or place of birth. If you believe that illusion, then you must also believe that we have no future as a species – in your mind, nature will always win out over culture and human potential; humanity can never progress far from its ape-like origins. However, I recognise there is a comfort in believing that nature governs our actions – it removes responsibility from us.

Humans are an adaptive species. If we weren't then we would have stayed living in the plains and jungles of Africa all those millennia ago. Just like the giraffe and gorilla.

This chapter will explore the changing self and the changing workplace, and also explain how neither are fixed and settled but in constant flux. What this means is we have some influence over both. We are not simply biological organisms programmed to think and act in a certain way. We are creative, adaptive, imaginative and intelligent. Which is just as well; otherwise we could not embrace the concept of Total Inclusivity – we'd still be believing that everything is functionally fixed, and there is nothing we can do to change that fact (Illusion No. 1).

[That is the first Illusion to let go of if we are to move to Total Inclusivity – there are several more illusions which humans like to hold on to, each disabused in this chapter and summarised in the conclusion.]

NO 'ONE'

No fixed identity, no illusions that the world is predictable, no holding on to ideas of biology as destiny.

In which case, what are we left with?

We are left with hope.

And that hope rests on a single truth: that the individual can make a positive difference to the world around them. So long as they make the effort. It is in our hands to bring about the change we'd like to see, no one else's.

That may sound rather utopian if not unrealistic. On the contrary, it is highly realistic. The world of humans has always been subject to change and never more so than at this point in history. We just have to accept our potential to improve.

So how does positive change come about? It occurs because humans are constantly evolving new and better ways of being; their actions, beliefs, ideas, expectations have advanced phenomenally and are continuing to do so. Look around you; how different is the world today to that of even 25 years ago, never mind 25,000 years ago?

Take the UK, for example: when I was a child, in the 1950s, gay sexuality was illegal, lesbianism wasn't even a recognised sexuality, a trans person had no hope of changing their gender identity, women were refused mortgages and bank loans without a man's support and it was considered a scandal for a single woman to end up pregnant. Indeed, many such single mothers had their child removed by the authorities – they could even find themselves committed to a mental health institution. Guest houses regularly posted explicitly racist notices. And unless you were male, white and comfortably middle class, your chances of going to university were less than 1%.

If you read that and are surprised, astonished or merely angry such injustices could occur in a supposedly 'civilised society' consider where we are today. Positive transformations in human society can only happen because human identity is not fixed and predictable; to use a sociologist term, there is no essential self. We are now educated to recognise and accept social justice and reject inequality and challenge injustice. We have learned that women's and men's roles are not fixed for eternity by some higher power and that the world is a lot more diverse than we ever imagined (Illusion No. 2).

Of course, whatever progress individuals and human society have made over time, we cannot afford to be complacent about assuming continuing social improvements. Just look at the rapid global rise of fascism during the 1930s, and just look at the torrent of hate, violence and prejudice still with us to this day and which, in some locations, is worsening.

Yes, we are constantly evolving, but what into is for the individual to decide.

You can look at yourself in the mirror and you'll recognise the image in front of you. But then look at your photo of, say, a decade ago; do you recognise that person in the photo? Yes, you'll recognise it is you, but you'll not be able to go back and inhabit the mind of your younger self. As you age so will that distance between current and past selves lengthen. Your memories may still be strong and vivid, but when you reflect on your past you are doing so from the present; your past is indeed another country.

If your identity is a work in progress, with no end date, how is it you feel complete? Where does that sense of Oneness come from?

It comes from the human capacity to create a feeling of being One, a whole individual. This is a very healthy state to be in mentally. Just don't imagine that the One you feel today is the same One you felt decades ago.

The human brain is a receptor; it receives information and stimulus. It reacts and as it does so it grows, learns, accumulates, develops, interprets, matures. Neuroscientists term this 'brain plasticity': you weren't born with this mental computer full of all the information it needed to live and thrive in the world. That information came later. It still is coming, every hour of every day, and every hour of every day we are changing.

> the intertwining jungles of your brain work themselves into something slightly different from what they were a moment before. These changes sum up to our memories: the outcome of our living and loving. Accumulating over minutes and months and decades, the innumerable brain changes tally up to what we call you. Or at least the you right now. Yesterday you were marginally different. And tomorrow you'll be someone else.
>
> (Eagleman, 2021, p. 8)

We have the power to use that information, our brain plasticity, to good or negative effect (ibid). We can build our life based on inclusivity, a sense of belonging and community, or we can choose to build it on isolation, anger and discrimination.

> What we are today comes from our thoughts of yesterday, and our present thoughts build our life tomorrow: our life is the creation of our mind.[1]

In Chapter 5 I explore language and meaning, not because I intend to delve deeply into the Derridean[2] world of multiple meanings so much as to highlight the power and politics which emanate from certain words, phrases, terms. But language is not just about conveying information and knowledge, albeit wrapped up in political rhetoric and contested subjective interpretations.

Language both reflects reality and helps constitute it.

Language can be arbitrary, signifying, ambiguous and fictive, but that does not diminish its power to inform our sense of self.

This One you imagine yourself to be is nothing more or less than the constitutional elements which language and socialisation have, over time, created in your mind. A process which began in the womb and accelerated from the moment you were born, influenced by environment, place, relationships, culture, social systems, experience, education and occasionally chance.

If you are born in Shanghai to middle-class Buddhist Chinese parents, that fact may not determine who you will become, but at the very least it provides the point of departure for your life journey.

If you are born in Louisiana to white working-class Christian American parents, that fact may not determine who you will become, but at the very least it provides the point of departure for your life journey.

If you are born in London to wealthy English professional-class parents both of whom are agnostics, that fact may not determine who you will become, but at the very least it provides the point of departure for your life journey.

Credit Line: Cartoons drawn by Advanced Standard Group Co., Ltd.

From the writings of philosopher Frederick Nietzsche to psychologist Jacques Lacan, from the theories of sociologist Michel Foucault to deconstructionist Jacques Derrida, a single over-riding and compelling notion emerges: that the idea of a grounded, fixed self is a convenient fiction which humans hold on to because it is too risky to recognise the existential gap which opens up below us the moment we stop seeing ourselves as a One (see Sarup, 1993).

The message here is therefore simply this; by all means hold on to that fiction of a permanent self (a One) if it makes you feel existentially secure and ontologically grounded. Just don't imagine your One is the only One that counts (Illusion No. 3).

THE END OF THE 'GENITALIA AS DESTINY' ILLUSION

One way to illustrate how (relatively) fast beliefs and assumptions can change is to give a current and stark example.

Ever since the Babylonian king Hammurabi (cc.1770BC) devised his Code, establishing judgements intended to ensure 'social order', so have religions, governments, bureaucrats, monarchs and dictators been following suit (Harari, 2015). A central tenet to virtually all these rules has been the control of 'Others', notably women; the marginalisation of LGBTQ+ people; and the acceptance that some races and classes of people are worthier than others. In other words, men get elevated, and rich men get elevated to the very top.

> How far back this erosion of female power went [. . .] is unclear . . . What we do know is that masculinity, often expressed through sexual violence, became part of the dynamics of [historical] imperial expansion.
>
> (Graeber and Wengrow, 2021, p. 371)

The week that I started writing this book, the horrific kidnapping and murder of Sarah Everard took place in London. A male Metropolitan Police officer was subsequently convicted of her murder. Such murders of women by men are not uncommon. Indeed, they are depressingly familiar. But for whatever reason, this murder struck a chord in British society. A number of powerful and prominent women subsequently made pronouncements on the continuing problem of male violence, including Baroness Jenny Jones, Green Party peer. She suggested that 'introducing a curfew for men would make women a lot safer' and that setting such a curfew at 6 p.m. would be a necessary move to ensure fewer women are murdered, assaulted, raped by men.

In other words, it is now time to regulate men.

Recognising that this proposal will never be legally enacted (well, unlikely), the point is the dramatic shift in attitudes regarding understandings of male identity. With few apparent exceptions (Graeber and Wengrow, 2021), for 3,700 years there was barely any noticeable change in terms of male hegemony in most parts of the world as humans grew in number, expanded geographically, built and destroyed empires, became urbanised. Indeed, even 30 years ago few people other than dedicated sociologists were minded to critically examine men and their masculinities, including male violence (see, for example, Connell, 1996; Whitehead, 2002). Today, male identity and the problems that can come with it are headline news.

And what has changed in this dramatically short time span? Attitudes towards gender identity and, especially, types of male behaviour which are threatening, abusive and destructive. Suddenly, there is a growing global realisation, among women especially, that what has been considered 'natural' male behaviour down the ages can no longer be tolerated. Such views are backed up by research: in 2019 the American Psychological Association issued new professional guidelines for mental health professionals declaring that traditional masculinity is 'harmful' to boys and men. This was no mere knee-jerk reaction to yet another example of male violence, but based on 40 years of research into men and their masculinities (APA, 2018).

What we are witnessing here is the end of an illusion – the illusion that 50% of humans should get a pass for being abusive, violent and murderous on account of them having a penis (Illusion No. 4).

YOU AND OTHERS

In order to embrace Total Inclusivity, it is first necessary to let go of not just the illusion of biological determinism but also those seductive but simplistic binaries, dualisms and dichotomies which serve to pull us apart, not bring us together.

For example:

The gender/sex binary:	male and female
The sex dualism:	his and her roles
The racial dichotomy:	Black and white

Take the gender binary and the idea that humanity is divided into two genders. Firstly, 'gender' is a term used to describe the social expression of a sex label which has been assigned at birth by a doctor based on the genitals you're born with. But gender is a social performance based on how you feel inside and how you express those feelings. There are many ways to express one's gender identity – it is not fixed in biology. Consequently, it is multiple, not dual. There are as many differences in the categories 'male' and 'female' as there are between these two categories. Similarly, there are multiple expressions of masculinity just as there are multiple expressions of femininity (Illusion No. 5).

If you look at sex binary identity (male and female) then you might assume you are on more solid ground in thinking in terms of a binary. Wrong. Based on chromosomes, there are at least six biological sexes; not all men have a penis or XY chromosomes, and not all women have a vagina/uterus or XX chromosomes. There are, in reality, tens of millions of people who are neither male or female, an even greater number who self-identify as trans, plus an unknown number who are intersex (Kennon, 2021) (Illusion No. 6).

Eventually, even the Olympic Games is going to have to become Totally Inclusive and recognise that having only male and female categories is an exclusive classification.

> Maybe we can't necessarily shoehorn everyone into these two categories? So it's not that trans people are the problem . . . it's the structure we currently have.[3]

The sex dualism of his and her roles is one which has held sway over humanity's lifestyles, probably since Stone Age men supposedly first went out to hunt, leaving females to look after the kids. It doesn't hold sway any longer. The male-breadwinner family began to disappear as a dominant social model around the time The Beatles were singing 'Nowhere Man'. Notwithstanding, a lot of men still have to catch up with the fact that they are equally responsible for the ironing. Which could be one of the reasons fewer women are choosing marriage (Illusion No. 7).

Nothing confuses or energises humans more than race. The differences may only be skin deep, but we invest much more in them than simply melanin, eye shape, hair colour, size of nose or whatever else we consider separates us from our fellow humans. Black, white, Asian, Western,

European, African, American, these are social identity realities, but they don't tell us who we are. You are more than a label simplistically imposed by a society too lazy to see beyond a dichotomy (Illusion No. 8).

And finally, there is the illusion of monosexuality, or as sociologists describe it, 'compulsory heterosexuality'. If any illusion has taken a battering over the past few decades it is the idea that we are all born to be 'naturally' fancying the opposite sex when it comes to sexuality. The more we mature as a society and become civilised towards one another, the more we are going to have to embrace sexual differences such as pansexuality, bisexuality, panromantic, polysexuality, polyamory and for many sociologists the most intriguing of all – asexuality and celibacy as a lifestyle option[4] (Illusion No. 9).

Sexuality is multiple, and how we express it is strongly influenced by social norms and conditioning. Sure, hormones will have a lot to do with it, especially your level of sex drive and desire, but . . .

> When it comes to who you go to bed with, do so with consent, and open your mind to everything else.

If you want clear evidence of the falsity of all binaries, dualisms, dichotomies and biological certainties then all you need do is look in the mirror.

You not only see a changing face and body, you see an individual of multiple identities. How many of those identities conform to social stereotypes?

Do a 'simple' test; Identify who you are. List the primary and secondary components that go to make 'You'.

Where do you start? Only you can say. Is it religion which is your primary identity, or is it your sexuality? Does your gender identity weigh more heavily in your consciousness than, say, your national pride? Do you see your sex identity as immutable but your racial identity as dispersed? And what about age, class, culture, language, education, family, relationships, professional identity? Where do these additional variables fit into who you are?

How deeply hidden is your 'authentic' self? Too deeply even for you to find. Authenticity is simply feeling good about who one is; or as they say, 'comfortable in one's skin'. Authentic identities are not fixed in biology (Illusion No. 10).

It is too confusing to even begin to unravel the Gordian knot of factors which make up just one human being, never mind 7.7 billion of us.

INTERSECTIONALITY

What is being revealed here is the intersectionality of human identity:

> Intersectionality . . . recognises that each life and each individual identity
> exists in the intersections of many aspects of self and social powers;
> encourages the recognition that gender intersects with, for example,
> race, sex, sexuality, ability, ethnicity, age, culture and class to 'produce'
> the individual.
>
> (Whitehead et al., 2014, p. 41)

Humans are not a single, unchangeable entity; they are an ever-evolving kaleidoscope of social elements, mixed in with hormones and chromosome to produce an individual, a person who is always in the process of some degree of metamorphosis.

However, it gets even more complex; having begun to identify the primary and secondary components that constitute your identity, we then complicate matters further by trying to address the different power relationships that operate between these diverse ways of being.

> Intersectionality investigates how intersecting power relations
> influence social relations across diverse societies as well as individual
> experiences in everyday life. As an analytical tool, intersectionality views
> categories of race, class, gender, sexuality, nation, ability, ethnicity and
> age – among others – as interrelated and mutually shaping one another.
> Intersectionality is a way of understanding and explaining complexity in
> the world, in people, and in human experiences.
>
> (Hill Collins and Bilge, 2020, p. 4)

Black is not simply an identity variable – it is a statement of power or, in racist societies, an absence of power. Where does the power of patriarchy come from if not from the subordination of women? Remove that subordination and the historical relationship between male and power is eliminated. Social classes (and caste systems) are nothing more than the imposition of an artificial social hierarchy by a society attempting to differentiate 'Us' and 'Them' in order to benefit 'Us' at the expense of 'Them'. When members of a society claim that a certain group of individuals are 'ill' because their sexuality doesn't correspond with their beliefs, one has to ask which group is actually in need of mental health advice, those who are oppressed or those doing the oppressing?

No single individual has pure insight into the lives of those around them. Indeed, rarely do people fully understand what is going on in their own lives, their own heads. But what people can feel, and very immediately, is when their identity is being rejected, discriminated against, marginalised, negatively judged, stereotyped, anonymised, silenced and violated.

The most toxic form of identity is the one imposed on you by those with power over you, not the one which you have agentically fashioned through your own experience and imagination.

The fundamental objective of any organisation that aspires to be a Totally Inclusive Community must be to provide shelter for all identities; eliminate power advantages and privileges historically associated with any identity; and encourage understanding and appreciation of the richness and beauty of human diversity.

CHANGING WORKPLACES

So far, this chapter has focused on the fluidity, multiplicity and contingency of identity.

But in today's complex, globalised, hyper-competitive world, it is not only identity which is changing; so is work. And when work changes, so does identity. Work is not 'out there' revolving around us like a distant, remote planet. Work is in our minds and in our hearts. It is not removed from our subjectivity, emotions and consciousness – work influences our very sense of self; it is a key if not dominant aspect of identity and directly informs our relationship to others, our place in society.

Work can be who we think we are, and it can certainly have a direct impact on how we see ourselves and the value we put on others. But that doesn't make the relationship between self and work automatically benign and inevitably positive.

I could now veer off into a lengthy treatise on the changing nature of work since 1945, not least the decline of industrialisation and the rise of post-industrialisation in the West especially. But I won't. For one thing, others have covered this topic much better than I can. But what I do want to draw attention to is the way in which paid work has become more intense, individualised and competitive, especially since the early 1990s, and one of the key reasons for this is 'performativity'.

Performativity can be a tricky concept to grasp, but when applied to work organisations and their cultures it is all rather simple and easy to identify:

> [Performativity is] the trend in organisations to measure and quantify every aspect of employee performance (e.g. targets, assessment, performance indicators, appraisal, success measurements) . . . The belief in the veracity of apparently objective systems of accountability and measurement rather than the subjective judgement and specialized knowledges of an individual.
>
> (Whitehead and Dent, 2002, p. 2)

By sheer coincidence, on the very day of writing this section a graphic example of performativity showed up in the UK.

The *Daily Telegraph* newspaper is apparently actively considering 'linking some elements of journalist's pay to the popularity of their articles' (The Guardian, March, 2021), using a "stars" system which scores stories published online to factors such as subscriptions and clicks. Not unreasonably, the *Daily Telegraph* journalists are expressing some concern at this suggestion their pay and career prospects should be dictated by an algorithm (Illusion No. 11).

Whether you agree with this particular proposal or not, what is unarguable is that it marks a change in workplace culture, and not towards a greater sense of community. Performativity culture is, indeed, the very antithesis of community in that it encourages a silo mentality based on competitiveness between employees. It also enables leaders and managers to exert 'hands-off' control over staff by applying pressure via imposed targets; the so-called performance indicators.

If you are an employee of any major organisation (or perhaps even a small one), all this may read as rather familiar to you. Very likely you too are caught up in a changing workplace, where an avid and relentless focus on targets undermines a feeling of togetherness and association. But it wasn't always like this. The whole concept of performativity in workplace culture and practice didn't emerge until the early 1990s in the UK and USA. Since then, it has gone global.

But performativity is only one example of how organisations and workplace cultures are changing, attempting to maintain a competitive edge in a world of immense and largely uncontrollable change. We could add 'zero-hours' contracts, the rise in automation and artificial intelligence;

low-paid immigrant work; Zoom and all the rest; the gig economy; degree inflation and credentialism; the demise of the high street and the rise of online shopping; hybrid work; internships; telecommuting, flexible work shifts.

In short, whether you are in work or out of work, you better try and think and act like an entrepreneur, because eventually someone is going to come along with a scorecard and 'objectively' assess your contribution to the bottom line. And that 'someone' could well be a smiley-faced robot.

Trying to find the community element or its potential in such a work environment is clearly a challenge. But we have to try, because otherwise not only will Total Inclusivity remain a distant dream, our emotional association with work will become singularly toxic and damaging, leading to people distancing themselves from their organisation: As I put it in Chapter 3, 'turning up for work but not being there'.

The pressure on workers is now enormous, creating a 'burnout epidemic'. That this, in turn, is leading to what is now being described as the 'great resignation', with millions quitting their jobs, especially in the USA (Cassidy, 2021), should not surprise anyone, especially the bosses and company owners. The combination of performativity and COVID creates mental and physical exhaustion – and the realisation that 'work is not your god' (Malesic, 2022).

While it is relatively easy for organisations to implement restructuring programmes, bring in 'streamlining' of delivery, enforce 'flexible working', invest in AI, it is much harder for the individual employee to adapt, especially if they have invested their sense of self in the 'old ways' of doing things or quite reasonably wish to retain a healthy work–life balance.

Of course, what has been outlined above is just one side to a very complex scenario. There is another side – you and your expectations.

For at least five years now, global research on 'what millennials really want from a job' has been producing answers around a single theme: they want to be valued, involved, partners more than employees, expecting reciprocity between employee and employer, and they want their jobs to mean something (TechRepublic, 2018, 2020).

Key points which emerge from these studies reveal the following regarding millennials and employment/organisations:

1 Give feedback, don't expect them to be motivated by silence.
2 Listen, they want to be heard.
3 Money isn't everything; they want to feel passionate about their jobs.

4   Equality of opportunity; a meritocratic work culture, not 'jobs for the (white) boys'
5   A feeling of being part of a community and belonging
6   A positive and healthy work–life balance

It would be wrong, therefore, to assume that there is only one direction of pressure on organisations – global competitiveness. There is another pressure – the expectations of the younger generation. These combined pressures not only raise challenges for all of us, employees and employers, they remind us not to underestimate the transformation in workplace culture and practice which is now bearing down on society and organisations from all directions.

It is from within this dynamic, unpredictable scenario that Total Inclusivity emerges – not as a panacea for all organisational and identity ailments and problems but as the basis for establishing a singularly beneficial workplace culture which everyone, regardless of their stake in the organisation, can recognise, accept, want to protect and contribute to.

Employees are first and foremost humans – they are only resources if they choose to be (Illusion No. 12).

BUBBLES

There are many ways to understand and theorise identity. Back in the 1950s, sociologists such as Talcott Parsons saw society and the individuals within it as functional, 'naturally' orientated to organising society based on apparently eternal principles, e.g. the 'biologically' differentiated roles of men and women. By the 1960s, Erving Goffman's theory of symbolic interactionism had taken hold, with those same gender roles being interpreted as performance, impression management, the individual's attempt at conforming, giving the appearance of authenticity. Then along came the critical gender theorists (feminists) of the 1970s. Not surprisingly, they raised the question as to how predictable and 'natural' these sex and gender roles really were and who was benefiting by perpetuating them. By this time, Freud was getting a severe hammering from critical theorists and, not unreasonably, being questioned about his fixation on the penis. Come the 1980s, and theories of identity were increasingly trapped between structure (blame it on patriarchy, capitalism, ideology) and agency (let's all become Sartrean existentialists). During the 1990s, there were various attempts to break out of the trap (e.g. Anthony Gidden's theory of structuration; Michel Foucault's 'discursive subject'; and Jacques Lyotard's postmodernism).[5]

But then along comes the new millennium and suddenly all that sociological, philosophical and psychoanalytical intellectual navel gazing starts to look rather passe. Somebody spins it all up in the air and down comes crashing all our previous certainties.

For the sake of brevity, let us call these certainties, 'bubbles'.

For centuries, 'big' thinkers (mostly men) have been in search of the grand paradigm, the single, over-arching theory which 'answers all questions'. Immanuel Kant thought he'd found it; so did Sigmund Freud, and certainly Karl Marx did. Turns out, they were simply reflecting their own worldview – their own bubble (Illusion No. 13).

There is no singular worldview, and yet nor is everything reduceable to a morass of competing, relative worldviews.

Each view has, in its turn, something to offer, and we must take from it accordingly. You don't need to be a paid-up Marxist to recognise that paid-up feminists such as Andrea Dworkin have a point when they argue that men (of all classes) can be oppressive and violent and a threat to women. Nor can you reject Max Weber's theory of the 'iron hand of bureaucracy' when you apply it to the contemporary workings of organisations and the state. As for social media, who would argue against theorising Facebook and the like from the perspective of Jean Baudrillard's 'hyperreal, radical postmodernism'? Finally, setting aside the musings of (mostly) dead white males, try instead to get connected to the thoughts of Judith Butler, bell hooks, Patricia Hill Collins, Heidi Mirza, Chandra Mohanty and Kimberle Crenshaw (see Whitehead et al., 2014, for introduction to these theories and a timeline).

Actually, it is Kimberle Crenshaw who gets especially connected to in this book, because she is the feminist theorist who is credited with developing the concept of intersectionality (other key theorists are Beverley Daniel Tatum and Richard Delgado – more on their critical race theory in later chapters).

But back to bubbles.

Bubbles are certainties, and we all love a certainty, not least the intellectuals among us. Unfortunately, being bubbles, these certainties cannot survive exposure to multiplicity – more bubbles. Well, they can, but then all these bubbles (ways of seeing the world) end up like the froth on your cappuccino.

And perhaps that's how it has to be. Maybe, in the final analysis, all we are is a single minute bubble on a damn big cup of coffee. Without these bubbles there'd be no cappuccino, so even in our disputable subjectivity and our contradictory relativism, it all adds up to something, in this case, humanity.

Total Inclusivity is not asking you to step outside your bubble, because that bubble protects who you are, who you have become. What Total Inclusivity requires is that you expand your bubble – allow it to grow. Embrace thoughts and ideas which may have lingered in the back of your mind for a long time but now have the chance to see the light of day. Be challenged, maybe even be deeply challenged, but don't let go of that single message, which is that Total Inclusivity protects us all.

CHAPTER 2: REFLECTIONS, GUIDANCE AND COMMITMENTS

Reflection Exercise: 'Who am I?' Try and answer that most difficult of questions but do so from an intersectional understanding by recognising the multiplicity of variables which serve to produce you. Which of these variables are primary, and which are secondary in your life and being?

Guidance for Implementation: Consider what you want from your work and employment, now and/or in the future. How does your identity relate to, for example, your professional status, your job? Look more closely at how your organisation is changing and what impact this is having on your association with that organisation and to work in general.

Commitment: Everyone you work with is living in their own bubble, partly self-made, partly created by circumstance and environment. Commit to better understanding and empathising with the different realities of your work colleagues while recognising that each of them, like you, no doubt sees themselves as occupying a singular, authentic and valid identity.

REALITIES, NOT ILLUSIONS

1 The world of humans is not biologically predictable – we are more than DNA, chromosomes, hormones or any combination of essential, unchanging components. Humans and their potential are not reduceable to some biological sound bite.

2 Life can improve for humans, and in the past decades it has done for most of us. Though this is not inevitable – as COVID-19 has reminded us.

3 We each might see ourselves as the 'centre of the universe', but the fact is we are not.

4 Your genitalia in no way determine how you'll think and behave.

5 There are at least three dominant masculinities in the world today: traditional, progressive, collapsed. And at least an equally diverse range of femininities (see Chapter 8).

6 We don't know just how many humans are neither male or female, how many are neither straight nor gay or how many are intersex. But it is more than you ever imagined. And you've met them. Indeed, you may be one.

7 Men can be househusbands; women can be CEOs and prime ministers. Indeed, there are examples of each all around us. So stop thinking in terms of binary sex roles.

8 Humanity is complex, which makes describing individuals difficult – we are each unique. Just don't swap complexity for simple-mindedness.

9 We can never fully answer the question as to what turns us on sexually. Who knows? Moreover, so long as the sex is consensual, does it matter?

10 Your authentic self is only in your imagination. Which is where it should be.

11 Employees are not motivated by threats to their job and professional identity. Managers/leaders who think otherwise should reflect on what motivates them.

12 Humans are not pawns to be deployed by the powerful – they are individuals with their own agentic capacity to say yes or no.

13 Searching for 'grand paradigms' is merely another way of assuming that we can control the world. Humans need to focus on ethical values and less on finding 'answers' to every conceivable question. We should embrace not knowing – and accept that some things we will never know.

NOTES

1 Ascribed to Buddha.

2 Jacques Derrida's theory of deconstruction and the recognition that meanings are multiple, language signals unclear and that language itself is a temporal process.

3 Dr Lynley Anderson, bioethicist, discussing the current debates over trans rights in (Olympic) sport and quoted in *Lunar*, South China Morning Post, 25th June, 2021.

4 There is some evidence that celibacy is growing in popularity, becoming even a lifestyle choice for many Generation Z and young millennials, www.theguardian.com/lifeandstyle/2021/mar/21/i-dont-want-sex-with-anyone-the-growing-asexuality-movement.

5 For discussion and introduction to all these theories see S. M. Whitehead, A. Talahite and R. Moodley (2014), *Gender and identity: key themes and new directions*. Oxford: Oxford University Press.

Three

DOI: 10.4324/9781003244073-3

FALLING IN LOVE

There is a fundamental flaw in humans, and it is not greed, lust or self-ishness. It is the need to be loved. Whether you are a newborn baby or a wrinkled centenarian, nothing is more likely to bring you comfort and joy than someone giving you love and affection.

But why is this most basic of needs a flaw?

Because it puts you at the mercy of your emotions and more riskily, at the mercy of the person expressing the love.

If you've ever been in love then you know the feeling of stepping out over a chasm, with the only thing stopping you plunging to the depths being the continued expression of love by your beloved. That's a lot of trust, a massive amount of faith and a galaxy of hope. No wonder it all too often ends up with us crashing down into misery.

But at least when we put our trust and emotional well-being in the hands of another human being, then we have the chance to measure, assess and evaluate the risks.

None of that applies if we put our trust and emotional well-being in the hands of an organisation.

One of the most common mistakes we all make when imagining, thinking about or working in organisations is to render them real. Organisations have no ontological identity. They are not existentially functioning beings with all the characteristics of humans. Organisations may have a website, an HQ, a thousand employees, a worldwide image and huge profits, but they do not have minds, nor do they have emotions.

Indeed, organisations don't even have a centre. The centre of an organisation only exists in the mind of the individual stakeholder of that organisation. The CEO and the cleaner both work in the same organisation, but those two individuals relate to it through their own experience and subjectivity, one in the executive suites, the other in the loos. Which of those subjective relationships to the organisation is the real one? Both are.

The takeaway here is that organisations cannot love you. Even though you can love them.

How one-sided a love affair is that?

All love requires an act of magic, whereby you conjure up in your mind and imagination that which you love. We don't only do this with other humans, we do it with animals, places, objects and our work.

Some years ago, I was delivering leadership coaching to an international school in South East Asia. The head of the school was particularly concerned at the deteriorating relationship between her and another senior manager. Nothing she tried seemed to bridge the growing gap between her and this other woman. Both were highly professional, capable and experienced individuals, though the head was much younger. After talking to the senior manager it became clear she was deeply upset at not being promoted – she felt her 25 years working in the school and especially her devotion to the organisation were not just unrewarded but largely unrecognised.

The senior manager was in love with her job, and she was in love with the school, the whole organisation. It had become her life to the point at which she was emotionally vulnerable to any act by the organisation which could be interpreted by her as 'a lack of love'. Her work and the organisation itself had over many years acquired a central place in her life, in her sense of self, in her understanding of herself as a woman, a professional, a person respected, valued and appreciated for her devotion to the organisation.

That is a lot of emotional investment in an entity with no heart, no mind and no feelings.

When I explained to the senior manager the difference between loving her job and loving the organisation, making the point to her that the organisation could never love her back no matter how hard she desired that love, it changed her whole relationship to her job. Well, at least to the extent that she very quickly became a lot happier. The 'barrier' between her and the head disappeared, her health and mental well-being appeared to improve and she was a lot more involved and productive.

Just as humans can deposit a whole mass of unrealistic and unachievable expectations onto other humans (especially romantic partners), so can employees do the same with their employing organisation.

This is not a new phenomenon, but it is exacerbated by the changing nature of relationships. With so many of us now living single lives, part of an extended-family network and largely communicating with friends and loved ones via social media, where do you think we are most likely to look for that elusive love contract?

Yes, in our job. In our work. In that unfeeling organisation.

FALLING OUT OF LOVE

The temptation to invest our happiness in work and organisations is immensely powerful though largely unrecognised even by sociologists and psychiatrists. Trawl through any of the great texts on organisational behaviour and you'll come across a host of jargon, theory and analysis, most of it evidentially reinforced, but one word you won't easily find is 'love'.

The reality is that any organisation without some sense of love in it, between employees and between employees and their work, will never become a community. It will remain a sterile, cold and distant environment, only good for earning a living in, no good for spending part of a life in.

What is being stated here is not revolutionary but merely common sense, a reflection of reality.

Which makes it interesting that people still keep falling in and out of love with their organisations.

When we apply for that new job we invariably do so with great hope and expectation. If we get a job offer then it can be as if a whole new and exciting dimension has opened up in our lives. And perhaps it has. But just as love is fleeting, so is that honeymoon period at work.

Just as humans tend to be besotted with the idea of the One being out there, a soulmate waiting for them, so we can become besotted with our jobs. Naturally, bosses like their employees to be devoted to work – it makes them easier to motivate for greater productivity.

But there is a very fine or invisible line between loving our job and loving our organisation. Both emotional investments are risky, though at least your job can give instant satisfaction and a feeling of accomplishment. Organisations can only relate to you through systems, missives and directives. Ultimately, they are anonymous, and the bigger the organisation the more impersonal it is.

Love requires trust and respect, not fine words or mission statements. It requires embracing all aspects of a person's character and all aspects of the work community. The risks of disillusionment between lovers and between worker and organisation are massive. And just as most of us experience pain and disillusionment in romantic love, so we can experience very similar emotions with paid work.

Professional development, a kind and sympathetic boss, away days, good pay and perks, a sense of empowerment and agency, plus a quality work–life balance all help to mediate the potential sterility of organisational culture and improve staff-retention rates. But each of us has our own relationship to work and organisations, and if/when that day comes when we fall out of love, then like a doomed marriage, not much is likely to save it. Hence the 'great resignation', the mass exodus of employees that is happening around the world at the time of writing (Cassidy, 2021).

Like a marriage or any other committed relationship which is heading for the rocks, something starts to happen to us long before we cut the cord, phone the divorce lawyer, walk out with just our laptop and bad memories.

We stop being involved. We cease to contribute. We emotionally and physically distance ourselves from that which we've fallen out of love with.

Some organisational theorists have identified this as the 'empty raincoat' syndrome. Office workers leave their raincoat on the back of their office chair to make it appear as if they are still in the building, still working. In truth, they are heading for home. It can also manifest itself as inauthentic performance, whereby the employee makes all the right noises about commitment, effort, enthusiasm for the next big marketing push, but in their mind, they've switched off – they are playing the part but no longer being the part.

They are still turning up, but they've stopped being there.

The irony is – in some cases it is even a tragedy – most of us yearn to be wanted by the organisation which has said it wants us to be a part of it. This statement of desire by the organisation translates into our minds as a statement of need for us. And who doesn't want to be needed? We all want to belong, and work is one place where we can get a great many positive emotions and well-being from belonging.

Yes, we can dismiss these emotional connections as unrealistic, maybe even juvenile, but who among us hasn't felt that pull of belonging to something bigger than ourselves? Indeed, as research shows, belonging is fundamental to well-being and happiness:

The most striking revelation from an 80-year old Harvard study of health and aging is that close relationships are what keep people happy throughout their lives and these relationships with family, friends and community delay mental and physical decline. These social ties are better predictors of our happiness and longevity than social class, IQ, or genetics.

(Buck and Hardwick, 2021)

And what is a key component of that social tie – the workplace:

This year's U.N. World Happiness Report showed that although people think being well paid is the most important driver of being happy at work, actually our belonging at work is the most important contributor to happiness (by far).

(ibid)

Work organisations have the capacity to validate our sense of identity, reward us for our love and devotion to them and give us a feeling of belonging which is surpassed only by family and partners. What they don't have the capacity to do is love us.

WHICH ORGANISATIONS ELICIT LOVE? WHICH ELICIT LOATHING?

Just like people, some types of organisations and workplace cultures are easier to love than others. For example, if you are working for the biggest global corporations then finding them loveable might be a challenge – they are just too anonymous, rigid and bureaucratic. Amazon is one such company, with employees complaining of "timed toilet breaks", "never-ending targets" and "a horrendous record of injuries on the job" (BBC News, March, 2021a; see also Chapter 10). Though on the plus side, Amazon does create a lot of jobs.

However, as I discuss, a company's size does not automatically equate to sizeable problems for employees. It all depends on the leadership styles, work culture and how effectively a feeling of community gets generated between all employees.

As is explored in Chapter 4, where an organisation is situated on the TI Organisation–Community Continuum is the most important variable in determining whether or not it will be loveable. If you find working for a heartless, performative-fixated, racist, sexist organisation to be emotionally and physically crushing, then you only have one option, and that is to leave. If you can afford to. Unfortunately, such organisations tend to exploit the fact that you won't leave – precisely because they offer paid employment to those who otherwise would be unemployed. Is this unfair? Absolutely. Which is why governments around the world bring in laws to ensure companies at least follow the minimum regulations regarding pay, health and safety, holidays and other forms of workplace protection of staff.

It is, therefore, important to recognise that no government has brought in laws to ensure Total Inclusivity (at least not yet). So what is being recommended in this book is at one level above and beyond what all companies are legally obliged to do, but at a humanistic level also what every company should be willing to do without being forced. If the organisational leadership cannot see the value in Total Inclusivity then the problem lies with them, not with governments or employees.

Below are examples of two very contrasting workplace cultures, one which tends to elicit loathing in its staff and one which tends to elicit love. You'll know which you work in, and you'll also know which you prefer to work in.

The Expendables

Visit any city in Asia and one thing you will immediately encounter, along with the stifling heat, is a motorcyclist. Not one or two but millions of them. Hanoi and Hoh Chi Minh City are but two extreme examples of how the motorcyclist has come to dominate travel in countries like Vietnam, making crossing the road as risky as crossing a crocodile-infested river in East Africa in a leaky canoe. In neighbouring Taipei and Singapore, more prosperous and organised cities, there may be fewer motorcyclists, but those that are around ride much more powerful bikes and go faster.

Around 2018 a new member of this motorcycling fraternity emerged, invariably wearing an orange or green jacket and toting a pizza or KFC pack of chicken legs. Today it is impossible to travel to most any city in the Asian region without coming into (hopefully not physical) contact with the gig economy, zero-hours, flexible workers. They are also visible in London, Paris, Tokyo and New York.

These Expendables are modern-day coolies: not quite slaves but not quite free either.

The so-called 'coolie' first emerged in the early 19th century, with streams of migrant labour from Asia travelling to the Americas and European colonies seeking work, thereby filling the gap left by the end of slavery. These men and women built the railroads, picked the cotton on plantations, sweated in mines and ensured the docks were kept clear of cargo. They cut, carried, carved and cultivated.[1]

Credit Line: Cartoons drawn by Advanced Standard Group Co., Ltd.

What they didn't do is earn a decent living working in a Totally Inclusive Community.

And nor do those now working for the ubiquitous delivery companies.

Recognising that at time of writing the UK's Supreme Court has ruled that Uber drivers must be treated as workers rather than self-employed, and therefore entitled to minimum pay, pensions and holiday pay, the world of the gig economy remains very much the world of the 21st century Expendable worker: poor, transient, stressful, insecure and most definitely not a community of belonging.

I do not intend to examine the ethical issues surrounding the employment conditions of the new global Expendable worker. I merely draw attention to the fact that there are ethical issues to be examined as well as issues of inclusivity and diversity.

Of course, an obvious riposte is to claim that such low-quality jobs are available to anyone – therefore being inclusive and diverse by both definition and design.

My response? Well, if the only organisations offering 'inclusivity and diversity' are those at the bottom of the employment ladder then that is a very sad state of affairs and an indictment of organisational and societal progress. Moreover, as is examined in Chapter 4, there is a lot more to being a Totally Inclusive Community than simply offering all applicants, regardless of their identity mix, low-paid, insecure, exploitative employment.

The Expendable worker symbolises, as it always has done, exploitation. The harsh and unethical working conditions are permitted only because a society has decided it benefits from millions of workers being thus employed and therefore, at some minimum level, socially and economically contributing.

What Total Inclusivity offers is something rather different: a higher aspiration for workers, bosses, stakeholders and all organisations that consider themselves to be positive contributing members to the wholesome and sustainable fabric of society.

Total Inclusivity is offered not simply as the right of individuals to feel they are valued and worthy of society but for the organisations who employ them to do so from the standard of community, not from the baseline of 'freelancing', which in reality translates as the 'employing' organisation claiming to have no responsibility over those people whose task it is to ensure the company stays in profit.

It should not be necessary to make the point that socially responsible organisations must have a higher aspiration than the bottom line, but unfortunately the reality requires such a point to be made and consistently.

And I write this not as a Marxist ideologue with some extreme political agenda but as a sociologist, educator and businessman who maintains that organisations cannot claim to be outside of society but must operate always as essential parts of that which holds society together. Because organisations *are* an essential part of that which holds society together.

However, is it unrealistic to expect an Expendable working in the 21st-century gig economy on a zero-hours contract to be investing anything of their self in their job, their organisation, especially a multi-billion-dollar corporation claiming to have no responsibility towards them other than to ensure they receive their allotted percentage of every delivery fee?

Surely, if you are a Expendable then you are not belonging, you are merely turning up – correct?

Yes, you are just turning up, and it would be unrealistic to expect it to be otherwise.

So where does that leave the Expendable worker? It leaves them devoid of any felt attachment to their work. Not for them even the barest flicker of job association other than when they happen to meet up with other helmeted and jacket-branded Expendables similarly waiting outside fast-food restaurants or shopping malls for their product to deliver.

Does it have to be like that? Is that the extent of the connection between organisation and worker? No. It can be better, more secure, more fulfilling and certainly more rewarding, both existentially and materially.

The recent UK Supreme Court has ruled on the legalities of ensuring fair material rewards.

It is now for the organisations to act on the ethics of ensuring a Totally Inclusive Community.

Who knows, engendering feelings of belonging within employees might even filter through to the bottom line.

The Googlers

If the Expendable is one extremely negative example of 21st-century organisational life (we could include the internship as another, plus the ridiculously long working hours demanded by some investment banks and law firms), then where are the exemplars of a more inclusive, healthy and balanced organisational workplace?

As the title to this section suggests, one company persistently at the top of 'best companies to work for' lists is Google. In 2020, and for the fourth consecutive year, Google was named the best company to work for by *Fortune* magazine. This book is not the place to advertise the benefits of working for Google, as the company is well able to do that for itself, but what I will do is draw attention to what employees of the 'best companies to work for' say about such companies based on employee reviews (Liu, 2019; Greatplacetowork.com, 2019).

"They truly care about empowering employees and improving the entire community in which we are involved."

"A lot of companies claim to be diverse and support equality, but I have never seen them do anything beyond write about it. Here at *** we live it every single day."

"The culture here is focused on what is doing right by our clients, the firm and associates. Knowing that the most important thing to do is the RIGHT and ethical choice, makes me feel good about my work here."

"This is a place that truly embraces team members as individuals. You don't have to cover your tattoos, you can wear your hair how you want, your race and sexuality have no bearing on your success. I can bring my whole self to work every day."

"I love the fact that we are diverse, inclusive, and progressive and I'm proud of the ways we support our community. I've made friends here who are more like family."

"There is an emphasis based on inclusion that just isn't lip service."

"We have a human-centric approach that stays tight to our core values which truly differentiates us from our competitors. People feel empowered to be their best selves."

"I can truly be myself here. It feels like you're coming to work with a bunch of friends every day!"

"This company instils an environment that encourages all professionals to bring their authentic self to work, and one that supports the integration of work and personal life."

"There is inclusion and respect for individuals and the unique talent they bring to the company. This company is not a 'boys club' [we] work to provide opportunities to all regardless of gender or race."

Not surprisingly, Google employees appreciate the very same values: 'the premium Google places on employees happiness . . . Google also encourages its employees to become teachers and coach one another to help build a more creative, satisfied and intimate community of employees.

(Gillet, 2016)

This selection of comments (all from different companies) is in the public domain and linked to specific companies. I am not confirming that these companies, or indeed Google, are Totally Inclusive. They may be or they may not; I have no qualitative or quantitative evidence to prove the case either way. What I am claiming is that any examination of positive employee comments, as per the selection, points to several consistent themes:

1   Caring, compassionate, empathetic and sincere
2   Strong and consistently reinforced ethical values
3   Inclusive, diverse and encouraging 'authentic selves'

4   Togetherness, support, belonging and strong feelings of association
5   A good work–life balance
6   Working in and for a community

This is how *employees themselves* define a 'good company to work for'. They don't say they want a Totally Inclusive Community, but the characteristics which define a Totally Inclusive Community are what stand out as being most desirable.

It doesn't take a leap of faith to assume that employees of these companies are not simply turning up for work, but committed to their jobs. They feel they belong.

The intelligent and sensitively led organisation does not need fancily worded mission statements, logos and social media marketing to engender 'belonging' in its employees. All it needs is to treat individuals with respect and ensure Total Inclusivity is the dominant value system throughout the operation.

In other words, all such organisations need do is tap into the innate desire to belong which most every employee (both Expendable and Googler) has within them.

People want to belong. They need to belong. We humans have a deep and persistent existential desire to be part of something, to associate, to be in a place which values our sense of self, our unique identity mix. We want to be with others who validate us and who we validate in return. What we don't want is to be isolated, marginalised, discriminated against or otherwise rendered vulnerable and threatened. Organisations led by those who either do not understand this fundamental human trait or choose to disregard it are culpable in diminishing their employees to little more than a functioning Expendable.

Belonging is not about exploitation, either materially or emotionally. Belonging can only occur where the individual's unique identity and sense of self are embraced, nurtured and respected.

Creating such a culture requires a particular leadership style, and this I explore in Chapter 11. But for the moment the key message is that there is no one dominant and authoritarian leader in communities. Everyone participates and contributes on a shared and equitable basis.

DEGREES OF SEPARATION

I am not suggesting you should love your organisation in order to get the most out of your work. Indeed, if you are minded to spread your love around then best reserve it for living beings, including humans, not faceless organisations. But I am suggesting that commitment to your work role, to your responsibilities can be healthy and beneficial so long as you keep it in balance.

Whether you are only turning up for work or have a deep sense of belonging to the organisation/community that pays you is simply a matter of degrees of separation.

The mistake that many unaware leaders make is to equate effort and commitment with physical presence. The worst examples of this occur where there is a strong and seductive culture of presenteeism.

The term 'presenteeism' is usually defined as 'turning up to work while sick' (Gillet, 2016). However, for the purposes of Total Inclusivity define presenteeism rather more broadly, as:

> Consistently attending at work beyond one's contractual obligations because job insecurity and the dominant work culture demands it.

As we have seen with the Googler and the comments of highly satis-fied employees, there is a symbiotic relationship between inclusivity and work–life balance. This occurs through the psychological contract that exists in all relationships, including between employee and employer.

> The invisible or implicit set of expectations that employees have of their organizations and that their organizations have of them but are not laid down in the formal contract of employment.
> (Knights and Willmott, 2007, p. 543)

The Totally Inclusive work community will not demand its employees work unreasonable and unhealthy hours, and it will recognise the value in employees having good physical and mental health; strong, mutually sup-portive public/private selves; and in ensuring loyalty, flexibility and trust arise through the quality of the community culture and working climate, not through written directives.

To demonstrate this as a working model for readers to follow and relate to, I offer the Five Degrees of Separation as follows:

1 My job and the organisation I work for are fully and healthily integrated into and supportive of all other aspects of my life and enable my authentic self to flourish.

2 I love my job but despair of the organisation. So long as I can work with my immediate teammates, then I am happy.
3 My work provides me with the necessary material benefits to ensure my lifestyle is comfortable but nothing more. I feel no emotional connection to my job or the organisation.
4 I turn up for work because I have to. I have no investment in this job or in the organisation.
5 I hate my job and I hate the organisation. I actively resist getting involved and distance myself from work as much as possible.

Most readers will be able to identify where they currently are on that spectrum, and most will have experienced being on the different levels during their careers.

Presenteeism is one example of how employees can appear committed but actually are not. 'Resisting through distancing' is another – where the employee makes all the right noises about being committed, but in reality, they distance themselves from work and from their responsibilities, ensuring only that they exhibit the minimum requirements of their contractual obligations.

Indeed, employee resistance is an interesting area of study within leadership and organisations (Clegg et al., 2005), revealing the multiple ways in which employees can appear committed, obedient and indeed dependent on the continuing benevolence of their employer while actively working to subvert the organisation's objectives.

The question that arises, however, is whether these intransigent employees joined the organisation with the deliberate attempt at corporate sabotage – a bit like members of a terrorist group applying to work in a nuclear power facility – or whether they became 'terrorists' through their experiences of working in the organisation.

Notwithstanding that there may well be subversive groups strategically united in destroying the 'evil capitalist empire' and its organisations, for the most part this seems unlikely or at least is not the focus of this book. Much more likely is that organisations create resisters and subversives, not that people apply for jobs simply in order to cause their boss sleepless nights of worry.

As is stressed in this chapter, most employees don't apply for work in order to undermine or destroy their employer. They apply for jobs because (1) they need the material benefits which accrue and (2) they desire the existential opportunity to invest their sense of self and emotional well-being in something bigger than themselves – a community.

The Totally Inclusive Community pays as much attention to motivation No. 2 as it does to motivation No. 1.

WHAT DO YOU EXPECT?

Much has been written about the expectations of Generation Z and millennials, and for the most part I would concur with the findings, previously referred to in Chapter 2.

There is little doubt that a new, better educated, more globalised and more socially aware generation is now in work and applying to organisations around the world. Indeed, this is a global phenomenon, not confined to Californian tech companies, multinational hotel companies or corporate consultancy companies. Go to Taiwan, Mexico City, Shenzhen or Bangkok, and you'll see the same expectations of a more inclusive approach to work and employment being visibly expressed by younger employees as you'll see in New York, London or Berlin.

Taking the long view, what might be described here is a new and vivid politicisation of identity meanings within young people is not a movement, it is not even always coherent, but it is certainly alive, and it is incredibly vocal. I am a baby boomer, and I've not witnessed anything similar in more than seven decades, not even during the supposedly 'revolutionary' sixties.

In the final reckoning, what both baby boomers like myself and millennials expect is identical: to be valued and appreciated not just for the job they do but also for who they are. If we are learning one lesson from this current time of global turbulence it is that the personal is political, and the personal is a lot more multiple than our ancestors ever appreciated.

Total Inclusivity allows for that appreciation of diversity within the organisation/community and across society.

It is not for any organisation to try and divide its employees (or society) into Us and Them. History has shown that humans are only too ready and able to do that for themselves. Organisations, in becoming communities of belonging, offer unity and belonging, albeit with a very reasonable expectation that if you are accepted into that community then you contribute accordingly.

The question as to what you expect as an employee (of whatever professional status) is for you to decide, though if it didn't include acceptance of who you are as a person, an individual, then I'd be very surprised indeed.

Recognising that organisations may well have a culture (or cultures), what they don't have is identities or minds. In which case we cannot expect organisations to think and act as human beings. But then, that is why they have humans who are leaders and members of senior management teams.

If you are a leader who is happy for your employees to simply turn up and demonstrate no involvement with their job beyond that, then you are going to be 'employing' an awful lot of people who are physically attending at work but emotionally distancing. If, on the other hand, you are a leader who has a vision for their organisation beyond simply exploiting the 'human resource' for as much profit as possible, then you must embrace Total Inclusivity.

All your community members (from baby boomers to Generation Z) are entitled to expect nothing less.

CHAPTER 3: REFLECTIONS, GUIDANCE AND COMMITMENTS

Reflection Exercise: 'What makes me feel like I belong?' What are you seeking from an organisation/community which offers you a job? How important is belonging to you when it comes to paid employment?

Guidance for Implementation: How to recognise where you can and can't find belonging (and why) and how to look in the right places to find a sense of belonging. Start by doing the exercise 'degrees of separation' in this chapter and which, if any, organisations you've worked for have managed to offer you the No. 1 slot. Make a list of the strengths and weaknesses of your current organisation in terms of its ability to engender a feeling of belonging rather than simply you just being there – turning up.

Commitment: To reappraise your relationship to your work, your organisation, and identify areas where you'd like to see it improve and become healthier. Make a commitment to helping the organisation improve.

NOTE
1 https://en.wikipedia.org/wiki/Coolie.

Four

Having established the importance of working for a community rather than an organisation, the next question is which are you currently working for – community or organisation? In this chapter I identify in more detail the fundamental differences between the two workplaces and how these get played out in practices, values and culture.

One vivid way to see these differences articulated is in Figure 4.1, which shows the key markers on the journey from discriminatory organisation to Totally Inclusive Community (from Aow et al., 2022; see also Whitehead and O'Connor, 2022).

What the aspiring Totally Inclusive organisation is working towards is a community culture, and this is distinguishable both in its systems and in the ways in which individuals relate to each other. Systems and behaviour combine to create culture. And cultures, in turn, create an organisational climate.

Organisations quickly generate their own 'feel', and one can instinctively pick it up when walking through the entrance, and that feel increases the more you encounter the organisational atmosphere or climate. No matter what the mission statement on the wall may pronounce, what you feel can be very different. What you are sensing when you walk into a workplace is whether you are entering an organisation or you are entering a community. One can detect the difference almost immediately. It is an intangible sense but can be very powerful. But how to create a positive workplace climate?

As is explored in this chapter, organisational members can make it real by ensuring communality, association, compassion, belonging, trust and respect. All of which become generated by Total Inclusivity, with no individual left behind, marginalised or unaccepted.

DOI: 10.4324/9781003244073-4

DISCRIMINATORY ==> REFLECTIVE ==> TRANSFORMATIVE ==> TOTALLY
INCLUSIVE

*Perpetuating Deliberate and/or Unreflective Privilege ==> Recognising and Reflecting on Privilege ==>
Reacting and Rebuilding towards Inclusivity ==>Climate Totally Inclusive*

Figure 4.1 The Stages of Development
Credit Line: from Aow et al. (2022)

Which all sounds like a fine an honourable objective for any organisation to work towards, but is it measurable? How can an organisation and
its members determine whether the Total Inclusivity principles are being
followed and if an organisation is well behind the inclusivity objective or
heading towards it?

There are two approaches, both valid. One is to undertake a formal
assessment or audit. This approach is more objective and works well
if you have set criteria to measure against. The second approach is
reflective, whereby you consider your feelings towards your job, workplace culture, sense of belonging – this approach is subjective and
engages the emotions. In this chapter, I offer ways in which to engage
both approaches.

For the objective approach, a Totally Inclusive assessment (or more
formalised audit) can be undertaken. And the tool to enable such is
provided with our Total Inclusivity Assessment Continuum (TIAC).[1]

HOW TO USE THE TIAC TOOL

If you are very familiar with your organisation, then you can probably
hazard a guess where it is currently placed on the following six stages:

1 **Actively Discriminatory** – a failing organisation
2 **Tokenistic** – a rhetorically correct organisation
3 **Reflectively Unsettled** – a contradictory organisation
4 **Tentative** – learning to become a community
5 **Rebuilding** – transformative and advancing
6 **Totally Inclusive** – an equitable and just organisation

While your sense and feel for the organisation is valid and important,
the TIAC tool also easily identifies the criteria that combine to constitute

where an organisation is placed on the continuum (or journey) toward becoming a Totally Inclusive Community.

One word of warning, however, and that is larger (global) organisations may well have different divisions or operations which themselves are at different stages, depending, for example on country, region and local leadership. If that is the case, then you can only really undertake the assessment based on your firsthand knowledge. You cannot be sure where other divisions or operations are on the continuum.

The advice to leaders of corporations, companies with many locations and potential work cultures is to undertake a Totally Inclusive workplace assessment in each operation and have the same individuals do this assessment.

While you are checklisting your organisation against the criteria listed in what follows, keep asking yourself a key question – 'Do I feel I belong?' That subjective assessment is the only one which really matters for the individual. If you answer that question positively, then the second question is 'How am I encouraging others to feel they belong too?'

THE TOTALLY INCLUSIVE ASSESSMENT CONTINUUM

THE SIX STAGES

1   Actively Discriminatory (A Failing Organisation)
   - Intentionally and publicly excludes or segregates by race, ethnicity, gender, sexual orientation, class, disability, age, language and religion. This includes discriminations over marital status, pregnancy, health needs.
   - Intentionally and publicly enforces a monocultural, 'masculinist' (Chapter 8) status quo throughout institution.
   - Institutionalisation of racism, sexism and homophobia includes formal policies, practices and decision-making on all levels.
   - Openly maintains and encourages a white-, male-, heterosexual-dominated leadership.
   - Employment and recruitment systems and policies designed to identify 'others' as undesirable.
   - Views privilege as entitlement and seeks to substantiate it in all policies and practices.
   - Actively resisting liberalisation and progressive attitudes.

- Toxic work environment prevails; there is a culture of fear and a lack of accountability, especially of the leaders.
- Leadership actively resistant to LGBTQ+ identities at all levels of the organisation.
- Leadership and management teams actively support each other both covertly and overtly in maintaining a discriminatory climate.
- Employees treated as 'resources' to be exploited to maximise 'efficiency' and profit.
- Employees have no opportunity to participate in the decision-making process.
- Employees controlled by performative measures, reinforced by unbalanced appraisals and bullying tactics.
- Sexual harassment and other forms of gender violence are commonplace across the institution and embedded in the masculinist, male-dominated, managerialist culture.
- Staff at all levels may experience bullying and intimidation.
- Hierarchical, top-down model of leadership and management, with lower levels having minimum input and working to strictly regimented systems and imposed targets while being made fully accountable for success or failure.
- No professional development beyond that strictly controlled by the organisational leaders.

Summary: This organisation is not only making no attempt to become inclusive, it may well relish being discriminatory and hierarchical in character. The only identity that can thrive in such a culture is white, male and explicitly heterosexual. It is a 'boy's own' culture (Kerfoot and Whitehead, 1998) in which a masculinist ideology dominates, not a workplace where 'others' are welcome, other than as resources to be used and exploited. Indeed, 'exploitative' is the best word to describe this type of organisation. The overall climate is oppressive, and bullying is common and may well be a sanctioned method of control over employees. All new hires will quickly find they must accommodate and assimilate into the dominant culture (emulating or being accepting of the discriminatory behaviour and language) or leave. In short, not a nice place to work and dangerous with it.

Next Steps: It will probably require a major overhaul of the senior management before the organisation can begin to make any progress toward Total Inclusivity. Merely introducing one or two professional development and awareness-raising sessions on, for example, racism and sexism at work won't cut it. Nor can the required change come from only one or two employee TI Advocates – individuals who demonstrate a clear commitment to TI and have the skills and knowledge to initiate it in the organisation – though that is how it will probably need to start. High-profile social media complaints from previous/existing staff and customers can get the ball rolling, though ultimately, the organisational bosses will need to undergo a major re-evaluation of their attitudes, practices, values and leadership skills.

Examples of next-step initiatives include (from Aow et al., 2022):

- Implicit bias training that includes exploration of openly aggressive and microaggressive behaviours that marginalise cross sections of the organisation's population.
- Analyse current policies using a DEIJ lens and identify all terms and concepts requiring shared understanding.
- Begin having open conversations across the workplace about DEIJ and which involve all staff and students.
- Train the leaders to understand the implications of their power and behaviour (Bishop, 2021).
- Ensure that open conversations are protected spaces for individuals to share their experiences of, for example, bullying, sexual harassment, sexual violence, intimidation and aggression.
- Begin to research the workplace culture – and feed back findings and recommendations to all leaders and employees.
- Leadership to acknowledge past DEIJ failings and publicly declare responsibility for changing the organisational culture towards TI.
- Begin identifying TI Advocates from within the staff and provide them with support and training.
- Begin to establish a Total Inclusivity team, which is given power and resources to raise corporate awareness and undergo and ultimately deliver professional development.

2   Tokenistic (A Rhetorically Correct Organisation)

- Tolerant of a limited number of 'token' Black, Asian, minority ethnic people, LGBTQ+ people, women, but not in positions of authority or power.
- Uses progressive rhetoric in public presentation of organisation, but systems and culture remain unchanged and discriminatory.

- Uses notion of 'meritocracy' to justify filtering and excluding, thereby ensuring continuation of existing power groups (e.g. white men).
- Decision-making processes and recruitment practices remain under the control of an unrepresentative and self-sustaining cohort.
- Has adopted anti-discriminatory policies due to legal requirements to do so.
- Leadership covertly discourages discussion of diversity and inclusivity (e.g. prohibits use of terms such as 'racist', 'sexist', 'feminist', 'white privilege').
- Leadership overtly resists liberalising measures by prohibiting professional development in diversity and inclusivity on the grounds of cost and priority.
- Continues to intentionally maintain white/male power and privilege through its formal policies, practices and decision-making on all levels of institutional life.
- Key individuals declare, 'We don't have a problem'.
- Monocultural norms, policies and procedures of dominant culture viewed as the 'right way' and 'business as usual'.
- Engages issues of diversity and social justice only on 'club' members' terms and within their comfort zone.
- Claims 'stakeholders don't want inclusivity and diversity' and that any discrimination originates from attempting to meet the (prejudiced) requirements and expectations of paying clients.
- Professional development for staff in areas of inclusivity and diversity are actively discouraged, and PD remains unreflective, monocultural, exclusionary and orientated towards biological determinism.
- Key actors within the organisation deny terms such as 'white privilege' and 'unconscious bias'.
- Little or no attempt to relate to identities, politics and concerns of staff.
- Attempts to shut down staff complaints of discrimination, either past or present.
- Leadership adopts an instrumental approach to diversity and inclusivity.
- Operational (management and leadership) systems and culture mirror those of the 'discriminatory' level, albeit with more effort to appear inclusive and democratic.

Summary:While continuing to adopt the male club culture of the overtly discriminatory organisation, this tokenistic organisation has moved to present itself as 'inclusive' to its market, largely for reasons of image. Many organisations operate in this style, especially now that more DEIJ public scrutiny is directed towards organisations and their leaders. The leadership style will be unreflective and weak in emotional intelligence. The 'feel' of the organisation climate will be cold if not oppressive. One can consider this stage as emergent towards Total Inclusivity, but only if there is a subsequent awakening by the leaders. Otherwise, the work culture will remain fundamentally discriminatory, indeed dangerous for some staff, with only the appearance of inclusivity and largely for media / public image reasons. This is a very tempting stage for discriminatory organisations to get stuck in, and it requires determined leadership and powerful TI teams to move it forward.

Next Steps: Usually only a change of senior leadership will move the tokenistic organisation along the path to Total Inclusivity. The level of resistance is deep while also being unrecognised by those doing the resisting. So the best policy is a TI audit. Yes, this will be a brutal experience for the leaders especially, and it may trigger even more resistance, but staying silent is not an option. Who will instigate the TI assessment? Ideally, the owners — if they recognise the risks to allowing the organisation to continue being discriminatory in practice if not in image. TI Advocates again will play a role and need to be brave enough to be vocal when required, not silent.

Examples of next-step initiatives include (from Aow et al., 2022):

- Create opportunities for interactive participation in which voices are valued in decision-making.
- Facilitate intercultural understanding workshops that shift understanding from token surface level actions to a deeper understanding of how individuals attend to difference.
- Create up-to-date and inclusive policies collaboratively with all stakeholders.
- Seek the help of DEIJ experts who can expand thinking and help inform how to be a more effective ally.
- Engage in deep reflection and actions that have been co-constructed with various stakeholders.
- Ensure there is a strong and open feedback loop from the TI Advocates and other TI supporters to the organisational leadership and that public commitments are made by leaders to further progress and address issues.
- Begin strategic planning for TI implementation across the organisation within agreed time frames.

- Ensure there are sanctions imposed on individuals who persist with toxic workplace behaviour.
- Hold all organisational members responsible for implementing and supporting TI as strategy and practice.

3   Reflectively Unsettled (A Contradictory Organisation)

- Makes official policy pronouncements regarding multicultural, sexual, gender diversity.
- Sees itself as an inclusive institution with open doors to Black, Asian and minority ethnic people, LGBTQ+, women.
- Carries out intentional inclusiveness efforts, e.g. diversity hiring on committees and at middle-management level.
- Expanding view of diversity includes other socially oppressed groups, especially LGBTQ+.
- A minority of staff and leaders begin their own reflective journey towards total inclusivity, both personally and professionally.
- A minority of staff and leaders begin to recognise their own privilege and how this has fed into a sense of entitlement.
- Women leaders emerge in the organisation but are pressured to adopt masculinist styles of leadership.
- The Black, Asian and minority ethnic people and women leaders experience schizogenic identity – e.g. meeting dominant contra-cultural expectations while trying to maintain an authentic self.
- Black, Asian and minority ethnic people and LGBTQ+ staff experience toleration rather than acceptance.
- Black, Asian and minority ethnic people and LGBTQ+ staff experience bullying and discrimination.
- Open dissent towards the organisational leadership is actively discouraged and 'those who make waves' marginalised.
- Little or no contextual change in culture, policies, and decision making.
- The majority of staff remain relatively unaware of continuing patterns of privilege, paternalism and control.
- Token placements in staff positions must assimilate into organisational culture – no attempt to encourage 'authentic selves' at work.
- Gender-based violence and harassment remain a problem but are hidden behind the culture of male privilege and managerialism.
- Diversity and inclusivity training is limited and restricted to overcoming 'unconscious bias'.

- Key organisational actors continue to resist progressive change but do so covertly.
- Organisational leadership attempts to retain control and overall direction of the progression towards full inclusivity and not fully recognise diverse views and experiences.
- Staff diversity and inclusivity forums are allowed to exist but remain separate from the primary workplace processes and therefore have little influence on the organisational climate.
- Leaders may genuinely believe the organisation is totally inclusive but have failed to audit the reality of this and have failed to undergo training in order to recognise the contradictions and tensions inherent in the organisation.
- Leaders accept the need for inclusivity but are reluctant to engage in this process personally, certainly if it results in what they see as a diminution of their power and authority.
- Employees sense the contradictions between (inclusive) rhetoric and (exclusive) reality but may well accept the organisational leadership is attempting to improve.

Summary: The hallmark of this stage is disruption, which means to get through it the organisation must be prepared to face its weaknesses. The tension arises because employees (and maybe some leaders) really want to bring about positive change but are up against the historic work culture and pockets of strong resistance within the organisation at all levels. Overcoming this resistance isn't easy and will require determined and committed leaders and advocates. Part of the problem is simply ignorance about Total Inclusivity — and this can be overcome by suitable professional development and training, especially of the leaders. The other key problem is that some identities (e.g. male, white, straight) will recognise they won't necessarily be beneficiaries of the changes in climate and culture which are starting to bubble under the surface. This is why no organisation can get through this stage on its own. It needs help, and no matter what resistances are expressed (especially by those who feel threatened by the process), the push towards a Totally Inclusive Community must begin here.

Next Steps: The organisation is slowly starting to move in the right direction, but it still needs focus and energy behind it. This is the point at which the TI Advocates and teams really start to matter. So the most effective policy initiative is to further empower the group of TI Advocates from within the staff and give them authority and resources to introduce regular awareness-raising sessions from leadership through to part-time support staff. It will be rough at times, but don't waver and make sure the TI Advocates are supported and protected. These TI Advocates should then lead the second-most-important initiative, which is to undertake regular internal research into employee and leadership attitudes, understandings and DEIJ values. These research findings are discussed openly at meetings with action points agreed.

Examples of next-step initiatives include (from Aow et al., 2022):

- Commitment from all senior post-holders to actively engage in learning about patterns of privilege, paternalism, protectionism and control and how to be culturally proficient and equity focused.
- Strategic implementation which is committed to sustainable development over time and reinforced by DEIJ training and awareness across the organisation.
- Establishing ways to measure growth over time and holding all stakeholders to account for planned initiatives.
- Greater transparency and democratic decision-making in which reasons for decisions provide legitimacy; the process of decision making is transparent and visible to all. People who are impacted by decisions have opportunities for participation and play a role in the process.
- Work to overcome resistance, overt or covert, by making it clear that a totally inclusive, equitable and just organisation is now inevitable and won't be compromised. Examples of tools that can be used to achieve clarity include the organisation's mission, guiding statements, strategic plan of actions, policies, community agreements, code of ethics, safeguarding policies and more.
- Hold all organisational members to account for behaviours and actions that are not aligned with Totally Inclusive beliefs and values.
- Introduce DEIJ achievements into staff appraisals/assessments and promotion systems so that all employees are fully aware that their career pathways within the organisation must now align with TI.
- Undertake DEIJ research across the organisation and ensure the findings are made transparent to all stakeholders, with action duly taken.
- Set a realistic and achievement time frame for moving towards TI across the organisation and within different departments. This strategy needs to be overseen by the directors and TI Advocates.

Be open and transparent about the problems and the hurdles to be overcome.

- Ensure that all staff have undergone TI training and awareness raising, and have as many of these sessions as possible led by corporate leaders who have themselves trained in TI.
- Check that 'uncivil' behaviour within the organisation is not being tolerated. Leaders set the tone for behaviour at work.

4   Tentative (Learning to Become a Community)

- Leadership have begun to strategise diversity and inclusivity into the training, professional development, systems, planning and recruitment processes.
- Growing understanding of racism, homophobia, sexism, masculinism, ableism, classism as barriers to effective diversity.
- Develops analysis of systemic racism and all forms of discrimination.
- Sponsors programs of diversity and inclusivity training
- New consciousness of institutionalised white power, privilege, entitlement.
- Develops intentional identity as a totally inclusive institution.
- Begins to develop accountability to oppressed communities, socially/economically/racially disenfranchised communities.
- Increasing commitment to dismantle racism and eliminate inherent white advantage.
- Actively recruits and promotes members of groups which have been historically denied access and opportunity.
- Identifies Totally Inclusive Advocates within the organisation and who work with a Totally Inclusive Committee containing staff, management, administration representatives.
- Institutional structures and culture that maintain white (male) power and privilege still intact and relatively untouched, with evidence of continued resistance by some staff at different levels of the organisation.
- Employees may still experience bullying, racism, discrimination, gender-based violence and harassment.
- Workplace and management culture remains performative and target driven, with outcomes privileged over processes.
- Senior management teams now starting to work towards Total Inclusivity and with genuine intention but also having to counter covert negativity, ignorance and resistance at different levels.

Summary: *This is a stage all organisations need to go through if they are to become Totally Inclusive. But it is not easy. It requires vision, strategy, sensitivity and determination, especially from the senior managers. Employees can, however, do much to contribute to the emerging positive organisational climate, not least by voicing their opinions, encouraging a culture of empathy among staff and working to ensure their authentic selves are heard. The gap between what leaders perceive is going on in their organisation and the reality for the typical employee can still be quite large, though it is starting to become bridgeable. Often, the organisation will need outside help to get it through this important transitional stage. So long as the leaders remain open-minded and are prepared to be guided by experts, then the organisation will feel a powerful upward turn in its culture as the sense of community and belonging starts to emerge at all levels. The whole organisation will need to re-evaluate its value system and work culture and subject it to critical but transparent scrutiny.*

Next Steps: Co-opt an experienced TI Advocate onto the senior management team (SMT) and/or board of directors as an advisor. This person need not have voting rights, but they act as and represent, the 'collective conscience' of the organisation in respect of Total Inclusivity. Ensure this person is given full support and resources as necessary. If there is already a strong and vibrant TI Advocate group operating effectively in the organisation, then it is a good idea to regularly rotate the person attending SMT meetings. This ensures a good free flow of ideas and suggestions to and from SMT. At the same time, the responsibility for ensuring the organisation moves towards a TI community rests with the SMT and Directors. Continue to undertake regular internal Total Inclusivity audits and research and disseminate findings throughout the organisation.

Examples of next-step initiatives include (from Aow et al., 2022):

- Differentiated professional learning opportunities across the organisation related to DEIJ impact on work culture, systems and practices.
- Require all stakeholders, students and staff to commit to the organisation's TI policy and practices.
- Ensuring that there are safeguarding measures for all stakeholders.
- Coaching, mentoring, sponsoring and supporting diverse advocates for DEIJ initiatives.
- Identify how to measure impact in specific areas, working out the best method for data collection and establishing baseline measures to track growth.

- Continuously engage in professional inquiry to seek understanding and to co-construct equitable practices.
- Engage in systems and design thinking to spark new ideas and to stimulate disruption where needed.
- Ensure there now is a critical mass of DEIJ/TI-aware leaders at various levels of the organisation.

5 Rebuilding (Transformative and Advancing)
- Commits to process of intentional institutional restructuring, based upon Total Inclusivity values, ethics, aims and objectives.
- Audits and restructures all aspects of institutional life to ensure full participation of Black, Asian and minority ethnic people, LGBTQ+, women and different social and economic groups, including their worldviews, cultures and lifestyles.
- Strategically and openly pursuing a vision of an institution and wider community that has overcome systemic racism and all other forms of oppression.
- Identifies where masculinism continues to linger in the institution and addresses it.
- Implements structures, policies and practices with inclusive decision-making and other forms of power sharing on all levels of the institution's life and work.
- Commits to struggle to dismantle racism, discrimination, prejudice in the wider community and builds clear lines of accountability to all oppressed communities.
- Total Inclusive intercultural diversity becomes an institutionalised asset which is understood, accepted, recognised and practiced by all staff and managers.
- Redefines and rebuilds all relationships and activities in society based on anti-racist, Totally Inclusive commitments.
- Professional development and training in Total Inclusivity is strategic, progressive, and led by trained internal Advocates.
- Professional development and learning processes support the voices of the community and all its members.
- Organisational leadership is committed and engaged in creating a Totally Inclusive Community, and this agenda is supported and understood by all staff.

Summary: By the time any organisation reaches this stage, it will have a culture and work climate which has matured beyond all recognition compared to where it was in the past. The sense of community is tangible, and the momentum is only in one direction – towards Total Inclusivity. This can be an exciting time to work in an organisation – there will be a lot of positive energy around, a feeling of progress and togetherness, and any staff who previously worked in less advanced organisations will appreciate having their voices heard and the feeling of commitment this generates for them. There may still be some pockets of resistance, and the leaders will have to take care to ensure progress is maintained, especially by careful hiring processes and ongoing training and development. But overall, there are fewer barriers to stopping the organisation moving to the final stage, a Totally Inclusive Community.

Next Steps: Your organisation has come a long way and made excellent progress, but you cannot take that progress for granted. You need to ensure you are not becoming complacent and thereby losing energy and vision. Power must now be more clearly devolved throughout the organisation and no longer coalescing at the top. A good way to avoid future miring (in which TI initiatives get bogged down by unreflective leaders) is to introduce leadership succession planning (see Lee, 2021, for discussion). If you can home-grow your leaders from within the community the whole operation is much more likely to become fully TI much more quickly.

Examples of actionable next steps include (from Aow et al., 2022):

- Community visioning to build shared understandings of the DEIJ agenda and what a liberated organisation looks like, including clear definitions of terms, roles and responsibilities.
- Identifying where discrimination continues and addressing it as an institution.
- Modelling, valuing and highlighting behaviour and practices that provide learning stories for growth and affirmation that a liberated state is achievable.
- Professional learning opportunities led by trained internal Advocates who can contribute to sustaining learning over time in the organisation.
- Continuing to actively reach out to all stakeholders and valuing diverse voices and their contributions to decision-making processes.
- Continuing to advocate for and develop new initiatives to meet the needs of marginalised identities.
- Continuing to hold individuals to account for their behaviours and the institution to account for employees' sense of belonging and success.

6 Totally Inclusive Community (An equitable and just organisation)

- Institution's life and culture reflects full participation and shared power with diverse racial, sexual, gender, cultural and economic groups fully participating and represented equitably.
- Leadership and staff work in harmony in ensuring a Totally Inclusive mission, structure, constituency, policies and practices.
- Members across all identity groups are full participants in decisions that shape the institution and inclusion of diverse cultures, lifestyles and interest.
- A sense of restored community and mutual caring.
- Allies with others in combating all forms of social oppression.
- Actively works in larger communities (regional, national, global) to eliminate all forms of oppression and to create intercultural organisations.
- Ensures Totally Inclusive agenda, principles and values are embedded in the community and regularly monitored for effectiveness.
- The community has confidently and openly identified its present and future as a Totally Inclusive organisation and regularly imparts this reality to all stakeholders.
- Community undertakes regular Totally Inclusive audits to ensure all aspects of the community maintain alignment with these aims.
- The leadership and staff are fully familiar with Total Inclusivity and ensure this value permeates and informs all practices and behaviours.
- Community climate ensures the well-being and safety of all, regardless of sexual, racial, class, ethnic, gender identity.
- Leaders and staff recognise and support intersectionalist understandings, values and principles.
- Where appropriate, professional development actively promotes understanding of intersectional identity as a means of appreciating and valuing diversity.
- The community recognises and accepts that diversity is a fact, a right and an important resource.
- The pursuit of Total Inclusivity takes precedence over all other aspects of the operation and defines the mission.
- A Totally Inclusive Community has been established which is therefore able to act as a model for other organisations to follow.

- The physical and mental well-being of all Community members is held paramount, and this includes ensuring a healthy work–life balance and protection of employment rights (e.g. paternity and maternity rights).
- Employees and work teams develop their own project and work objectives with support and guidance from leaders.

Summary: If you are working in a Totally Inclusive Community, then you won't need this assessment device to confirm it. You will know for yourself. It will be evident in the systems, vision and especially in the climate. As an employee you won't feel like an employee; you'll feel like an equal part of a thriving enterprise, where humanistic values prevail and take priority over profit. There will be no need to discuss efficiency, because a Totally Inclusive Community is, by definition, operating at maximum. How? Through having enabled and developed the unique skills and attributes of all its members. Empathy, support, trust, respect and all the intelligences combine to make such organisations not only strong but great adaptors, able to weather whatever changes emerge in their market.

Next Steps: The best policy initiative you can possibly adopt is to commit to spreading the TI word to other organisations. You have the leadership, the people, the values, the practices and the experience. You also have the bruises! Share that with other organisations similarly committed to becoming TI communities. Not only will you be helping others, you'll be helping yourselves by learning through doing.

Examples of sustaining practices (from Aow et al., 2022):

- Honest and open feedback mechanisms.
- Evaluation protocols to monitor progress and to recalibrate for continuous organisational improvement.
- Quality-assurance protocols are selected for their embedded DEIJ values. These are chosen to help guide, monitor and evaluate growth.
- Deep implementation across systems, structures and policy is evident through consistency of practice, collective efficacy, skill development and continuous reflection.
- Distributive leadership models encourage voice, choice and ownership of learning. Rigid hierarchical leadership structures have been dismantled.
- Maintains a reputation for being a totally inclusive organisation and is able to act as a model for other organisations to follow.

USING THE TOTALLY INCLUSIVE ASSESSMENT CONTINUUM

What the TIAC offers is an accessible and easy-to-interpret measurement, which you can use to firstly, quantify what makes such an environment and secondly, identify what needs to be in place to move from discriminatory to inclusive. You may well add more variables/assessment points as you see fit. Indeed, any organisation aspiring to become a Totally Inclusive Community starts with this continuum and develops it further, perhaps adding/replacing criteria depending on the type of operation, its history/culture, the business it is in and feedback from employees.

For example, in my books *Creating a Totally Inclusive School* (Aow et al., 2022) and *Creating a Totally Inclusive School* (Whitehead and O'Connor, 2022) we use the above continuum but include the needs of educators, students and parents. If you are a corporate hotel operation, then clearly, you'd include the needs of your guests, which are somewhat different to those of students. Likewise, if you are a social media company, then you will need to reflect on the degree to which your organisation is enabling inclusivity or diminishing it. And if you are leading an NGO, establishing a Totally Inclusive Community will require careful examination as to the positive and negative effects of your operation on the fabric of the cultures and societies in which you are operating.

In our estimation, none of the above criteria are negotiable, though every organisation will need to decide its priorities, strategy and timeline for progress. Always staying true to the principle underpinning Total Inclusivity:

Total Inclusivity means recognising, valuing, protecting and nurturing diverse identities, including those of race, gender, sexual orientation, class, disability, age, religion and language.

That is your start and end point.

If this principle is not being met, then you are leading or working for a discriminatory organisation and therefore have a long way to go before you get to even Stage 3: 'Reflectively Unsettled'.

However, some criteria may need to be flexibly approached under certain circumstances, and accordingly, the six stages of TI progress may have different criteria and strategic objectives attached to them.

An example would be those working in hospitals during a global pandemic. As we've seen from the COVID-19 situation, the pressures such a pandemic has put on nurses, doctors and ancillary staff in hospitals, care homes and the like have been immense. Similar pressures have been placed on teachers. In which case, is it feasible to ensure a healthy work–life balance within such crucial organisations when humanity is suffering millions of dead and ailing and accepted social and support systems have broken down?

Clearly not. Different priorities emerge for different organisations in extreme circumstances.

However, that is not the same as saying such organisations and professions should expect to be subject to lesser levels of Total Inclusivity as a matter of course. On the contrary, given that society clearly relies more heavily on some sectors (e.g. hospitals, schools and care homes) than others, then it is even more important that those it is reliant on are Totally Inclusive Communities because being so will strengthen the bond between management and staff and strengthen the working climate and culture of the operation, thereby making it more likely the organisation can survive the stresses it will be subjected to during any a tidal wave of change (e.g. emergency).

We now turn to some key questions which also need to get raised when using the TIAC. These questions can be addressed separately to the TIAC, or they can form part of the overall assessment within an organisation.

1. VOICING

Q: Is your voice heard and listened to?

A strong indicator of where an organisation is positioned on the Totally Inclusive Continuum is to assess the quality and level of communication. If people feel silenced, are afraid to voice opinions contrary to the dominant organisational discourse and have limited ways of expressing their authentic selves without fear of consequence or retribution, then clearly the organisation cannot become a community.

And the only way to get everyone's voice heard is to allow them to be heard. For a great many organisational leaders, that could feel very threatening – they risk being told truths and having realities exposed to them that they'd hitherto conveniently ignored or been blind to.

Nevertheless, voicing has to be undertaken.

Here are some further questions which you can put to all staff but especially those most at risk of discrimination – they can be applied to any organisation, and the answers are revealing as to whether the Totally

Inclusive culture is rhetoric or reality. Virtually all these questions are objective in character, though some reflexivity will be required to answer one or two.

1 Are all LGBTQ+ employees 'out'? The 'all' is important here because research (McKinsey Quarterly, 2020) shows that it is easier for LGBTQ+ senior leaders to come out at work than it is for women and junior employees. It is also easier for Westerners to come out than those from other regions.

2 How often do LGBTQ+ employees have to come out? According to the McKinsey survey 50% of LGBTQ+ respondents reported having to come out at work at least once a week – they are forced to constantly reaffirm their identity because other staff don't recognise it or understand it.

3 Are Black, Asian and minority ethnic, disabled, LGBTQ+ employees regularly passed over for promotion and much less likely to be given the opportunity to represent the company externally?

4 Does the company provide benefits for domestic partners and offer trans-inclusive health care?

5 Does the organisation have gender-neutral toilets?

6 If an important company client complained that a gay, trans, Black or minority ethnic person was on their project, how would the company respond? Back down and accept discrimination or stand firm and explain that Total Inclusivity was a hallmark of the company's culture?

7 What safeguarding measures are in place for women and LGBTQ+ employees who may have to travel to or work in countries where their identity is threatened and their emotional and physical well-being at risk?

8 What are the types of microaggressions experienced by LGBTQ+, disabled, Black, Asian and minority ethnic group employees and junior women employees? Do these get reported, and what are the actions taken?

9 Do LGBTQ+, Black, Asian, minority ethnic, disabled and women employees feel they are seen solely as diversity representatives, being used by the organisation to burnish its progressive credentials?

10 Is any reverse mentoring taking place in the organisation? This occurs where, for example, a Black, minority ethnic, disabled or

LGBTQ+ person would mentor a senior leader in order to provide that leader with more direct experience of the issues faced by minority groups.

11 Is the organisation sponsoring LGBTQ+ events such as Pride, using same-sex couples in its advertising, highlighting its Total Inclusive message to every current and potential stakeholder?

12 Do Black, minority ethnic, disabled, and LGBTQ+ employees feel respected, or do they have their 'otherness' reinforced at work?

13 Does the organisation have recognised Total Inclusivity Advocates, part of whose job is to provide training and development in diversity and inclusivity to all staff?

14 Is the organisation promoting itself as a Totally Inclusive Community during recruitment road shows, etc.? And if so, who is leading on this?

15 How is the company ensuring its hiring and retention processes are Totally Inclusive? What onboard training is being given in Total Inclusivity? How is the company tackling drop-offs of Black, Asian, minority ethnic, disabled and LGBTQ+ employees, and what interventions are taking place to reduce this?

16 Does your organisation voluntarily disclose the racial and gender makeup of its workforce? If not, why not?

17 Are the organisation and its leaders relying on meritocracy to bring about inclusivity in the workforce, or are more direct and powerful interventions being made? This is not creating bias in the workplace, it is removing bias in the workplace.

18 Have full facilities been created for disabled persons?

19 Does the organisation have staff who know sign language and regularly utilise this in meetings, videos, promotional activities?

20 Does the organisation recruit graduates mostly from a select exclusive number of universities, or is the recruitment process more open and diverse?

Employees and leaders can use these questions to indicate how far along they might be on the journey to Total inclusivity. These questions are not definitive of all questions that might get raised, but they are good indicators of what needs to get voiced. How they are answered, if at all, will open doors into the cultural heart of the organisation and perhaps expose a reality which is way beyond what leaders imagine their organisation to be like.

2. EMPATHISING

Q: How would you assess the emotional intelligence of your organisation?
One way is to compare it to a lit candle:

* Flame completely absent
* Flickering but weak
* Bright so long as there's no wind
* Stable and bright under all conditions

Organisations which lack diversity, equity, inclusivity and justice and have no desire to improve are clearly absent of emotional intelligence – and can therefore be risky places to work, because no matter your employee status, you'll never belong, you'll never be secure and you'll be under constant critical (performative) scrutiny. As is discussed in Chapter 9, these can be physically and emotionally unsafe places for employees.

Not only is this a material threat to the individual, it is an emotional threat – we all need relationships of some description, and in today's world of increasing singleton lifestyles, the relationships we are most likely to have are at work.

As is stated in Chapter 1, employees spend more of their time at work than they do at home with their families. Sure, the COVID-19 pandemic has upended whatever was left of the 9-to-5 job for countless millions of us, but nevertheless all the pandemic has done is place more scrutiny on employee well-being and emotional intelligence in organisations (Tucker, 2021).

Central to any analysis of emotional intelligence is empathy.

Like all human characteristics which engage the heart and brain, empathy is learned. While it can be argued that men are less likely to openly demonstrate empathy than women, this is not because they lack empathy but because they are often born into a (masculinist) culture in which males are not expected to demonstrate emotional intelligence, including empathy. So there is a masculinity gender issue here which organisations may not be able to tackle directly (see Chapter 8). However, they can tackle it indirectly, and that is through encouraging empathetic responses in the workplace.

Emotional intelligence (EI) is a notoriously tricky concept to measure, though if we stay close to our feelings and are prepared to be reflective, then it is possible to identify just how much the organisation culture has EI embedded in it.

Here are some indicators for spotting whether or not your organisation has an absent or strong candle of emotional intelligence:

1 All employees feel comfortable being open and vulnerable, sharing more of themselves and learning how to support one another.
2 The work culture stresses that it is fine to not always be okay, with time and space allocated for people to share their feelings, positive or negative.
3 Employees are encouraged to have boundaries that help them feel safe and comfortable in their workplace relationships with both colleagues and bosses.[2]
4 Colleagues and leaders are supportive and engaging; they ask questions as to how people are coping, what distractions they may be experiencing and what challenges they are facing. This is not about them being nosey, it is about showing a caring spirit.
5 We all listen to what our colleagues are saying and especially if they appear to be experiencing anxiety or stress. If a colleague needs supportive members, that support is readily available and from professional counsellors if needed.
6 There are few if any microaggressions in the culture. Sexist and racist 'jokes and humour' are proscribed formally, though they don't need to be because colleagues wouldn't use this language anyway.
7 There is a strong trust relationship between colleagues, within teams, across departments and from leadership onwards.
8 Compassion for others, both within and beyond the organisation, is expressed in multiple ways, e.g. charity events; active support for the marginalised, abused and discriminated against; awareness-raising activities, both individual and organised.
9 We feel respected not as clones of the organisational corporate image but as individuals with our own unique identity.
10 Mental health issues are not hidden away, silenced and avoided, but where necessary and appropriate, counselling and guidance is available to employees.

You can score the above on a scale of 1 to 5 (with 1 being completely accurate representation of the workplace culture, 5 being the extreme opposite).

If you are a team leader, manager or boss, then the demonstration of empathy is a key to your success and that of your team. In Chapter 11 I explore in more detail the practices and interventions that leaders can

Credit Line: Cartoons drawn by Advanced Standard Group Co., Ltd.

reinforce in order to create a Totally Inclusive Community within which is embedded emotional intelligence.

3. ADDITIONALLY IMPORTANT QUESTIONS TO ASK

Accepting that no two organisations are exactly alike and that they are complex, changing environments, there are additional questions which you can ask in order to answer the bigger question as to whether you are working for a community or an organisation. Some of these questions get explored in more detail in later chapters, but for the moment use these questions as indicators as to where your organisation is on the Totally Inclusive Assessment Continuum and, equally importantly, how far it has to go to become Totally Inclusive.

Q: How does it feel to be managed and led in your organisation?

1   I feel disempowered
2   I feel empowered

Q. How emotionally safe do you feel while at work?

1   Not safe
2   Safe sometimes
3   Totally safe

Q. How much bullying goes on in your organisation?

1   Constantly
2   Sometimes
3   Never

Q, How much sexual violence, harassment, coercion goes on in your organisation?

1   Regularly
2   Sometimes
3   Never

Q. How performative is your workplace culture? (see Chapter 2)

1   Totally target driven
2   Targets important but not obsessive
3   Targets devised by employees not leaders

Q. How does it feel to be accountable in your organisation?

1   We have no power but lots of accountability.
2   We have a good balance between power and accountability.

Q. Would you describe your organisation as a 'learning organisation' (see Chapter 10)?

1   No professional development whatsoever
2   Limited professional development
3   Regular professional development

Q. Do you consider the leaders 'recruit in their own image' (see Chapter 9)?

1   Yes
2   Sometimes
3   Never

Q. How would you describe the employee retention rates?

1   Appalling
2   Average
3   Good

Q. From your perspective, do you think your colleagues enjoy being at work?

1   No
2   Some
3   Yes

Q. Is your organisation a 'listening organisation' (see Chapter 11)?

1   No
2   Depends on the situation
3   Yes

Q. If you have a problem (either personal or professional) and which might negatively impact your ability to do your job, do you have a line manager or boss whom you can talk to in confidence to seek guidance, without fear of repercussions?

1   No
2   Not sure
3   Yes

ORGANISATION OR COMMUNITY?

What I have tried to do in this chapter is bridge the gap between the objective and subjective in addressing the question as to whether you are working for an organisation or a community. The TIAC provides a more objective approach in so much as it lists a range of criteria which you can check against your knowledge of the organisation – most of these criteria can be answered by facts, not feelings.

However, feelings count. Our workplace relationships engage our heart as much as our head. Indeed, I would argue that if your workplace doesn't feel like a community to you, then no matter how many TIAC criteria it is positively identifying, it is not a community – at least as far as you are concerned.

Which is, in many respects, the ultimate test – how do you feel about your workplace? Because as stated at the beginning of this book, you are the champion of this story, no one else.

This chapter cannot ask all the questions that might possibly be asked about organisational climates and culture, but what has been identified are the most important ones especially in terms of focusing on race, gender and sexual identities.

Finally, the question as to who is responsible for engendering a Totally Inclusive Community.

We should certainly lay a lot of emphasis on the power and authority of leaders – and this issue is explored in Chapter 10. But it is not all about them. It is about each and every member of the workforce. Individuals make the difference. Indeed, people create the culture; the culture is not created by mission statements, market forces or marketing sound bites.

If you seek positive change then you have to be that positive change.

CHAPTER 4: REFLECTIONS, GUIDANCE AND COMMITMENTS

Reflection Exercise: 'Am I working in a community culture or an organisational culture?' 'How do I feel about my job, workplace, the organisation that pays me?' 'What contribution am I making towards engendering a community culture at work?'

Guidance for Implementation: Use the TIAC and questions listed in this chapter to begin a conversation at work about what Total Inclusivity means and why working for a community is a whole lot healthier than working for an organisation.

Commitment: Begin to identify those areas in which you can take positive action to help engender the community aspects and potential of your workplace. Identify where your organisation is on the TIAC and commit to moving it forward towards a community, one step at a time.

NOTES

1 For a more detailed TIAC (designed for schools), see A. Aow, S. Hollins and S. Whitehead (2022) *Creating a totally inclusive school*. London: Routledge.

2 For more on setting healthy boundaries, see N. G. Tawwab (2021) *Set boundaries, find peace*. London: Piatkus.

Five

DOI: 10.4324/9781003244073-5

In any major conflict the first casualty is truth. The winners get to write the history; the losers have to live with it. Eventually, all that is left standing is the word, because those who actually witnessed the deed are long dead – their version of truth eternally silenced.

But how reliable are those words left standing? Not very when we look closely.

Even taking what appears to be an unquestionable truth turns out, upon examination, to be highly questionable. For example, when did World War II begin? There is no definitive answer. Many might answer 1 September, 1939, when Hitler invaded Poland. Long-view historians might suggest 28 June, 1914, when Archduke Franz Ferdinand of Austria was assassinated by a Bosnian Serb nationalist. The Chinese and Japanese would perhaps proffer 7 July 1937, the date of the Marco Polo Bridge incident in Beijing (Frank, 2020). And if you want to be really provocative, how about sometime during the 15th and 16th centuries – the Age of Discovery and the rise of the European empires?

This is just a simple example of using words to try and answer an objective fact. That we cannot settle on a definitive answer is telling. All we can achieve is to add to the discussion. In the end, you'll have to decide for yourself when World War II began.

If humans cannot even agree on history how can they ever agree on the present? It is estimated there are still around 7,000 languages in the world, even though most of us speak only one. Each of those languages is not only a means of communication, it is the tool we use to make sense of the world and our place in it.

Seven thousand languages, spread among 7.7 billion humans.

The possibility of universal understanding diminishes rapidly when faced with the reality of human diversity, difference and multiple (and shifting) interpretations.

Reality is not an objective experience; it is only what you feel, hear, speak, see. We live in our heads, but our ability to connect with other heads comes through the word.

In the past, communication was just verbal utterances. No one read or wrote anything during the European Dark Ages, well, other than a handful of cloistered monks. The first book wasn't published until around 850 AD, in China. Today there are more than 6 million ebooks on Amazon alone.

Those sounds made by our ancestors and enhanced over countless millennia became invested with meaning, and multiplied beyond all human comprehension. They also became politicised. It is no surprise that those who seek to control society first try and control language – burning books, eliminating the intelligentsia, dictating school curricula.

Hitler, Stalin, Pol Pot and Mao all tried that. What would they make of the internet? They'd do what the Myanmar junta is trying to do as I write – shut it down.

Not much chance of that, fortunately. The internet has been doubling in size every two years since 2016. Trying to imagine the size of the internet today, and the volume of words going through it at any one time, is like trying to imagine the number of stars in the known universes. Don't even bother; it will just give you migraine.

This chapter is certainly not designed to give you migraine. The aim is to help you appreciate the multiplicity of meanings in the spoken word together with the politics of those utterances. Because Total Inclusivity is about what we, you and everyone else, defines it as, and that definition requires words, along with a mutually accepted appreciation that words count.

POLITICAL INTERPRETATIONS

On 16 March, 2021, exactly ten days before I began writing this chapter, a 21-year-old white man from Georgia (USA) shot and killed eight people at three Asian-owned businesses in Atlanta. These murders, which left six Asian women dead, the latest victims in a growing list of random massacres in the USA by white males, were immediately linked to the rise in hate crimes directed at Asian Americans.

The fact that hate crimes against Asians are on the rise in America (and the UK, Canada, New Zealand, Australia) is not in dispute (Haynes, 2021). But what can be disputed, if you are minded to do so, is defining and explaining these attacks.

For example, a police captain in the Atlanta police department, speaking at a news conference a day after the shootings said:

The attacks were not racially motivated. He (the perpetrator) apparently has an issue, what he considers sex addiction, and sees these locations as something that allows him to go to these places, and it's a temptation for him that he wanted to eliminate . . . He was pretty much fed up and kind of at the end of his rope [that Tuesday] was a really bad day for him and that is what he did.

(quoted in Gostanian and Ciechalski, 2021)

Here we have an example of words being used to deflect a particular truth — that the killings were racially motivated. At the same time the words make linkages which are at best pejorative and at worst racist. At the very least, they attempt to justify that which cannot be justified, ever. The statement raises the possibility of mental illness in the shooter, the women victims are implied to be sex workers, the businesses as locations for prostitution; even a religious rationale is hinted at whereby the murderer was acting to 'eliminate temptation' which had been placed before him by those who are bad and immoral — the victims. And who hasn't been 'at the end of their rope' and 'had a bad day' on more than one occasion? Those words are used to reach out to the audience, to garner their sympathy, to connect to their reality and move the discourse away from racist attacks on Asian Americans by a white male. There is a clear attempt at creating an alternative discourse, one which still leaves the shooter as a murderer but tries to close the door on issues such as race, masculinity, misogyny and 21st-century American culture.

One person who is offering a very different truth is Vicente Reid, CEO of the Arizona Asian Chamber of Commerce:

I am frustrated for my community, my parents, my children. This was an act of domestic terrorism, and too many leaders have been silent about the atrocities that have happened to our community. We cannot ignore the significance of this act and others in recent weeks.

(quoted in Molina, 2021)

The term 'domestic terrorism' takes the meaning of the attacks into an altogether different realm to that presented by the Atlanta police captain. There is no attempt to offer an explanation for the killings other than as further evidence of something toxic, sour and deeply rooted in American life. However, even Reid is being circular in his statement. He makes no mention of Donald Trump, for example, though one can speculate he had Trump in mind when he said 'leaders'. The inference being that Trump's 'mocking and vilifying of Asians', describing COVID-19 as 'kung flu' or the 'China virus', served to worsen whatever racist discrimination existed towards Asians prior to the pandemic.

The bullets killed eight innocent people, but the battle for truth began immediately after the killing ceased.

One of the few benefits of having leaders like Trump is that sociologists and critical linguists do not have to interpret layers of narrative designed to conceal what is actually going on in that person's mind. It was always very clear what Trump's value system was – because he told you in language that brooked no misunderstanding. You didn't have to be a psychologist to decipher it. More reflective and cautious politicians, if they are to survive, quickly learn the art of narrative dissembling. Indeed, democratic societies have gotten so used to having their leaders avoid giving a straight answer, telling you what they really think, that when a character like Trump comes along it can be quite a shock to the system. We tend to react in one of two ways – appalled or impressed. In short, the words spoken become divisive, and people immediately take sides.

Is that the intention of the politician or leader? Who knows, but it's probably safest to assume so.

One of the most (in)famous speeches ever made by a British politician, and one germane to this book, was that given by Enoch Powell, MP, on 20 April, 1968. Intended, Powell claimed, simply to draw attention to what he saw as the problems of mass immigration (by Black and Asian people to the UK), the words he spoke were inflammatory.

As I look ahead, I am filled with foreboding: like the Roman, I seem to see the River Tiber foaming with much blood.

The so-called rivers of blood speech caused an immediate social and political uproar. It was ugly, provocative, rhetorical – and popular – at least with those British voters fearful of Black, Asian and minority ethnic immigration.

However, compared to some of the speeches made in the past few years by the likes of Trump and many right-wing European politicians, Powell's speech on race relations was little more than a gentle tickling of the prejudices of the masses. Though tickled or not, the speech resonated; more than 50 years later, US and UK politicians are still using it to promote a racist (or 'anti-immigration') agenda. All they need say is that 'Powell was right', and they don't need to say any more – the audience gets the message.[1]

GETTING THE MESSAGE

If you'd arrived as a tourist in Thailand prior to around 1995, one word which you wouldn't have come across is 'gay', other than as a description of being cheerful and rather colourful. The Thai word used to describe 'men who have sex with men' was *kathoey* (which today gets translated by Thais and foreigners as ladyboy, third-sex person, transgender, trans). Using 'gay' to denote male homosexuality only became common currency in the West around the mid 1970s. Prior to that you were a 'homo'. The Thai LGBTQ+ community duly adopted the word 'gay' as part of the globalisation (West to East) current sweeping over Asia from the early 1990s especially (see Jackson and Cook, 2000, for discussion).

The point being, until Westerners arrived en masse as tourists, Thailand, like most of South East and East Asia, didn't even have a word for homosexuality – presumably they didn't need one.

Today, 'gay' is used as a shorthand term to define men who have sex with men most anywhere in the world.

Over the past few decades, the human race has had to learn a lot of new words and forget others.

Most laypeople would struggle to list, never mind explain, the plethora of terms found under the LGBTQ+ banner.

It wasn't until 1992 that the World Health Organisation declassified same-sex attraction as a mental illness, by which time many in the LGBTQ+ community began to emerge publicly not only in the world of arts and entertainment but also in politics.

Nearly a quarter of a century after the Stonewall riots in America and the formation of the modern LGBTQ+ liberation movement in the USA and elsewhere, the WHO is finally getting the message. A decade later, that message is inscribed in law, with the UK Employment Equality (Sexual Orientations) Regulations Act (EER, 2003), making it illegal to discriminate against LGBTQ+ people in the workplace.

These changes in law, culture and acceptance of what is correct language and terminology to describe a person's identity may have seemed inexorably slow if you've been waiting all your life for positive change to occur. However, in the span of human history this is but a millisecond. We should not be surprised, nor unduly critical therefore, if many people find it difficult to keep up with the changes taking place in gender, sex, sexual and racial identifications.

IDENTIFICATIONS

Sex/Gender/Sexuality

At the time of writing it seems as if every few weeks or months a new identification emerges which people have to try and factor into their language. Indeed, Facebook now lists more than 50 gender options for its users. Is it reasonable to expect that we all know what these are and should keep track of them as they presumably multiply? Of course not.

Below are the most common terms now in global circulation and related to sexual identity:

Gay: *Same-sex attraction, usually used to refer to men only.*
Straight/heterosexual: *Opposite-sex attraction e.g. male to female, female to male*
Bisexual: *Sexually attracted to both male and female*
Lesbian: *Same-sex attraction, women attracted only to women*
Pansexual: *Sexually attracted to people regardless of their sex or gender*
Polyamorous: *Open to more than one romantic/sexual relationship at a time*
Cisgender: *Having the same gender identity as that assigned at birth*
Trans/transgender: *Having a gender identity or expression different to the one assigned at birth*
Asexual: *Lack of or total absence of sexual desire towards others*
Non-binary/genderqueer: *Umbrella term for gender identities that are neither male or female*
Monosexual: *Exclusive attraction to a single gender*
Polysexual: *Sexual attraction to many but not necessarily all genders*
Queer: *An umbrella term for sexual and gender minorities who are not heterosexual, not cisgender*

To this list one should add the variability which exists with sex identity. This is discussed in Chapter 2, where I highlighted the fact that within the key chromosome patterns humans might have, there are not two but six prominent sexes plus intersex identity.

All this multiplicity can be confusing, even for the experts. Gender and sexuality identifications are a minefield – so step in cautiously. One famous person who didn't do so is the *Harry Potter* author J.K. Rowling – accused of transphobia after mocking 'people who menstruate' headline (Madani, 2020; see also Whitehead and O'Connor, 2022).[2]

With so many people no longer automatically identifying with the sex they were assigned at birth, it is safer to ask people which pronouns they prefer. Not all of us are using he, she, her or him. Increasing numbers are using 'they' or 'them' (Moor, 2019).

Race and Ethnicity

Next, we turn our attention to racial and ethnic identities, noting that these two terms overlap and can mean the same thing.

Ethnic tends to relate to cultural and social distinctions; in every country there exist side-by-side numerous ethnic groups, and most are not physically distinguishable from each other. In any large UK city, for example, there may be more than 100 different ethnic groups; Irish, Welsh, Scottish and English being just four of them. Each ethnic grouping has its own sub-culture, festivals, language, associations, rituals, traditions, which serve to provide its members with a sense of belonging. Some estimates suggest there are in excess of 5,000 ethnic groups around the world (Historyplex, 2021).

Credit Line: Cartoons drawn by Advanced Standard Group Co., Ltd.

Racial identifications can also encompass ethnic factors but are more likely to be identified by physical differences.

Black, for example, as racialised classification, can be interpreted as both a racial and ethnic identity, but 'Black' also encompasses different social identities (e.g. Black American, Afro-Caribbean, Black Canadian, African American, African, Black-Asian, South Asian, Black British). In some countries, the term 'black' is used to describe persons who are perceived as dark-skinned compared to other populations.

One might argue that the term Black (capitalised for political distinction) does not exist as a social or politicised category outside of white-dominated Western cultures. For example, would designating yourself as Black have any distinct meaning if you were born and lived in Africa?

Ask any white British citizen where their ancestors originated from and its unlikely they'll be able to tell you. After several millennia we are all so mixed up, racially, culturally, ethnically, that not only is it impossible to find our 'beginnings', what's the point of doing so anyway?

The only point is if our identity is politicised by a dominant social group, and that group occupies the hegemonic position within our home country.

So if we live in the West, and we have a dark skin, then we are going to get designated as Black whether we like it or not. Our identity becomes politicised. No surprise, therefore, that Black people feel politicised. And the roots of that politicisation lie in racism and racist stereotypes.

In Chapter 2 I discuss the sociological concept of intersectionality, and this is especially helpful for understanding the power dimensions of Black identity:

in a given society at a given time, power relations of race, class, and gender, for example, are not discrete and mutually exclusive entities, but rather build on each other and work together; and that while often invisible, these intersecting power relations affect all aspects of the social world.

(Hill Collins and Bilge, 2020, p. 2)

This statement reminds us that we all live with identities, coalescing to produce the 'I', but we also have to live with the political and power consequences of those identities. I may be a Black, gay, Jewish, working-class woman, but which of those identities matters most? While only I can possibly answer that, the identity that will stand out will be Black, because that is what people will see first – my skin colour. If I choose to do so I can conceal my Jewishness, my sexuality, even my femininity, but not my skin colour. No matter our religion, culture, education, sexuality, sex, class or gender, skin colour trumps them all as a signifier. It is the most visible marker of difference. Though only in those countries where it is politicised. If we were all black or brown skinned, there would be no marker of difference between us, at least not in skin colour.

For a Black person, one may or may not embrace their Blackness as a marker of difference, but no matter; others are going to do it for them. At that point their identity (albeit only by virtue of skin colour) is politicised for the rest of their life.

Complex and powerful – and we have only looked at Black identity.

How much more is there to be said about Latino, Asian, European, American, Chinese, Arab, Jewish, Scandinavian, Christian, Muslim, Russian, Australian identity?

VERBAL (MICRO)AGGRESSION

It is not necessary to embark on a trawl through the most damaging terms and words which humans use to denigrate and racially and sexually abuse each other. If you want that information then it is readily visible on most social media. One would also expect that any organisation aspiring to become a Totally Inclusive Community has in place safeguards and protocols for addressing racist and sexist language (see Chapter 9).

However, verbal aggression may often be concealed behind ignorance and lack of empathy. Below are some examples of how Black women may experience microaggressions from white people (Ira, 2021).

'But you are not like other black girls'.
'I find black women so sexual, they have this earthy primitive sexuality'.
'You mean you don't wash your hair every day?'
'I bet you sing and dance amazingly'.
'You don't sound black'.
'Black women are naturally erotic'.
'Your ethnic name is too hard for me to say, do you have a nickname?'

As one Black British woman put it to one of us in a communication on this topic, having to deal with these microaggressions on a daily basis is a terrible trial that no one should have to suffer:

I read somewhere about how black women were put on blocks naked and sold, with some women having their genitals kept as remnants for display. Identity is politics and people are fighting for their identity, who they are not who society says they are. I am not to be pigeon-holed, compartmentalised. I know who I am and that's why I am exhausted – it's a constant fight against others' dangerous assumptions of who I am.[3]

These may only be words, but their power is immense. Words matter because they label, they express power, they diminish, and they segregate.

Individuals have to live with the consequences of other people's words.

There is only one way to test whether or not your words are hurtful to others:

By their very name, microagressions seem small, but in reality, they have major repercussions on people's lives. To test whether or not a particular comment is a microagression, one must say it to oneself and see how it makes one feel. If it sounds right, then chances are it is okay to say it. As a general rule, however, be empathetic and kind.

(Stevens, 2021)

LEARNING AND UNLEARNING

By the time an adult applies to work in your organisation they'll already have experienced and/or expressed bullying, sexism, abuse, violence, misogyny, racism. They'll already have imbibed and/or had thrust at them the central stereotypes around gender and sexuality, race and ethnicity.

There are no innocent adults.

Innocence gets swept away very fast and very young.

By July 2021 more than 50,000 accounts of sexual harassment, abuse and assault in UK schools had surfaced on the campaign website Everyone's Invited.[4]

This campaign has all the indicators of being another MeToo movement and Black Lives Matter movement, in which case by the time you get to read this, the campaign will likely have gone global and tens of millions of students, and ex-students around the world will have identified many hundreds of thousands of schools as sites of racism, sexual abuse, rape and discrimination. And even if it hasn't gone global, the campaign gives a horrifying insight into what is very likely to be a global problem in schools.

The matter of how *To Create a Totally Inclusive School* is addressed in my co-authored book of this title (Aow et al., 2022). However, the starting point for any organisation intent on becoming a Totally Inclusive Community is to recognise and accept the political dimensions of language and the empowering and corrosive power of words.

This means that the organisation has to put respect for the individual first, and secondly, it must ensure there is appropriate professional development and learning with regards to Total Inclusivity.

Inevitably, individuals must at times be challenged on their language and on any negative racial or sexual assumptions they have learned over their lifetime.

The organisational members and especially the leaders cannot risk assuming that individuals always understand the power of their words. Nor can the organisation assume that employees have been taught how to behave correctly, speak correctly, towards people with different identities. Right now, this teaching is, unfortunately, not taking place in schools. Hopefully it will, but no organisation can assume all its members have this knowledge and awareness. In which case, the employer must provide it.

No single book can provide all the learning and support which every organisation is going to need on its journey to becoming a Totally Inclusive Community. But then again, no single book needs to, because there are vast amounts of knowledge and experience out there already. All it takes is embracing the intent to become a Totally Inclusive Community and then having the strategy and determination to move it forward.

This process will require learning new words and terms, especially around sexual identities, and unlearning words and terms which are racist, sexist and discriminatory.

Here are some tips on how to proceed:

1 Start with respect for the individual. That comes before all else. If you want to know how Black, Asian and minority ethnic people feel about being racially stereotyped, racially discriminated against, ask them.
2 Similarly, if you want to know how LGBTQ+ people feel about being sexually stereotyped and discriminated against, ask them.
3 Listen to what people say and how they say it – allow them to express themselves in a healthy and positive way.

4 Do not permit microaggressions in the workplace, especially those which are racist, sexist, ableist. And this includes proscribing against racist humour and having sanctions in place for when it occurs.

5 Help and support people as they go through this process of unlearning and relearning. As I say above, if there is good and genuine intent on the part of the individual to learn new, more positive ways, then help them do so.

6 Most people will be unsure about what is 'correct' and what isn't in terms of language and words, so help them by getting all individuals in the organisation to 'name their identity' and state how they'd like to be addressed. This also links to the use of pronouns in the work-place discussed earlier.[5]

7 Don't ever assume the organisation has completed this process of learning and unlearning. Society is not static; it is moving, and to keep it moving in a positive direction, organisations need to step up and help ensure this happens. So professional development and training cannot ever cease.

8 Create a trusting, respectful, safe and open workplace culture. Do not hide behind authority and power. Everyone counts, just as every-thing they say counts. All must be able to speak to power equally and without fear or prejudice.

9 Some employees will have been badly hurt (physically and emotionally) by racist and sexist actions and words, hopefully not in your organisa-tion, but in the past. Ensure your organisation has access to a qualified counsellor who can support such individuals if it becomes necessary.

10 Always work towards openness whereby individuals can express their fears especially with regards to 'saying the wrong thing'. Best to get these fears out in the open and then guide people into saying the right thing.

RESISTANCES (TO NEW WORDS)

While some [institutions] have seen some positive progress [towards diversity, equity, inclusion, and justice] others may be facing resistance or greater discord resulting from their efforts. Institutions experiencing challenges with their DEIJ efforts must understand that this is part of the process of growth . . . If we wish to create environments where all identities represented in our communities can thrive, we must stay focused on this work and it will eventually pay off. DEIJ is not about a destination but rather a journey of continuous improvement.

(Nyomi, 2021)

One of the biggest fears with any organisation looking to become Totally Inclusive is that in doing so it will leave some (valued and loyal) employees behind. I have seen this reaction firsthand when delivering inclusivity and diversity training in schools, colleges and universities. It is not necessarily the case that people do not want to learn but that they are afraid to learn. This is a very palpable fear, and it will bring forth resistances, especially over language. No organisational leadership wants to create a revolution, upend years of 'stability', even if within that stability there has been festering discrimination, bullying, racism, sexism and marginalisation of 'others'. But a revolution is what needs to take place. Much better for the leadership to lead this revolution by choice and strategically than to have it forced on them by the complaints, actions and accusations of their staff and stakeholders.

Toxicity can exist in an organisation but not necessarily be seen by its leaders. But once it is publicly exposed, then the organisational leadership can never unknow it. They must face reality. And one key aspect of that reality is recognising diverse identities and, as is outlined in this chapter, some of the terms and phrases which serve to positively reinforce those identities.

Following are listed the most common negative responses to professional development and training for Total Inclusivity in organisations in relation to language and words.

Political Correctness

Claiming that positive social change is 'political correctness gone mad' is a standard response by those who are seeking to distance themselves from the consequences of that change. They evoke a claim to 'madness' whenever a change presents itself which might force them to reflect on their long-held assumptions, biases, actions, language. This is driven by fear, not logic. The same response would have been made by many British middle-class men at the turn of the 20th century, when women were marching in the streets of London, demanding the right to vote. The same responses would have been made by many white Americans in the southern states during the 1960s and the civil rights marches for the end of racial segregation were taking place. No one today can claim that universal suffrage is political correctness nor that being anti-apartheid is political correctness. It is also highly unlikely that you would find an LGBTQ+ person denigrating anti-homophobic language as 'political correctness'.

Nor would a Black person cry 'political correctness gone mad' if a white person refused to use the 'N-word'.

The lesson from this is to recognise that only those with something to lose (notably dignity, respect, power, status, image and self-esteem) are going to claim that positive social change towards Total Inclusivity is 'political correctness gone mad'.

Freedom of Speech

There is no universal freedom of speech for all humans, and nor should there be. We each live in a community, a society wherein there is diversity and difference. More important than freedom of speech is respect and safety for all. This requires recognition that others have a right to exist but not at the expense of a dominant group. Certain words and phrases can only be used to hurt and harm. They are not used to create knowledge and understanding, remove ignorance and enhance empathy. If the so-called demand for 'freedom of speech' is simply a demand to be abusive, create hatred, generate misunderstanding between peoples, then this freedom of speech must be denied. It must be denied in societies and in organisations. The individual has rights, but not at the expense of the community. This is why we have laws and why a judicial system operates to ensure that hate is not perpetrated in social media and similar systems of communication. (For further discussion, see Whitehead and O'Connor, 2022.)

'I Was Only Joking!'

Humour can be positive and it can be negative. Anti-Semitic jokes, for example, are not jokes, they are racist statements disguised as jokes. Jokes against Black, Asian, minority ethnic people, LGBTQ+, immigrants, disabled people, all 'others' in a society are merely reinforcing that otherness and therefore are operating as political actions by a dominant group against a minority group. Maybe humour does 'work best' when it panders to stereotypes, but if those stereotypes are negative portrayals of those who suffer discrimination in a society, then that is not humour; that is a clear reinforcement of racism, sexism, ableism.

Cartoons/Images

At time of writing, a teacher in the UK is receiving police protection after online threats were made against him. And his 'crime'? Showing a cartoon of the Prophet Mohammed in class. Regardless of your opinions as to this particular situation, it needs to be recognised that religious cartoons have generated a great deal of anger in some communities, and this anger has to be respected. But we would make the point that behind the claim for 'freedom of expression' is often a misunderstanding of what freedom means in a global society. Freedom cannot come without responsibility. And that responsibility must be to contribute towards communal cohesion, mutual understanding and respect for all. We all must contribute, and we all must listen.

Distancing

Distancing is the most common form of resistance in organisations, and I've referred to it in previous chapters. People pay 'lip service' to the changes being brought in but they don't 'buy in' to those changes. Acceptance is only on the surface. However, one of the interesting things about language and words is how they quickly permeate an organisation. Once a new discourse (e.g. Total Inclusivity) gets articulated, explained, oxygenated into the system of the organisation and repeated endlessly by employees, it will take root not just in the language of the organisation but in the identities of the employees. Eventually, they will stop noticing that they are becoming Totally Inclusive in attitude. At that point distancing is not needed because the organisation is a Community, and no members are distancing themselves from that reality.

Deflections

Several decades ago, I was delivering equal opportunities awareness development to a department of lecturers in a UK college. The small team of lecturers was very strong and positive together, though this type of training had not been attempted before. The focus of the training was on Black awareness raising – 40% of the student body were Black and Asian. From the outset there was resistance expressed by several lecturers – each wanted to talk about their own experience of being subjected to prejudice (e.g. Irish, age related, class based). While these experiences were valid they were not about the key theme of the PD which was white attitudes to Black and Asian people. This was a form of deflection, using the comfort of the personal to avoid discussing the less comforting reality of white overt and covert racism towards Black and Asian people. There are times to put aside the comfort of the personal and embark on the riskier journey to explore the discomforting realities of 'others'.

SUMMARY

What is truth? Truth is how you see and experience the world. Truth is also how others see and experience the world.

That is a lot of 'truths'.

In this chapter I've attempted to bridge the gap between these perspectives as they apply to words and language. What I've tried to avoid doing is telling you what to say and what not to say. I believe you can work that out for yourself. As a responsible adult, a member of many communities, you'll know the words for love, bonding and togetherness, just as you'll know the words for hate, discrimination and separation.

If you are committed to a Totally Inclusive Community, indeed if you are committed to a totally inclusive life, then your language needs to reflect that, and it needs to strengthen the bonds between us. It also needs to remove any notion that some of us are 'others'. We are each of us centres of our own unique world while also being members of a global community.

Words and language which sever bonds, break up communities, deliberately intend to hurt and harm, engender loathing and fear should not be spoken. That is part of the commitment you, the reader, make to ensuring your aspiring Totally Inclusive Community becomes a reality.

REFLECTIONS, GUIDANCE AND COMMITMENTS

Reflection Exercise: Why is language important when it comes to Total Inclusivity? Which words reflect good feelings for you towards people you work with?

Guidance for Implementation: Explore how your work colleagues are reacting to the use of different pronouns to self-categorise, especially around gender and sex identities.

Commitment: To become confident at articulating Total Inclusivity to those around you, both at work and in your personal life. Finding the right words to describe and explain Total Inclusivity positively and engagingly.

NOTES

1 https://en.wikipedia.org/wiki/Rivers_of_Blood_speech
2 For discussion of 'free speech' and trans rights, see S. Whitehead and P. O'Connor (2022) *Creating the totally inclusive university*. London: Routledge.
3 A comment contained in an email communication with one of the authors of this book (16 March, 2021).
4 See 'Welcome – Everyone's Invited (www.everyonesinvited.uk).
5 See also, www.idealist.org/en/careers/pronouns-workplace-inclusivity.

Six

I introduce this chapter on the obstacles to TI with a brief email exchange that occurred between myself and an anonymised Western male during the time that I was writing this book.

It begins with a message sent to me via my educational consultancy website, www.whiteheadlee.com:

Message title: Online school for Filipino Students

I've been thinking about establishing an online school in the Philippines, one which focuses on the STEM fields. Can you advise?

However, I must say that I'm not interested in a "woke" school.

1. Filipinos are not interested in Marxist, critical race theory. They don't see themselves as "victims" oppressed by "white people".

2. I also don't subscribe to that ideology. I believe in merit (Lockean ethics), and I believe in treating people as individuals, not placing them into groups for some political end.

The word "inclusive" is one of those words that makes me cringe. The definition is harmless enough, but whenever I see that word on a website it immediately raises an eyebrow. It's often used by the "woke brigade" as a way to imply or suggest that they have been historically "excluded", which I don't think is the case. People are certainly excluded based upon merit. Harvard excludes about 40,000 applications a year, but that "exclusion" has nothing to do with skin color or income.

So yes, I'm interested in discussing it more. But I'm not interested in a woke radical school that tries to place individuals into groups based upon skin color, class, or otherwise. I'm not sure if that is your company's goal or not, but it certainly crossed my mind as a possibility when I saw that word 'inclusivity' on your website.

Regards,

Hi ***

We appreciate you confirming your ideological relationship to your proposed project. From your description, it would appear that WLA

DOI: 10.4324/9781003244073-6

would be too far apart from your standpoint in terms of core educational ideals to be able to help you in your project. For a more details of our value system please go to:

www.totalinclusivity.com

We wish you well in your endeavours.

best

Stephen

Hi Stephen

That website is pretty far to the left:)

I don't think that is a step forward; it's more or less a step backward.

It destroys individuality, self expression, authenticity, and creativity – all in favor of some dystopian version of homogeneity.

Quota based systems – and equality of outcome – also presupposes that people have no right to choice, and no right to determine their destiny. They are no longer rewarded for the quality of their work, their productivity, or their genius. Instead, their job prospects and careers amount to "filling a quota" based upon their "group identity". It will lead to gulags, concentration camps, or both!

In my view, it's a dangerous proposition.

Take care,

As I explained in the previous chapter, words matter and especially nowadays. We are living through what the Chinese dissident Ai Weiwei describes as 'a time when interpretation and judgement is changing'.[1] Values, attitudes, and especially identities are undergoing dramatic and profound reshaping. The upshot is that these are especially sensitive times. Not surprisingly, this can quickly lead to a polarisation of views.

I present the above email exchange because it neatly encapsulates the problem of a binary way of thinking – emotive and uncritical reactions to that which is not understood properly. The discourse adopted by the enquirer attempts to link 'woke' with 'left/Marxism'. Yet in reality, these two positions are not inevitably mutually supportive. One can be a capitalist and still hold on to Totally Inclusive values – and why not? But making this link is a rhetorical device increasingly being used by those who oppose inclusivity – or who are frightened of it. The lumping together and labelling as 'lefty' of all liberal-minded folk is a discursive shift now apparent in conservative political realms in the USA, UK, Australia and many other parts of the globe. As we see in the email exchange, the next leap is to link 'lefty' with totalitarianism, uniformity, loss of freedom, loss of individuality, social control and then on to the almost inevitable 'gulags and concentration camps'. It doesn't matter that this constructed connection is completely artificial; what matters is that it acts as a resistance against Total Inclusivity, indeed against any form of social action which demands equality, diversity, inclusion, social justice.

Please be assured, Total Inclusivity does not require gulags and concentration camps! Indeed, as history shows us, the only threat of such comes from a lack of diversity and equity and an absence of inclusivity.

However, getting that message across to all humanity isn't easy. As with the individual above, who fears it will all end badly (e.g. concentration camps), resistance is always present.

THE INTERSECTIONALITY OF RESISTANCES

Confronted by confusion and uncertainty people tend to respond in one of two ways – retreat to the safety of the known or embrace the new and unfamiliar. And perhaps that is one reason why the world, right now, appears divided into two groups; the so-called woke[2] and the rest. Because never in human history has so much change been experienced by so many and in so short a time span.

As is recognised in this book, change is unsettling. However, it is also inevitable.

I would expect that most readers will be self-identifying among the 'woke', which is fine. That is the anticipated readership. However, I also hope that many who read this book are among 'the rest'; those who do not feel comfortable with 'political correctness', LGBTQ+ diversity, social justice, the concept of 'white privilege' or even maybe the idea that females can aspire to be more than housewives (though being a house-wife is fine if that is what you aspire to).

If you are among 'the rest' or perhaps not sure where you are, well, first let me congratulate you on reading this far into the book. No, ser-iously, because to get this far you've had to navigate some pretty challen-ging concepts and ideas.

But hey, that's the point of the book. And it's the point of life – to try and keep thinking outside our little bubbles, our tiny boxes.

Yes, you are entitled to your resistances. But in holding on to them rec-ognise them both for what they are and why they are important to you. Perhaps by the end of this chapter, and certainly by the end of the book, you may even have joined the wokes!

In this chapter I will discuss the most common reasons individuals and organisations will openly (or covertly) resist Total Inclusivity. At the conclusion, in the Reflections section, you can undertake your own quiet and private self-analysis into which of these resistances are most active in your mind and in your workplace. Ideally, none will be present in either your mind or your workplace. But as we know, rarely is life ideal.

Although I present and examine these resistances as individual factors, in reality they connect, reinforce and combine to strengthen resistance to movements for social justice. In other words, just like identity, resistances are intersectional. They do not exist discrete of each other. Also, like intersectional identities, each resistance is powerful in its own way, impacting individual subjectivity and organisational climate and practices.

In other words, if you spot one resistance in your organisation, it is quite likely more will also be present somewhere. Likewise, if you recognise one resistance in your head, then look for where others may be lurking.

Credit Line: Cartoons drawn by Advanced Standard Group Co., Ltd.

But first let us get five common 'explanations' for anti-inclusive attitudes in people out of the way. I detail these five in what follows and, in so doing, dismiss them as false trails – they take us nowhere, are unhelpful in bringing about positive change and indeed can lead us in a circular route back to where we don't want to be – stereotyping people.

'EXPLANATIONS' WHICH ARE NOT

IQ

The concept of IQ as an innate, biological, predetermined and unchangeable human essence has a lot to answer for in both creating misunderstandings among the general population and damaging the education of countless millions of children. It is a flawed science, an outdated monocultural method which has over the decades encouraged educators to destroy human potential. It is the absolute enemy of Total Inclusivity. But however ridiculous, as a theory of human potential IQ still pops up like the proverbial bad penny. For example, you may have read somewhere that those who are racist, homophobic or misogynistic have a lower IQ than 'normal folk'. Complete rubbish. Just ignore any so-called 'explanations' based on intelligence levels. Intelligence or lack of it does not equate to a person's ability to empathise with others, those different to themselves. Moreover, there are multiple intelligences (Gardner, 2000). I have the intelligence to write books on TI; just don't ask me to explain quantum physics! If you have any doubts about this, just look at some of the most 'successful' people in history – there was little doubt they were intelligent, but were they the most empathetic, non-racist, non-sexist individuals on earth? No. IQ is not a simple consequence of genetics; it is a complex trait influenced by both genetic and environmental factors. Also, IQ levels are not constant – they can and do change. Expect to get smarter as you get older. Maybe after reading this book your IQ will go up a few points!

Education

First of all, do we mean compulsory education (schooling) or post-compulsory education (university)? Schooling (K–12) as it is currently delivered around the world is barely addressing the issues of Total Inclusivity. Which is why I have co-authored the book *Creating a Totally Inclusive School* – because education needs to change and become not only more inclusive but also ensure children adopt a Totally Inclusive mindset. Very few schools are addressing this. Which is why we have the problem of racism, sexism, violence, rape and sexual harassment in schools and in society. As for college and university education, there is some evidence that going to university and studying for several years does help young adults become more aware and embracing of equity, inclusivity and diversity. We can wire our brains to become more inclusive, and university-level education is a good way of doing it. But that doesn't mean everyone with a degree is 'woke' or everyone without a degree is prone to being racist (see Whitehead and O'Connor, 2022, for more on TI in universities).

Media

Any debates about the influence of the media over people ends up being a chicken-and-egg debate. Which comes first, the media message or the message from the people? You make your choice. But frankly, there is no definitive answer. For example, have Facebook, Twitter, Instagram and the like caused racism and misogyny in society? No. To assume otherwise would be to give the bosses of these media conglomerates far more credit for social control than they could ever be capable of, plus it requires ignoring human history. At the same time, are these companies completely innocent? Hardly. They certainly (mostly unwittingly) created a particular environment and added the fuel, but the fires of prejudice and hatred were already burning quite nicely and long before the internet arrived. The media can decide to contribute solutions to human and social problems, or it can choose to encourage those problems (e.g. fake news) for whatever reason, though usually it comes down to profit.

Class

I am British, well, English to be precise (a mix of Lancastrian and Yorkshire). I was born into a family which on one side was middle-class, the other side, working class. I've spent a large part of my life becoming unquestionably middle class, not least due to higher education. Born in 1949 to a lower-middle-class family (small shopkeepers), leaving school at 14 (11+ exam failure) with no qualifications, my first real career was as a pub landlord in Leeds. On the basis of my class, work experience and early education, there is no way I should have a PhD and even less chance of me becoming a writer and international educationalist. But that is the point of class – it labels and attempts to slot the individual into a pathway based on their social status. Just as well, then, that, encouraged by my family, I chose to ignore the prescriptive character of my class upbringing and take advantage of the growth in educational opportunities over the past decades. I imagine a great many people reading this will have experienced something very similar.

For social class to be the determinant as to whether someone was inclusive or racist, we'd have to look at which social class exhibits inclusive attitudes and which social class exhibits racist attitudes. If you can spot that one, please let me know, because I certainly cannot.

Maleness

As I have written elsewhere (Whitehead, 2021) traditional or toxic forms of masculinity are most definitely implicated in racism, sexism, violence, misogyny and indeed, most of the world's ills. However, toxic masculinity is only one masculinity out there. There are many others. The two most prominent alternative masculinities (ways of being a man) are progressive and collapsed. Therefore, it is important to avoid simply condemning all men and their maleness as a root cause of anti-inclusivity. Toxic masculinity is most definitely a major factor, but not all men have toxic masculinity (see Chapter 8).

Having rejected the preceding five variables as the causes of resistance to total inclusivity, we should turn our attention to those variables which are a problem: They are divided into the personal and the organisational.

PERSONAL BARRIERS TO TOTAL INCLUSIVITY

Stereotyping: Everyone stereotypes, and pretending otherwise is to fail to recognise the attraction of stereotypes – they make diversity appear 'simple' and 'explain' differences among us. Stereotyping means we don't have to think too hard about all the complexity around us – we just jump in the pool of stereotypes and come up with the one we prefer. Take the stereotyping of all gay people as camp. A few are, but most are not. But stamping the stereotype of effeminate behaviour on all gay men is an easy way of distinguishing gay from straight. The reality is, of course, that so-called straight men can and do have sex with men, while men self-identifying as gay can look the very opposite of camp. Moreover, a good many straight men can act in a feminine manner – look at young males in Japan, South Korea, China, for example – herbivore masculine performances (see Whitehead, 2021, for discussion). To move toward Total Inclusivity we have to first recognise any stereotypes we have about certain social, ethnic, racial and sexual groups in society – and then bin them.

Upbringing: If you are a white person born in Alabama the chances are you will be less 'woke' than a white person born in San Francisco. It's not inevitable, but the likelihood is higher. Upbringing is not destiny, but it comes as close to being so as any other variable in our lives. Who our birth parents are and how we get raised matter a lot in our journey towards understanding and open-mindedness. This is why education is so important; it offers a way of reducing bias in those who have been raised in environments where anti-inclusive attitudes and behaviours prevail. We can remove the problematic consequences of a problematic upbringing, but this cannot be done without some guidance and when we are mature enough and wise enough to recognise which aspects of our upbringing might be causing us problems. For a pithy take on upbringing read Philip Larkin's poem 'This Be The Verse'.

Religion: It is entirely natural for humans to want to look to some higher power for guidance, help, salvation and the promise of a better life in the next one than in this. Unfortunately, those natural inclinations always get taken over by non-inclusive organisations − religions. Christianity, Islam, Hinduism, Buddhism, Judaism, Mormons, Mennonites, Hamish, Scientology, they each contain some central belief or tenet which is anti-inclusive − commonly to do with women, LGTBQ+ and sexuality. This book is not the place to explore why this is, just the place to recognise that while being religious in no way precludes the possibility of someone adopting a Totally Inclusive outlook on life, if one follows the strictest and most inflexible interpretations of any religious text, then Total Inclusivity is unlikely to be an outcome.

Ignorance: One of the fascinating aspects of the human character is that when we put aside stereotypes and prejudices and actually get to know someone who is different to us and whom we might otherwise have stereotyped negatively, we invariably find we have a lot in common. We are all uniquely alike. Ignorance is only bliss if it protects you from unnecessary hurt. Ignorance is certainly not bliss if it means you continue to live in your miniscule comfort zone, afraid to look beyond into the wider world. So much racism, sexism and hatred of the 'other' in this world are simply born of ignorance.

Disassociation: Identity works as both association and disassociation − those who are like me are my compatriots; those who are different to me are strangers. At the most simplistically ridiculous level, that of nationality, we have people associating with others simply because they were born in a particular place and disassociating with those who were born elsewhere − it is even more ridiculous when we apply this to sports such as football and soccer, where lumps of men end up fighting each other because they wear different coloured scarves around their necks. These associations are not natural, they are human made ad therefore artificial. We can choose to be, for example, global citizens, or we can choose to retreat to our identity bunker, bolting the door on all those who look or sound different to us.

Biological Determinism: In Chapter 2 I list a number of illusions which people need to let go of if they are to embrace Total Inclusivity, and the first and arguably most important of these is biological determinism: the idea that humans are how and who they are because of fixed and unchangeable nature. Following this simplistic thinking, white people have a right to be racist over BLM people because there is a natural hierarchy of races with whites at the top; men are natural leaders, and women should stay at home raising kids; gay sexuality is unnatural and should be wiped out; and any attempt to become transgendered is simply to fly in the face of nature. One can understand why people are drawn to this type of simplistic thinking. During the 1930s, the Nazis did a good job in persuading many white people to hate Jews, Russians, Romanies and Black people, for example, using biologically deterministic 'theories' as a rationale for the ensuing holocaust and wholesale slaughter. But there can be no place for such ideas in Total Inclusivity or, indeed, in a civilised society.

Emotions: Feelings have origins; they don't simply arise from nowhere. So in terms of resistances to Total Inclusivity, feelings don't cause the problem, but they certainly can reveal the fact that we have a problem with others. The difficulty is separating our emotional responses from the root cause of those emotional responses. Even psychiatrists can fail to unravel this particular knot. One way to address this is through emotional intelligence development: empathy, understanding, sympathy. Unfortunately, one has to first be willing to submit to such development, and too few of us are. We prefer to wallow in our 'instinctive' emotional responses of anger, hate, and aggression, and so the cycle of intolerance and disassociation not only festers but increases. Eventually, some of us crack – we go crazy with an AK-47 and start shooting innocent strangers simply because our out-of-control emotions have overcome our basic humanity.

Fear and Insecurity: How is it that racism especially is driven by fear and insecurity? For sure, it is invariably the hegemonically and demographically dominant social group (e.g. white people in the USA and Europe) who will be racist towards Black people. What have these dominant whites to be afraid of? At a psychological level they are afraid of what Simone de Beauvoir refers to as 'the other'; that group of people (women, LGBTQ+ persons, Black people) who are physically and culturally different and therefore deemed 'unknowable' or lesser. This indicates how primitive a response racism is – not born of understanding and civilised behaviour but of a deeply rooted existential fear of having one's identity (and power) disturbed if not displaced by those who are not us. This fear may be deeply rooted, but it is easily uprooted – through association with those who look and sound different to us and through education and awareness raising.

Power: There are some sociological theories that suggest the number-one drive within humans is for power, leading to inevitable conflict.[3] This power is the energy which drives our search for status, resources, advantage. Whether or not this theory works in every case, every situation, there is no doubt that power is at stake when there is conflict between races, ethnic groups, etc. To take an example, one might argue that men who are misogynistic are so because they are afraid of the power of women – not only as an emasculating source but in terms of women's independence. If women don't need men, who needs men? Many men may well not rationalise it like this, but at a deeper level loss of male power fuels misogyny. Likewise, loss of white power fuels racism.

Bubbles: Bubbles are discussed in Chapter 1, and they are relevant here also. Call them bubbles, comfort zones, boxes, caves, whatever – essentially, they are places we retreat to for existential and ontological safety. This is entirely natural when we are five years old and want to be close to our mother and father, but it becomes a problem in the adult globalised world where difference is all around us and can no longer be ignored. Recognising that the cultures, belief systems, myths, illusions and notions we build up to create our bubble only exist in our head, not in everyone else's head, it still leaves these places as potentially dangerous not just to us but to others. For it is out of these bubbles, often fuelled by fake news, political propaganda, fear and insecurity, that really lethal actions spring. All the racists, homophobes and misogynists live in bubbles of deep fear and hatred.

Identity: At the core of all these resistances is identity – who we think we are or who we would like to be. We invest so much in being and becoming a person, an individual, that we too often fail to stop and reflect on what type of person we are actually becoming. Until one day we have a situation arise, perhaps a traumatic incident, which jolts us awake, causes us to critically reflect on our assumptions, beliefs, attitudes, fears and prejudices. Trauma can be good for us so long as we learn from it and become better humans as a consequence. And this reveals the interesting thing with identity – it is always a work in progress, never a final accomplishment. Because it is not invested in biology but environment, so our identity can change, but into what? That is the big question. We have the capacity to become better than we are, to learn more, open our minds, ask more questions and not assume we have the answers. We also have the capacity to reject becoming 'the better angels of our nature', to descend into the pit of anger and hatred. And as we have seen down through history, it is far easier for humans to hate and fear the 'other' than to embrace it. Total Inclusivity requires bravery, strength and imagination. Are you brave, strong and imaginative enough to embrace it?

ORGANISATIONAL BARRIERS TO TOTAL INCLUSIVITY

History: Chapter 10 looks at why non-inclusive organisations are heading for failure. And history is a signal reason. An organisation's history may well be celebrated by bosses and owners, but it should never determine its future, because the future is so much different to the past. Failure to adapt, evolve, develop brings stagnation, and this creates lack of faith and trust in the future of the organisation – employees remain because they have no choice, not because they see a future for themselves in the job. No organisations were Totally Inclusive back in the 1960s; indeed, most didn't even have an equal opportunities policy. If those same organisations are still around today then it's only because they have evolved and adapted, which means that the individuals in the organisation have evolved and adapted. But this evolution never ends. Any organisation looking to be successful now and in the future must be Totally Inclusive, not least to help ensure its own survival.

Cultures: Although organisations have no ontological identity they do have culture. In fact, most organisations have many cultures – related, for example, to departments, branches, locations, work specialisms. Work cultures arise when people gather together and create their own workspace dynamic, and the keys to that dynamic are the personalities and attitudes of the employees. Work cultures are not automatically anti-inclusive – they could be Totally Inclusive – but if you want to look for where resistance to Total Inclusivity might exist in a particular organisation, study its sub-cultures.

Power Blocs: It is a commonly held assumption that organisations are hierarchical, with fixed power held by the bosses and trickles of power filtering through to the base of the pyramid. This can be the case, but especially in larger organisations, power gets diffused. Power blocs exist which might have little or nothing to do with formal organisation authority and hierarchy but a lot to do with the charisma and personality of individual employees. These power blocs may or may not be orientated towards Total Inclusivity, but if they are not then it becomes a big problem for any organisation seeking to bring in positive change.

Performativity: Performativity was examined in Chapter 2 and for good reason, because this often-underestimated aspect of organisational life can be a major barrier to Total Inclusivity. Performativity creates internal competition within the organisation, and in turn, this generates a silo-mentality where individuals feel threatened and insecure and therefore are unlikely to cooperate and collaborate with their colleagues. There is no possibility of becoming a Totally Inclusive Community if employees are constantly at odds with each other over resources, etc., and competing to save their jobs.

Leadership: All organisations, whether Totally Inclusive or not, require leaders and managers. But what type of leader and what style of management? I explore this variable in Chapters 10 and 11 because it is one which will largely determine the character of an organisation. A bad leader won't automatically create a discriminatory organisation, but neither will they have the ability to turn it into a Totally Inclusive Community. A good leader is much more likely to have the emotional intelligence and ability necessary to steer an organisation towards Total Inclusivity. Can we distinguish between good and bad leaders? Yes, and I do so later in the book.

Fear of Disturbance: One of the most telling moments in doing professional development and training in anti-racism, and indeed, any aspect of Total Inclusivity within an organisation, is to see the fear arise in the eyes of the leaders when they finally grasp what is actually required to bring about change towards a Totally Inclusive work culture. This is the moment when the bosses awake to the deeply rooted character of change necessary. It will be disturbing and unsettling, and perhaps not everyone will want to be part of such a revolution. Yes, there may be casualties. Fear of disturbance means continuing as before and hoping it will all be okay. Or at best agreeing to take small steps towards Total Inclusivity, one at a time, and maybe over many years. In the end, the impetus will disappear, and the organisation and its culture will remain institutionally racist, sexist, systematically discriminatory. Don't fear disturbance; accept it as inevitable and embrace it strategically.

Rhetoric over Reality: Rhetoric is easy; action is the challenge. Rhetoric alone won't dismantle institutionalised discrimination towards minorities, but rhetoric can and does serve to present an agreeable image to the public. As is explained in Chapter 4, you can spot where your organisation is placed on the Total Inclusivity Assessment Continuum simply by noting how much of the organisational rhetoric of Total Inclusivity is translated into organisational reality.

Habit: Rituals, systems, bureaucracy, all the tedious but essential components which ensure any organisation is able to exist and function are nothing more than habits. They get started with probably good intent, and no one thinks to change them. Well, usually not until a crisis or two requires they do so. Habit is comforting. It means we go into work on a Monday knowing full well what lies ahead. Individuals invest a lot of themselves in these work rituals, from the way in which job vacancies are advertised, applicants chosen, new employees are inducted to how people get promoted. Of course, no organisation wants continual change, reinventing systems and practices every year, but moving any organisation towards Total inclusivity will require a constant and never-ending critical examination of those work systems to ensure that the values and principles of TI don't get compromised because people don't want to change and adapt.

Professional Development: I would always counsel any prospective employee to ask a simple question at interview: 'What professional development does your company offer me?' How that gets answered is a good indicator as to whether or not you should invest your time and energy in the organisation. And don't rely on the answer given to you at interview – ask current employees what PD they receive and what support they get for it. Total Inclusivity cannot arise without specialist professional development and training. Most organisations do not have the capacity, the skills, the awareness, nor the experience to introduce TI themselves. And nor do they have the self-critical reflectiveness. Often, only expert outsiders can bring about the change required, not by themselves but in collaboration with and in support of the organisation and its members, drawing on the positive, healthy intent that already exists and ensuring this develops into real momentum for change.

Profit: If profit is the purpose of all for-profit organisations and profit brings about positive change in such organisations because it generates more resources, why is it then that many of the most 'successful' organisations are also the least inclusive? I explored this phenomenon in Chapters 2 and 3, and the answer is that the pursuit of profit in and of itself is no reason to be in business. This may sound counter-intuitive to all those hedge fund managers, shareholders and bankers reading this (are there any?), but in today's globalised world where sustainability, humanistic values and social good are vital for society's healthy continuation, profit cannot come first, and it certainly cannot be allowed to displace human good. If it does then the organisation doesn't deserve to survive for the simple reason that it is acting as a leech on society – drawing more out than it is putting in. Which is why Chapter 10 introduces the concept of 'inclusive capitalism' and gives examples.

Silence: A healthy work culture will encourage and enable all the voices to be heard and listened to. It will not seek to silence individuals, and nor will it seek to silence debate and discussion. Trying to silence debate and discussion around, for example, institutional racism is tantamount to promoting racist attitudes. All employees should be encouraged to present their authentic selves at work, and this requires they have the opportunity and power to speak to that identity in a way which is true for them, even if it counters whatever dominant discourse exists in the organisation. The organisation must change and become adaptable and not fear doing so. Silence is a corrosive means of rendering individuals not only mute but invisible.

Awareness: In Chapter 4 I identify what makes a Totally Inclusive Community, and one of the variables is working to eliminate all forms of oppression, social injustice, discrimination. In short, if an organisation does not care about these problems then it does not care about its employees, its clients, its stakeholders. It only cares about exploiting them for maximum profit. Lack of awareness towards social injustice is nothing less than saying one does not care about social injustice. As is explained in this book, organisations are a fundamentally important element in the social fabric. Therefore, what type of culture and level of awareness is exhibited in that culture will matter. It has an impact, positive or negative.

Stress: Stress at work can be positive, though too much of it will make you ill. It will certainly act against any chance of the organisation becoming Totally Inclusive. Why? Because if employees become ill because of the work they do then that is a clear indicator that the organisation is not creating a healthy work–life balance – employees are not being protected and nurtured; they are being driven to the edge by a work culture which places results before people. True employee well-being can only be achieved in a Totally Inclusive Community. Stress can also lead to the next organisational barrier – violence.

Violence: Violence comes in many forms, from physical assault to murder; sexual harassment to rape; bullying to online trolling; slut shaming to revenge porn; stalking to ghosting. Racism, sexism, classism, ableism, homophobia are all forms of violence against the person and can be present in any organisation which has not achieved Total Inclusivity. Does your organisation promote violence or does it promote peace? If you answer that it promotes peace then violences should be absent from it, and when they do occur clear actions are taken, sanctions applied, to ensure justice and no repetition.

Vision and Ambition: Mission and vision statements usually get created by bosses and senior managers sitting around a table and writing them. This can be an organic process, or it can be stale. Accepting that most employees will be unable to recite the vision and mission of their organisation, nevertheless these statements of intent and purpose are important because they set in words the reason the organisation exists (beyond simply to make profit). If the vision and indeed the ambition behind the vision and organisation are not orientated towards Total Inclusivity, then not much chance of it emerging into reality.

CONCLUSION

The beginning of the Total Inclusivity journey lies in being aware of which direction one is going, and that requires a map. Like any good map, the Total Inclusivity one will point out the barriers, dangers and places to avoid. No single book can list all these for every organisation, but what I have done in this chapter is highlight the most common barriers or resistances to Total Inclusivity.

What gets in the way of Total Inclusivity is you, and it is others. Don't blame the organisation – remember, the organisation is not a living and breathing entity; it is only constituted by the people who work in it. We are all responsible for overcoming barriers to Total Inclusivity and for ensuring no barriers exist in the first place.

Do not displace responsibility for Total Inclusivity onto others. Do not make it the sole task of one or two senior leaders to bring in Total Inclusivity. They cannot do it alone. Every member of the organisation counts. Sure, some will have more power and influence than others, but in the final reckoning, Total Inclusivity is down to you.

Which brings us to the final barrier towards Total Inclusivity and one which is invariably trotted out as the 'reason I and my organisation are still acting in a discriminatory manner'.

Unconscious Bias: Firstly, let us recognise that 'unconscious bias' is no excuse for discrimination of any kind. For example, if you are Black, LGBTQ+ or a woman who is being given the cold shoulder or worse by people or by an organisation because of your skin colour, sexuality, gender, then you will not experience it as 'unconscious'; you'll experience it as very much overt marginalisation. Secondly, it would seem rather a thin excuse to claim a prejudice was 'unconsciously' performed given we've had many decades of global research and media examinations about all aspects of social injustice. If you've been living on a remote island in the South Pacific all your life, with no access to social media, then maybe these debates have passed you by. If not, it seems unlikely. Certainly, if you are in a profession such as education, health, social services or medicine, where issues of equity, diversity and inclusiveness are so strongly researched and voiced, claiming unconscious bias is stretching the limits of probability. Perhaps one can claim unconscious bias if one works in the uniformed services or any male-dominated profession, but only by virtue of that profession being decades behind the global curve in respect of recognising issues of social justice and inclusivity. And right now, even the uniformed services are in the public spotlight over their lack of inclusivity and active discrimination.

There may well be microaggressions or more overt acts of discrimination operating in an organisation and which the leaders of that organisation have not yet recognised as problematic for some sections of society. Examples would be in teaching, where the curriculum makes no mention of Black and Asian lives, history, perspectives, role models (for more on this, see Power, 2021). Or any profession where the unstated assumptions are that only males who went to Oxbridge or an Ivy League university should be considered for promotion. Any large organisation which does not offer gender-neutral toilets to its employees is also guilty of discriminatory behaviour. If your organisation encourages or passively permits acts of sexual harassment of staff or treats sexually predatory behaviour by managers as 'just blokes being blokes' then it too is guilty of discrimination. And if you work in the judicial system of any white-dominated society and find that more Black people are in your jails than were enslaved in 1850, a decade before the Civil War began, then clearly there is a problem somewhere (see for discussion Tatum, 2017).

Are these and similar behaviours all undertaken unconsciously? Not even an expert psychiatrist will be able to answer that for every individual. What we do know, however, is that research shows no more than 15% of Americans, for example, openly express discrimination against Black Americans (ibid). Which tells us that white people prefer not to admit to discrimination even, or especially, when they practice it.

If we are to assume that these material manifestations of discrimination are because our brains haven't registered them as discriminatory, then we have to assume that once our brains have been raised to a higher level of awareness then unconscious bias will disappear.

In other words, once something is known it cannot ever be unknown. Given we've had many decades, if not centuries, to address social injustices in humanity, then we should no longer be talking about unconscious bias/discrimination. We all know discrimination exists. We've all seen these manifestations close up. And if we haven't witnessed them firsthand then we've certainly read about them or seen them acted out on our TV screens.

We, as individuals, as organisations, as societies, can only hide behind ignorance and the 'unconscious' for so long. I respectfully suggest that it is now time to have a more open, honest and adult discussion about what might stop us moving towards Total Inclusivity.

Then we can overcome that final barrier.

REFLECTIONS, GUIDANCE AND COMMITMENTS

Reflection Exercise: 'How does my silence hurt me and others?' Reflect on the times you know you should have spoken up in defence of a colleague suffering discrimination or microaggressions and chose not to. How did it feel to know you let an injustice pass without challenge? Would you do it again?

Guidance for Implementation: Silencing is a passive form of aggression and is very palpable in non-inclusive organisations. Speaking up requires some courage but mostly it just requires you to know when and where speaking is demanded because it is the right thing to do. Have a look at each of the personal and organisational barriers listed earlier and consider which are present in your life, your work, and list them. Then pass that list to others in your organisation. Or better still, encourage them to read this chapter and list the barriers for themselves. Once a majority of people in the organisation feel confident about challenging injustices and voicing, so will Total Inclusivity become more of a reality and less of a dream.

Commitment: To effect positive change within your workplace by encouraging feelings of connection between colleagues and challenging a 'competitive silo' mentality.

NOTES

1 Quote from Al Weiwei in www.theguardian.com/artanddesign/2021/may/29/ai-weiwei-on-colonialism-and-statues-churchill-china-and-covid.

2 'Woke' is taken to mean alert to and seeking challenge, social injustices, especially those concerned with gender, sexuality, race, ethnicity and class. To be labelled as 'woke' is to be described as someone who is decent and fair-minded.

3 Conflict theory: Usually associated with the materialist (Marxist and functionalist) view of society as made up of competing groups, ideologies, entities, classes. In this eternal (everlasting?) struggle, tension and violence arises when resources, status and power are unevenly distributed.

Seven

The previous chapter examined what gets in the way of TI. One obstacle deliberately omitted is 'privilege'. Why? Because it is such an important, pervasive but contested term that it is deserving of its very own chapter. Very few of us feel privileged, at least not all of the time. If anything, we are more likely to feel hard done by, marginalised, stressed, disenfranchised, victimised, misunderstood, overworked, unpaid and rarely appreciated for our true worth. Explaining to such a person that maybe they are privileged in comparison to most others in the world isn't easy and can quickly lead to denial, rejection or worse. Yet the reality is that some identities are more privileged than others, even if the person inhabiting that privileged identity experiences it rather differently. This chapter will delve into the discussion around white privilege, straight male privilege and cultural capital privilege. It will open the door to a greater self-awareness and aims to trigger reflection in the reader as to why their identity mix may be elevated in certain social, organisational and cultural settings and situations. As with every chapter in this book, the discussion will come back to key questions such as 'why is this the way it is?' and 'what can I do to change it, make it better?'

To help get started on this discussion the chapter opens with examples of 'unrecognised privileges', because it is important to realise how this feeds discrimination and unconscious bias.

UNRECOGNISED PRIVILEGES

Several decades ago, I was a Further Education lecturer working in an inner-city college in the north of England. Around half the 1,500 or so students were Black or Asian. At any one time there were an estimated 30 different ethnic and racial groups in the student body, representative of the 80-plus ethnic and racial groups living in the immediate vicinity of the college; it was an area of strong and diverse community links but high levels of unemployment and poverty. Out of more than 200 lecturing

DOI: 10.4324/9781003244073-7

staff less than 10% were Black or Asian, and no ethnic minorities were represented at senior management level. 90% of the students were from a Black, Asian or white working-class background. The vast majority of the lecturers were white middle class, male. They worked hard, were stressed, underpaid, insecure, and invariably considered themselves under-appreciated by management.

How do you explain to such middle-aged white teaching professionals that their class and racial identity is a privileged one? With difficulty.

More recently, I was delivering race awareness training to the senior management of a very exclusive independent school in the UK. The school has a history going back more than 200 years. The senior managers, all white, 50% male, 50% female, were keen to understand why alumni of the school were complaining about institutional racism they'd experienced as students. These complaints, in writing, had been trickling in for a few years, though they spiked once the BLM movement kicked off. The school managers were concerned to address the matter. Firstly, the complaints took them completely by surprise; secondly, out of eight senior managers, only one openly recognised the concept of white privilege. These managers were dedicated professionals. Most had given their best working years to the school. They worked hard and were committed to the well-being of the students. They truly saw the school as one big family – students and staff working in harmony for the good of all.

How do you explain to such professionals that part of the problem stems from their lack of self-awareness? With difficulty.

When whiteness dominates it blinds.

Back to the FE college: One morning I was walking to the class to begin work, and I came across two of my Black female students in the corridor. They were deeply anxious and upset, and one was in tears. Obviously, I stopped and expressed concern as to what the problem was and asked could I help. It transpired the two students (both aged 19) had been verbally abused and harassed by police slowly driving past them in a marked police car as they walked to the college.

That incident prompted me to make further enquiries with the other students in the group. I learned that such racist actions by the British police were commonplace, at least for these students. For example, it was almost certain that should any of my Black students drive outside the city for any distance there was a high chance they'd get stopped by the police for a random check.

As a white lecturer, aged mid-40s, I had never once been stopped by the British police for a random check throughout my 25 years of driving.

Between 2016 and 2019, I held a non-executive director position for a successful international and independent school operation in Brunei. The schools had built an enviable reputation for quality and innovation. None of the teachers were white. All were Bruneian, Malay, Filipino, Indian, Sri Lankan or Chinese. The owners were Malay/Chinese. A significant percentage of the expat male international school teachers were gay, though not out. Despite being in a Muslim country, the gay teachers expressed no concern over their identity being compromised or threatened in Brunei – until April 2019, when the Sultan of Brunei enacted Sharia law making homosexuality, sodomy, adultery, and rape offenses punishable with death by stoning (BBC News, 2019a).

Within 18 months, most of the gay expat male teachers had left the school and Brunei. Which was a great pity, because they were among the best teachers in the schools if not in the country.

The examples above cover class, race, gender and sexuality. Inevitably, these 'Big 4 Identities' do not exist independently of each other. They intersect to form powerful vehicles for opportunity or, as we can see from above, lack of it. They all happen to be from the world of education, because that is the one I have personally experienced. No doubt you will have similar examples from your profession. If you haven't then it is likely because you haven't noticed them. And it is very easy not to notice them if you are not personally impacted, e.g. have a privileged identity mix.

But then it is very easy to miss our privileges – it's precisely because they're often unearned then we take them for granted.

Take, for example, one particular concept of identity which has emerged to prominence on the back of globalisation: the 'global citizen'.

There are now many thousands of international and independent schools around the world busily trying to develop this concept in the subjectivities of their students – preparing them for a good life, rich with material advantage, career opportunities and social capital.

But who teaches these global citizens of the future?

Mostly white, straight, middle-class professionals, led by white, straight, middle-class males.

If you are not white, not middle class and not straight then becoming a global citizen will be more of a challenge for you. It will mean you are always at risk of having your identity rejected, marginalised, threatened by your social environment.

Being a global citizen is a privilege and not one extended to the vast majority of people. But it is easy to forget just how many barriers there are to enjoying the opportunities and benefits which come with a globalised outlook on life; having the right skin colour, sexuality, education and, of course, passport.

To fully understand what it is like to be Black in a white-dominated society, LGBTQ+ in a homophobic or transphobic society or a woman subjected to a persistent patriarchal oppression, you have to live it.

And if you cannot live it then you have to open your mind to it.

Just don't say you 'know it' unless you have lived it.

Having a blind spot is a luxury. It is a privilege in itself. But it is not helpful to you in your journey towards enlightenment, awareness, understanding and Total Inclusivity.

Black students don't have any blind spots about racism in the UK. Why? Because they live with the consequences of it every day of their lives.

If you are born LGBTQ+ then you will have to be very careful where you decide to live and work. Not for you the freedom of being a global citizen when there is so much blatant, and often institutionalised, anti-LGBTQ+ behaviour and attitudes out there.

And wealth alone won't protect you from it. Having parents' wealthy enough to send them to an elite school in England didn't protect that school's Black students from the pain of racism.

Which leads us to the next issue invariably raised by those who discount the notion of privilege – meritocracy; if we have meritocracies, who needs TI?

MERITOCRACIES?

You will often hear those who are privileged and successful proudly declare that they 'got there on their own, without any help'. The inference being that if they can do it so can everyone else, regardless of their identity mix.

No one gets there on their own. We all need help at times. That help may be a coincidental meeting, a loan, a mentor, a scholarship or the right job opportunity coming up at just the right time. For many marginalised people, assistance often needs to be more structured, more formal and less discriminatory. Which is why many governments and organisations, seeking to increase the representation of marginalised groups, provide policies and practices which enable affirmative action, also known as positive action.

This is necessary because there are no true meritocracies. For there to be so society would need to have erased all disadvantages which accrue from NOT having been born to the right parents at the right time and having an able body and mind which can take advantage of all the opportunities afforded to those who automatically inherit high levels of cultural capital. Added to which there are the issues of skin colour, gender, sexuality and ethnicity.

We may never make the world equal, but we can make organisations Totally Inclusive, which would go a long way towards equalisation not least by virtue of removing barriers to opportunity.

One of the biggest barriers to opportunity is the selection process for jobs. Unconscious bias can play a big role in influencing our perspectives and opinions of others, and this inevitably contaminates any comfortable notions of meritocracy which one might assume are operating in an organisation.

To imagine you or your boss automatically always hire the 'best person for the job' is simply naïve. It is all too easy to unconsciously hire someone in one's own image,[1] and given the dominance of white (presumably straight) males in management it is no surprise that they are most likely to be the ones shortlisted for interviews.

If you doubt that or imagine you are immune from unconscious bias, then why not take the unconscious bias test developed by Harvard?[2]

This Implicit Association Test (IAT);

measures strengths of associations between concepts (e.g. black people, gay people) and evaluations (e.g. good, bad) or stereotypes (e.g. athletic, clumsy). The main idea is that making a response is easier when closely related items share the same response key.

The IAT includes the following diversity variables:

Gender
Asian
Weapons
Disability
Sexuality
Transgender
Religion
Age

Skin-tone
Weight
Race

For example, on Race ('Black –White' AIT) it requires the ability to distinguish faces of European and African origin. It indicates that most white Americans have an automatic preference for white over black. The Age ('Young–Old' AIT) test measures the ability to distinguish young from old faces. It indicates that Americans have automatic preferences for young over old.

The Harvard AIT is just one way of measuring your unconscious bias when it comes to those who are different from yourself and/or who draw down social stereotypes. But there are other questions you can ask of an organisation to see to what extent certain identities are being privileged over others:

1 Does an after-work drinking culture operate?
2 Do the same people always lead on the interviews?
3 Is the promotion process transparent?
4 Do people regularly send emails after work, during holidays, weekends?
5 Do job advertisements list criteria that could only be met by men?
6 Do job advertisements list criteria that could only be met by white applicants?
7 Do job interview selection panels ensure they have strong diversity representation?
8 Do you run CV blind interviews?
9 Do you instigate contextual recruitment processes – e.g. consider backgrounds?
10 Does the organisation have a buddy system for new recruits?
11 Does the organisation look to attract certain personality types?
12 Does the organisation prefer people who are of a certain faith outlook?
13 Are meetings regularly held early in a morning and/or at the end of the workday?

These questions are not simply there to be answered 'yes' or 'no'; they are offered as tests of the diversity and flexibility of the organisational culture and of the level of importance you might afford the answers.

For example, if you are a regular at the pub or bar at the end of the working day, drinking along with those colleagues of yours who likewise have no need or desire to return home to a family, have you stopped to think whether this negatively impacts the work culture – especially if that pub or bar is where important work decisions are getting make and networks being built?

If you are one of those responsible for the recruitment process, when you are looking at CVs do you go straight to the last job and perhaps the degree of the applicant? Or do you take the time to consider that person's background and what it took to get them from their starting point to where they are today?

What about the 'ideal candidate'? Do you have a mental image of them? E.g. white, smart looking, confident smile, dark suit, shirt and tie, 30 to 45, not too overweight and male? Does this image fit your 'brand'?

If you or your organisation have internalised what the 'ideal' candidate or employee looks like then you've already internalised unearned privilege and are consequently contributing to a lack of diversity in your organisation. You've also set up 'others' as lesser and therefore more likely to fail – not because they are programmed to fail but because the system, the perspective, the dominant culture actually expects it.

You see, privilege is a self-perpetuating prophecy. In many workplaces, 'white, straight, male' is the dominant culture and there is an unstated assumption that any 'others' won't last long in the job. If an employee with a marginalised identity decides to leave the workplace suddenly or after only a short period of time, most organisations which are not Totally Inclusive will not be bothered to ask the really critical question: 'Why did they leave so soon?'

So how can we examine these privileges in more depth? How do they operate and which often unseen or unrecognised dynamics serve to perpetuate them, especially in the minds of those who benefit from having identities which are privileged?

The examination that follows doesn't cover every possible privilege but it does cover three of the most pervasive: those relating to race, sexuality and class.

WHITE PRIVILEGE: RACISM AND COLOURISM

In this section I am going to intentionally mix up three important but rather different terms; white privilege, racism and colourism. These issues exist independently to some extent but still influence and draw nourishment from each other, often in a way which is unrecognised by those who perpetuate them. They are each, of course, massive concepts, and I cannot do justice to them in a single sub-section. But what I can do is illustrate how they connect to produce and 'validate' privilege.

The statistics on racism are stark and overwhelmingly depressing, whether it be the USA, UK, Europe or most anywhere else in the world. To imagine that being white does not carry with it some unearned privileges is to be simply in denial of the reality of racism.

So are all white people automatically racist? No, though all white people need to recognise how being white can contribute to the perpetuation of racism, not least by failing to recognise that white skin symbolises so much which is powerful – and negative in global society.

The reason being that racism is built on white privilege. It confers advantages based on the colour of one's skin.

As critical race theory emphasises, racism is more than prejudice, it is the power effects of that prejudice:

> racism, like other forms of oppression, is not only a personal ideology based on racial prejudice by a system involving cultural messages and institutional policies and practices as well as the beliefs and actions of individuals. . . . the system clearly operates to the advantage of Whites and to the disadvantage of people of color. Racial prejudice combined with social power – access to social, cultural, and economic resources and decision-making – leads to the institutionalization of racist policies and practices.
>
> (Tatum, 2017, p. 87; see also Delgado and Stefancic, 2012)

If you are white and in a position of power in an organisation then you have a particular responsibility to ensure that racial prejudice does not creep in through the gaps in your awareness and that of others in your organisation. And the first step in closing off those gaps is to recognise the reality of white privilege.

The IAT Harvard test referred to above includes a test on skin tone. The results may be different for you if you take the test, but the Harvard research shows that this test 'often reveals an automatic preference for light-skin relative to dark-skin'.

At one level this discrimination does operate simply at the level of skin colour. It is impossible to determine just how powerful this discrimination is, but one indicator is the global skin-lightening and -bleaching industry, estimated to be worth up to US$20 billion back in 2017 (Rehman, 2017). In India alone, the industry is valued at nearly half a billion dollars, with 60% of Indian women saying they use the products (Mwanza, 2019).

That is an awful lot of creams, all designed to make people's skin look less dark.

And the product sell is often blatantly racist:

> In the Indo-Pak subcontinent, a considerable chunk of this revenue is earned by Uniliver's best-selling 'Fair and Lovely' product. The adverts for the cream tend to follow a staid format, where a dark-skinned girl is unable to get a job or get married unless she uses the product and manages to lighten her skin.
>
> (Mwanza, 2019)

Taken to extremes, this fear of being dark skinned can lead to ridiculous, dangerous actions:

> Recently I heard that [Kenyan] women even use Jik bleach on their faces – it's a brand that's supposed to clean floors, drains and clothes.[3]

But ridiculous or not, the social, economic consequences of having a darker skin can be severe:

> Matrimonial advertisements in India and Pakistan openly specify that the prospective bride or groom be 'tall and fair'. Newborn babies with dark skin are massaged daily with herbal ubtan mixtures in order to make their skin fair.
>
> (ibid)

'Colourism' is one term for racial prejudice because behind the desire for a whiter skin is a desire to not be Black. When societies around the world are celebrating, promoting and privileging people with lighter skin tone over those with dark skin, then how can there not be a culture of unearned privilege operating as a system of power effects through all levels of society?

Even those in power are not immune from its corrosive and toxic effects.

Take a closer look at the political candidate posters which get put up on billboards and buildings and down highways and country lanes during any election in Asia, especially Thailand and Malaysia. Why is it all these candidates for election have light skins?

Yes, their photos have been doctored to ensure their skins look lighter than they actually are. Apparently, this aids their chances of getting elected by the populace, most of whom are born with naturally darker skin tones.

We can blame this obsession with whiter skin on Western colonialism, the media, globalised culture or centuries of class distinctions whereby the poor worked outside in the harsh environment while the rich and leisured stayed indoors. You can decide the reason for racism. What you cannot deny is that white privilege exists.

Pretending that white privilege does not exist is to help build the foundations of individual and institutionalised racism. That first, very basic level of awareness raising must take place in any organisation, and any individual, aspiring to Total Inclusivity.

STRAIGHT SEXUALITY PRIVILEGE

Straight sexuality privilege arises when a society, culture or organisation only recognises and only validates heterosexuality and either overtly or covertly creates barriers against any other type of sexual identity. Those barriers may be hidden within unconscious bias or made explicit through, for example, the death penalty. Any place where heterosexuality is made 'compulsory' is a place of risk for LGBTQ+ people. Indeed, no identity can be truly safe if some identities are deliberately rendered unsafe.

Why would some sexualities be privileged over others? Because clearly, they are. It is difficult to tell if, based on historical evidence, global society is becoming more or less open to lesbian, gay, bisexual, transgendered and queer identities. Much depends on which aspects of history you examine (e.g. Ancient Greece compared to Medieval Europe) and from where you gather your evidence.

On the plus side, 2019 (the year before the COVID pandemic), the top 20 global Gay Pride Parades (New York City, Madrid, Sao Paulo, Vienna, Amsterdam, Taipei, Zurich, Toronto, San Francisco, Cologne, Manchester, Los Angeles, Buenos Aires, Malmo, Seattle, Mexico City, Stockholm, Tel Aviv, Sydney, Dublin) attracted hundreds of millions of participants and spectators of every nationality, every race and ethnic group, all ages, all religions and every sexuality, including straight (Agoda, 2019).

These parades are both a global celebration of LGBTQ+ identities and a poignant reminder that such identities remain marginal to mainstream society.

In a world of compulsory heterosexuality, celebrating LGBTQ+ identities is essential, because coming out as LGBTQ+ is a risk, no matter where you live, no matter how open-minded your employer is or how supportive your family is.

How big a risk mostly depends on nationality and culture. The 2021 global ranking (Human Dignity Trust, 2021) of the most dangerous countries to be LGBTQ+, either as a citizen or a traveller, is as follows:

1 Nigeria
2 Saudi Arabia
3 Malaysia
4 Malawi
5 Oman
6 Jamaica
7 Myanmar
8 Qatar
9 UAE
10 Yemen
11 Zambia
12 Tanzania
13 Brunei
14 Afghanistan
15 Iran
16 Uganda
17 Algeria
18 Pakistan
19 Kenya
20 Indonesia

There are, at time of writing, 71 countries where homosexuality is illegal (Erasing 76 Crimes, 2021), and at least 10 of these implement the death penalty for gay sex. Dire as this situation is, it is an improvement on a hundred years ago, when homosexuality was illegal most everywhere, and most 'advanced' societies could not even contemplate bisexuality, homosexuality or transgenderism.

In the USA, a country that has been at the forefront of LGBTQ+ rights over the past few decades, a majority of Americans now back LGBTQ+

protections – 70%. Though worryingly, support has fallen since 2015. What appears to be happening is a polarisation of opinions, with many Republicans now hardening their views against LGBTQ+ people/rights (Fitzsimons, 2019). Similar anti-LGBTQ+ rhetoric and politics are trending in Poland, China, Russia, Ukraine, Georgia, Latvia and Serbia. As ever, the crux of the problem comes down to education, or lack of it:

> If homophobic attacks in Serbia are so often perpetrated by the young, blame an education system that teaches them nothing about gay rights, women's rights, worker's rights – or any other rights.
>
> (Kastelec, 2020)

To put this in perspective, have you ever come across an education system which promotes LGBTQ+ rights over straight male rights?

Similarly, it is unthinkable that a heterosexual person might have to consider where to live and work because of fear over their sexuality being discovered and discriminated against.

Credit Line: Cartoons drawn by Advanced Standard Group Co., Ltd.

It is unconscionable that a straight person would apply for a job and feel they have to hide their sexuality at interview or during the course of their employment.

It never happens that an 'expert' stands up and claims to have found a 'cure' for heterosexuality.

No one questions or raises an eyebrow when a 20-something straight couple decide they want to get married.

How often have you heard a religious sermon or read a religious text which condemns heterosexuality as 'evil' and 'evidence of corrupted society'?

I know of no countries where heterosexual marriage is illegal, criminalised, outlawed. Indeed, every culture and education system in the world celebrates heterosexual coupledom.

This is the true nature of compulsory heterosexuality. And it is why straight sexuality is an unearned privilege which in any decent, equitable, mature, learned, inclusive and open-minded society it would not be.

CULTURAL CAPITAL PRIVILEGE

If you'd stepped into a sociology department of most any decent university back in the 1970s, 1980s, 1990s, then very likely you'd quickly have gotten caught up in the lectures, discussions, debates, research to do with social class. That was the age of class revolution (at least rhetorically), and it encouraged many thousands of students and their professors to study it intensely. Most of these researchers would be drawing on some aspect of Marxist or neo-Marxist theory – from Gramsci to Althusser, Marx to Braverman, Marcuse to Weber, you had many theorists to choose from. Nowadays, those same departments are more likely to have researchers studying feminist poststructuralism, masculinism, post-colonialism, post-humanism and certainly intersectionality.

Yes, even sociologists have their trends, and the trend nowadays is to critically examine identity in all its manifestations.

In which case can we assume that social class distinctions have disappeared?

No, they have not. Though they are trickier to spot.

For example, gone are the days when the British working-class male smoked Woodbines, wore a cloth cap, worked in heavy industry or mining, drank his pints of bitter ale, watched a football match on Saturday afternoon and then went home to his back-to-back terraced house in some soot-stained inner-city suburb to have his dinner served up for him by his aproned wife.

Today, we are all part of a greater middle-class porridge, a mix of languages, values, beliefs, statuses and wealth. For at least 30 years now, the global middle class has been expanding like the belly of the working-class beer drinker – swelling outward in all directions. In 2018, half the world's population became officially middle class, some 3.8 billion people (Smigiera, 2021).

This global tipping point has indeed been disrupted by the global COVID pandemic, but certainly, Asia, and especially China and India, are pouring more and more families into the middle classes, leaving behind as they do a diminishing group of those who are poor and vulnerable (Brookings, 2018).

The story of the decline of the traditional working classes is not one for this book, but it is worth taking note of. Because what has replaced social class is cultural capital privilege.

The concept of cultural capital comes from the writings of Pierre Bourdieu (1984), who identifies culture as now the central means of acquiring wealth and status. But not just any culture. Bourdieu argues that the most powerful groups in any society have the power to 'impose meanings and to impose them as legitimate'. And this includes having the correct manners, style, language, grammar, all those complex and invari-ably unrecognised socialised behaviours which 'unlock' advantage in a globally competitive, capitalist society.

Sociologists see this as a hegemonic process, whereby the those from high-level cultural backgrounds grab more of the opportunities than those from poorer (or 'culturally deprived') backgrounds.

Wealth has a lot to do with it, but mostly it is about education. Developed countries such as the UK, France, USA, Germany, Australia, New Zealand and Canada are typically sending well over 50% of school leavers on to university education – with a degree inevitably becoming the normal, if not minimum standard, for employment.

The same pressure to acquire cultural capital, and the keys to a profes-sion, career, material advantage (and global citizenship) are now present across the world, from Brazil to China, Russia to Morocco.

But what happens to the 30% to 50% who don't go to university or on to further education?

If you are reading this book then you are likely already a recipient of cultural capital. Firstly, you can read and communicate in a global language – English. You can use a computer, and you have access to the internet. You can interpret the messages being presented in this book and analyse them based on your own subjective (professional and/or educational) experience. Some of this information and discussion will resonate with you; maybe some won't. But almost certainly you will be a member of the global middle class. Though likely you won't feel especially privileged as a consequence because you have to work hard, are under pressure, have deadlines and targets to meet and often feel very vulnerable and insecure financially.

But vulnerable and insecure or not, you are privileged. And are so by virtue of having acquired, maybe from birth and upbringing, perhaps from higher-level education and work opportunities, cultural capital.

This is, in effect, more important nowadays than material capital. You can lose a home, go bankrupt, lose your job, end up broke. But what you won't lose is your cultural capital privilege. It is always with you – a ready resource to be used whenever necessary. It may not in itself guarantee you a 'good life' – there are other factors and identity variables at play here, as I've discussed – but without it you've got a real uphill climb.

Not surprisingly, people who are poor and vulnerable in every country recognise the reality of this, perhaps more than the typically privileged individual. Which is why they are prepared to expend large amounts of whatever meagre disposable income they have on ensuring their off-spring get the best possible education. They spend this money not to ensure their children acquire knowledge of maths, science, history and languages but to acquire the cultural capital which will open doors, create opportunities and get them a foothold on the ladder going, hopefully, upwards.

Of course, if you've studied hard, worked diligently, been a little entre-preneurial and thereby lifted yourself out of an impoverished background and into a higher-level cultural status by your own efforts, then you are entitled to say that the cultural capital you've acquired is most definitely earned.

And one would not argue against that.

Only to reiterate – no one gets there entirely on their own merit. We all need a lift up at times.

CONCLUSION

This chapter has examined unrecognised privileges and the unearned privileges which lay behind them, notably white privilege, sexuality privilege and cultural capital privilege. I've evidenced how they connect to powerful but ultimately toxic forces in society, and in that respect, they adversely affect us all. Because one is safe unless there is Total Inclusivity, and there cannot be Total Inclusivity when individuals and groups are discriminated against, rendered invisible, violated, persecuted.

If you are white, straight and middle class and imagine all this doesn't concern you, then reflect on this poem:

> First they came for the communists, and I did not speak out because I was not a communist.
> Then they came for the socialists, and I did not speak out because I was not a socialist.
> Then they came for the labor leaders, but I did not speak out because I was a unionist.
> Then they came for the Jews, and I did not speak out because I was not a Jew.
> As one day became another and others disappeared, gypsies, mentally retarded, homosexuals, Jehovah's Witnesses, criminals, anti-socials and emigrants, I remained silent because I was not one of them.
> Then they came for me, but no one spoke for me because by then there was no one left to speak.

(Martin Niemoller, 1946)

REFLECTIONS, GUIDANCE AND COMMITMENTS

Reflection Exercise: 'How has my identity been shaped by privilege?' It will have been shaped by privilege somehow, though maybe not in an inevitable, predictable or consistent way. But if you are reading this book then you are most definitely privileged and more so than many millions of others (and I acknowledge my privilege in being able to write it and get it published). That may not feel like a very heightened privilege to you, but it will be in comparison to those who could not read the book or relate to its central messages. That is just the base line for reflecting on just how privileged you are.

Guidance for Implementation: How to recognise and challenge privilege in the workplace? Take your starting point as being a desire not to perpetuate privilege which is unearned. Spot where privilege is operating in your organisation and look to challenge it – assumptions surrounding sexuality, whiteness and cultural capital are a good starting point, though you can extend it to include physicality, religion, ethnicity and age. Maybe use this book as a source of discussion with a few like-minded work colleagues.

Commitment: To reflect on your privilege in different contexts and any assumptions that come with it. We are not asking you to renounce your privileges or to feel guilty about having them, only to try and ensure that you recognise that all these life benefits and bonuses haven't automatically arisen from a meritocratic situation but from advantages bestowed by society and culture.

NOTES

1 Diversity at work: hiring the 'best person for the job' isn't enough. Women in Leadership. *The Guardian*, www.theguardian.com/women-in-leadership/2016/jan/05/diversity-at-work-hiring-the-best-person-for-the-job-isnt-enough.

2 Take a Test, https://implicit.harvard.edu/implicit/takeatest.html.

3 www.businessoffashion.com/articles/beauty/profiting-from-the-skin-lightening-trade.

Eight

We are living through interesting times, and not just for the reason you might imagine. At time of writing humanity is still very much caught up in the full impact of the COVID-19 pandemic, so it is impossible to make predictions as to what happens next regarding this virus. By the time you read this book it may all be over, or we may be still dying in our hundreds of thousands.

But whatever the immediate future, one thing has changed forever: the pandemic has shattered the historic and largely unquestioned relationship between men and leadership.

Or to be more precise, and as is explained in what follows, between a particular type of masculinity and leadership.

Based on the evidence of how different countries coped with the pandemic depending on whether they were led by men or by women, it is certainly tempting to state that women make better leaders than men.

In an analysis of 194 countries published by the Centre for Economic Policy Research and the World Economic Forum in August 2020, Germany, New Zealand, Finland, Taiwan, Bangladesh, Belgium, Norway, Iceland, Denmark, Switzerland and Scotland all did noticeably better at handling the initial stages of the virus and reducing death tolls than did male-led countries such as the US, Italy, UK, Spain, Brazil and India (Bostock, 2020).

Commentators pointed to the lack of empathy and compassion and a desire to not upset the economic applecart exhibited by leaders such as Trump, Bolsanoro, Johnson and Modi.

The researchers discuss the hesitancy on the part of the US, UK, Brazilian and Singaporean male leaders, by way of illustration, to first admit the presence of the crisis, and to take timely and appropriate decisions. This led to unnecessary sickness and deaths. In contrast, they show how female leaders in Taiwan, Iceland and New Zealand recognized the implications of the outbreak, listened to experts, took

DOI: 10.4324/9781003244073-8

quick and effective decisions, and therefore were able to relax the restrictions sooner or avoid lockdown altogether.

(Thomas, 2020)

While I would concur with this analysis and indeed welcome the fact that the myth is being shattered that men make better leaders than women, it is important to point out that this is not simply a test of men's leadership qualities versus women's leadership qualities.

If we follow that line of thinking then we end up trapped once more in the gender binary, critiqued in Chapter 2.

For example, if we claim that all men make weaker leaders than women, then how does that account for the high quality of male leadership demonstrated by the likes of Gandhi, Mandela and Martin Luther King? How to explain the remarkable turnaround against COVID-19 seen in the USA once Joe Biden became president? The reality is, the only thing Biden has in common with his predecessor is that they are both male politicians in their 70s.

Their masculinities are very different.

As I explore in this chapter, herein lies the clue to understanding which types of leaders or styles of leadership are best suited to helping create a Totally Inclusive Community.

However, in order to undertake this exploration, it is, reluctantly, necessary to operate within the gender binary – male and female – and this actually illustrates the problem. Because the world is not made up of only male and female; it is a whole lot more diverse than that, with non-binary, gender-questioning and gender non-conforming people also part of the human tapestry.

WOMEN ON THE RISE

The relationship between men and leadership is one of those givens which most of us fail to see simply because it is so ubiquitous. By way of example, if, a decade ago, you'd have asked any cohort of MBA students to present contemporary icons of inspirational leadership and discuss, chances are at least 9 out of 10 would have come up with a male leadership icon. Indeed, that was invariably my experience as a director of a UK university MBA programme for the first 15 years of this century.

However, undertake that same exercise today and it is almost certain that a significant number of such students, whatever their gender, will present figures such as Greta Thunberg, Kamala Harris, Malala Yousafzai,

Alexandria Ocasio-Cortez, Nancy Pelosi, Jacinda Ardern, Oprah Winfrey, Angela Merkel, Melinda Gates, Sheryl Sandberg, Christine Lagarde, Jameela Jamil, perhaps even Lady Gaga and Beyoncé.

What is being signalled here is a deep and hopefully lasting discursive shift away from the inevitability of men as leaders. It is no longer the case that men are seen as the unquestioned gender to lead us. Women are now leaders in every area of society, and their value as leaders is being globally recognised. Though that fact does not lessen the other reality, which is that female leaders are still treated differently in the media, by male colleagues in government for example, as compared to their male counterparts.

Below are a number of quotes from global researchers, political leaders, business leaders and prominent women and men leaders from across the public and private spectrums:

> We live in a world that is increasingly social, interdependent and transparent. And in this world, feminine values are ascendant.
> A recent global survey of 64,000 people across 13 countries shows that traditionally feminine leadership and values are more popular than the macho paradigm of the past.
>
> (Gerzema, 2013; Gerzema and D'Antonio, 2013)

> Modern women use soft-power to get what they want and they wield it with precision. They're aware of the need for harmony between the genders . . . and for the public face of balance. [But] these women are not engaged in a battle and they rarely see their gender as a barrier. Quite the opposite.
>
> (Gage, 2015)

> Pay special attention to women. Women care for others much more than men. Men only care about themselves. Women are going to be very powerful in the 21st Century. Because last century people compared about muscle. This century people will compare about wisdom. Hire as many women as possible. This is what we [Alibaba] did. This is our secret sauce.[1]

> The gender balance in the [British] military will gradually improve over the next 10 years. And that isn't going to be a benevolent action, it's going to be by necessity, because the complexities that we have in defence are going to mean the big chap mastering commander skills

we think of as leadership are just going to fall away. We'll need people who can really manage complex programmes and projects and that's absolutely gender neutral.[2]

More women need to be put into positions of power because men seem to be having some problems these days . . . Not to generalize but women seem to have a better capacity than men do, partly because of their socialization.

(Mejia, 2017)

The macho image has to go . . . the issue for some [of the male firefighters] is that if a woman can do the job, then it isn't the big hero job it was. It de-machos their role. [which is fine]. We have to change the perception of a six-foot muscled bloke who can kick a door down.[3]

Supporting this research and comments is the following data (from Whitehead, 2017)

- Women business owners hire 17% more women than do male business owners.
- Women use their incomes more productively, devoting 90 cents of every dollar they earn to their families and communities.
- Small and medium-sized enterprises form the engine driving economic dynamism in Asia.
- Gender diversity doubles on corporate boards which have female leadership.
- Women entrepreneurs outperform their male peers by more than 60% in creating value for investors.
- ASEAN (Association of South East Asian Nations) women contribute 36.4% of the combined GDP. ASEAN economies can boost their collective GDP by US$370 billion by 2025 if existing gender inequalities are eliminated.
- More than half the stores on Alibaba's online platform are owned by women.
- Of every five companies in Malaysia, one is now owned by a woman.
- According to an analysis of thousands of 360-degree reviews, women outscored men on 17 of the 19 capabilities that differentiate excellent leaders from average or poor ones (Zenger and Folkman, 2019).
- The number of self-made women billionaires went from 1 in 2001 to 56 in 2017, and more than half of these are Asian.

- Women corporate leaders are outperforming men, raking in $1.8 trillion more profits (Nasdaq, 2019).

A number of questions arise from the growing global evidence that women make better leaders than men. But they come down to two rather simple ones:

1 How?
2 Why?

HOW DO WOMEN MAKE BETTER LEADERS THAN MEN?

In her study of female leadership first published in 1990, Sally Helgesen (also 1995; Helgesen and Johnson, 2010) found that women leaders in America stood out for the following qualities over men leaders:

1 Placed a high value on relationships
2 Have a bias for direct communication rather than following the chain of command
3 Put themselves at the center of the people they lead
4 Are comfortable with diversity
5 Are skilled at integrating their personal lives and their lives at work rather than compartmentalising

Five years later, Gallup research (Fitch and Agrawal, 2015) revealed the following:

1 Female leaders are better at engaging employees (both male and female).
2 Female leaders are rated higher at giving employees recognition.
3 Female leaders are better at connecting with the people they lead.
4 Female leaders are better at giving helpful performance feedback.
5 Female leaders are better at getting people into the right role so they will learn.

Fast-forward, and yet more research, this time by Zenger and Folkman (2019) proves the same point:

1 Takes initiative   women outscore men by 7%
2 Resilience   women outscore men by 5%
3 Practices self-development women outscore men by 5%

4	Drives for results	women outscore men by 5%
5	High integrity and honesty	women outscore men by 5%
6	Develops others	women outscore men by 5%
7	Inspires and motivates	women outscore men by 4%
8	Bold leadership	women outscore men by 4%
9	Builds relationships	women outscore men by 4%
10	Champions change	women outscore men by 4%
11	Establishes stretch goals	women outscore men by 3%
12	Collaboration and teamwork	women outscore men by 3%
13	Connects to the outside world	women outscore men by 2%
14	Communicates powerfully	women outscore men by 1%
15	Solves problems and analyses	women outscore men by 1%
16	Leadership speed	women outscore men by 1%
17	Innovates	women outscore men by 1%
18	Technical/professional skills	women outscore men by 1%
19	Develops strategies	women outscore men by 1%

Based on the overwhelming evidence that women make better leaders than men, you'd have to ask yourself what would encourage any organisation to choose a man leader over a woman leader.

However, while being a reasonable response this fails to address the second question: 'Why?'

Because once we explore a little deeper, we realise this division is not simply down to gender identity, but is a consequence of gender performance.

WHY DO WOMEN MAKE BETTER LEADERS THAN MEN?

One immediate answer to the question is because women are now generally better educated than men.

There has been a pronounced global swing towards women outperforming men across Higher Education at least since the mid-1970s. For example, today 57% of college students are women, while in 1972, 43% were. According to UNESCO's 2009 Global Education Digest, female students increased sixfold between 1970 and 2007, while males only quadrupled (UNESCO, 2009).

> UNESCO's survey found that in North America and Europe, a third more women than men were on campus. Latin America, the Caribbean as well as Central Asia also show high rates of female enrolments. In a number of countries, at least two females graduate for every male.
>
> (Superscholar, 2021)

Taking the UK as an example, women are now more than a third more likely to go to university than men, with the gap between the sexes at 'record levels' (The Guardian, August, 2017). This data is supported by UK university experts, who have observed:

> Women get better degrees, they are more likely to get jobs and they are less likely to drop out. Women just do better than men.
>
> (Times Higher Education, 2016)

Globally, females are outperforming males at all levels of education, from K–12 through to postgraduate study. Not only do they demonstrate better leadership qualities than males, they are therefore better qualified than males to be leaders.

So does this explain why women are outperforming men in the leadership stakes – because they are, overall, better educated?

Not quite.

Certainly, education is a big factor, but then there are still a whole lot of highly educated and highly effective male leaders working in industry, commerce, education, finance and politics.

Credit Line: Cartoons drawn by Advanced Standard Group Co., Ltd.

What is being tested here is the capacity of individual women and men to be effective leaders and to be so in ways which are inclusive, emotionally intelligent and supportive.

Earlier, we quote Barak Obama, who offers a simple-to-understand explanation as to why women make better leaders – 'partly because of their socialization'. In this brief but telling statement, Obama is avoiding the trap of biological determinism, and the gender binary (almost), by declaring that women learn to be better leaders as a consequence of their upbringing.

And I would agree with him – females are more likely to be socialised into higher levels of emotional intelligence, and these traits are readily transferable to effective leadership.

But it does raise an interesting question and one very relevant to any organisation aiming to become a Totally Inclusive Community.

Can men learn to be emotionally intelligent, empathetic and supportive leaders, just like so many women are?

We have to believe that men have this capacity; otherwise we are condemning men to no future whatsoever as leaders. However, unlike for women, for men to acquire this capacity they must have the strength of will, intelligence and opportunity to disregard and not be tempted into following traditional forms of masculinity.

Where this takes us, then, is into an inevitable exploration of masculinity. Because it is within male gender identity performances (not gender identity) that we will find the clues to what makes a man leader into a potentially Totally Inclusive leader – or not.

DIFFERENT MASCULINITIES, DIFFERENT LEADERS

The starting point for this examination is the recognition that there are multiple masculinities, not one. Sure, as I will explain, there is a dominant type of masculinity, but there are at least two other types now apparent globally.

Unfortunately, it is the dominant (or most globally common) type of masculinity which is the problem, and any man who demonstrates it is not going to be able to engender or lead, a Totally Inclusive Community.

But first, how to define masculinity:

Masculinities are those behaviours, languages and practices,
existing in specific cultural and organizational locations, which are

commonly associate with males and thus culturally defined as not feminine.

(Whitehead and Barrett, 2002, p. 15;
see also Whitehead, 2002)

As you see, this is by necessity a fairly broad definition. But it is important because it signals not just the multiplicity of masculine identities but also their contingency and the fact that they emerge not from a biological imperative but from socialisation.

In that respect, masculinities and femininities are no different. What is different is how societies and cultures define 'what it means to be a man' and 'what it means to be a woman'. These definitions are constantly adapting, evolving and changing according to wider social and environmental factors and pressures. These gender performances are not fixed, and they are not predictable.

Indeed, they have perhaps never been less predictable than at this point in human history.

I now define and categorise global masculinities into three types. This is based on research I've undertaken and published over a 30-year period (Whitehead, 2002; Whitehead, 2021).

1 *Traditional Masculinity:* This is the most common type of masculinity, and it is the one which is a problem, not only for women and LGBTQ+ people but also for the men who exhibit it. No man with traditional masculinity will be able to lead a Totally Inclusive Community. Because to do so he will have to reflect so deeply upon himself – on his masculinist ideals, assumptions, attitudes, beliefs, very sense of power and superiority as a man – that it will demand levels of emotional intelligence he just doesn't have. Some can achieve this with help, but only if they are open to it.

That said, as I have explained elsewhere (Whitehead, 2021), there are different levels of traditional masculinity, from the mildly toxic to the extremist male fundamentalism exhibited by incels and highly violent, racist and misogynistic males. Clearly, no organisation would wish to be led by a man who professes to be a misogynist, incel, racist, male fundamentalist. In which case, we can dismiss this type of extreme traditional (toxic) masculinity from the start – though it does raise the question as to how an organisation can ensure such men do not get employed in the first place and, secondly, most definitely do not get promoted.

137 **How Is Gender Implicated in Leadership?**

As the title suggests, traditional masculinity has been around a long time. Back in the 1980s sociologists first named it 'hegemonic masculinity' and defined it as follows:

Hegemonic masculinity [is] a form of male behaviour and expression of male identity that seeks to reinforce men's power and patriarchal values. Based on characteristics such as competition, ambition, self-reliance, physical strength, aggression, and homophobia.

(Whitehead et al., 2014, p. 22)

The image of masculinity that is perpetrated [by hegemonic masculinity] involves physical toughness, the endurance of hardships, aggressiveness, a rugged heterosexuality, and unemotional logic.

(Barrett, 2002, p. 81)

More recently, mainstream discourse has identified it as 'toxic masculinity'.

Within many masculine cultures and value systems, male aggression is not considered problematic; indeed, it is actually lauded. Criminal gangs, the armed forces, militaristic and totalitarian societies are where we are most likely to witness and experience 'toxic masculinity': that is, aggressive male behaviour that is fundamentally corrosive to society and to individuals, including those who perform it: such behaviour continues to be expressed by, indeed attracts to it, males of all ages, cultures, ethnicities and social statuses.

(Whitehead et al., 2014, p. 246)

Toxic masculinity is now widely discussed and in common everyday usage. Which is positive, because the only way to eradicate it is to first identify it and then examine it publicly.

So today, there are three names given to the dominant, problematic type of masculinity:

Traditional
Hegemonic
Toxic

In effect, they refer to the same mental condition in males — a way of being a man which draws on power over others for validation of maleness and seeks to achieve this through aggressiveness, avid competitiveness, physical and/or emotional violence and emotional distancing. Arising from this condition will be racism, sexism, homophobia, extreme religious/political ideologies, misogyny and various forms of mental health problems, notably emotional dysfunctionality, lack of empathy and an absence of reflexivity and ability to communicate feelings.

Not a healthy state to be in for any man.

Which is why, in August 2018, the American Psychological Association did something extraordinary. For the first time in its 127-year history it addressed issues arising from male identity work. It published a 36-page report designed to help psychologists specifically address the problem of traditional masculinity:

> Traditional masculinity ideology has been shown to limit males psychological development, constrain their behaviour, result in gender role strain and gender role conflict and negatively influence mental health and physical health . . . [Masculinity ideology] is a particular constellation of standards that hold sway over large segments of the population, including: anti-femininity, achievement, eschewal of appearance of weakness, and adventure, risk and violence. [these behaviours link to] homophobia, bullying and sexual harassment.
>
> (APA, 2018)

In effect, the APA is finally confirming what gender sociologists have long recognised, which is that traditional masculinity is a damaging and toxic political gender ideology, not a biological state. This simple but profound statement by the APA throws the 'gender as biological destiny' myth out the window.

Consequently, any organisation aspiring to become a Totally Inclusive Community must first understand what traditional masculinity is and, second, ensure its leaders do not have this condition. And if they have, then they must be removed from positions of power, or they must agree to undergo counselling – because traditional masculinity is a mental health condition.

At this point you may well ask 'can women catch toxic masculinity?' I look at that interesting question in what follows.

2 *Progressive Masculinity*: If toxic or traditional masculinity is the worst form of gender performance both for individual males and for organisations, which is the best? Indeed, is there a best type of masculinity?

Yes, and it is called progressive, for obvious reasons.

These are the primary and secondary indicators that a man has progressive masculinity (from Whitehead, 2021).

The 10 Primary Indicators

1 He does not feel threatened by women's power or powerful women.
2 Feminist: supports LGBTQ+ rights and the MeToo movement
3 Liberal-minded and open to alternative cultural expressions
4 Anti-racist
5 Reflective, able to recognise and express his emotions positively
6 Negotiates and shares child-care duties with partner
7 Negotiates and shares household duties with partner (may be househusband)
8 Pro-choice (abortion and birth control)
9 Approaches intimate relationships from the standpoint of equality and equity
10 Masculinity not threatened by partners with higher professional status or earning power

The 10 Secondary Indicators

1 College/university educated
2 Seeks personal improvement (emotionally and intellectually)
3 Ambitious but also aims for a good work–life balance
4 Not avidly following any single religion but possibly spiritual
5 Can articulate his feelings and thoughts
6 Not prone to outbursts of aggression or violence
7 Comfortable with new technology
8 Considers himself a global citizen with an international mindedness
9 Has developed emotional bonds and friendship networks with straight and gay men
10 Uses online social networks in an engaging and supportive, non-violent way

I consider the most critical variable to be the first: *the man is either a declared feminist or he is comfortable with and therefore unthreatened by the power that women are acquiring and expressing today.*

Following which, my personal criteria for being a feminist, of whatever sex or gender, is are follows:

> If you believe in equality for women, are pro LGBTQ+, consider that all societies must challenge male abuse and de facto, educate males into less violent and damaging forms of behaviour, then you are a feminist.

If a man cannot meet this benchmark then he is very likely to be still embracing traditional/toxic masculinity, at least to some degree. Any man who has become more entrenched in his anti-feminist stance and allowed it to spill over into misogynistic attitudes, including trolling, abuse and violence towards women and LGBTQ+ people, will have slipped into male fundamentalism. Not all men with toxic masculinity will become male fundamentalists, but all male fundamentalists will have toxic masculinity.

If you know anything about men then you'll know that only a minority have progressive masculinity. It is impossible to put an estimate on the global percentage of men with progressive masculinity, though you are more likely to find them among the educated, middle-class, liberal-minded, younger generation of males (Gen Z and millennials especially). They can be working in any profession, and this masculinity is not a condition of race, nationality or ethnicity.

It may still be a minority masculinity when compared to toxic/traditional masculinity, but it is global. It has come to prominence over the past few decades and is rising in popularity. But no man who has progressive masculinity has gotten there on his own. He's had help, most likely from a partner, parent or educator.

There are a number of questions which arise from this masculinity and they are explored in depth in Whitehead (2021) *Toxic Masculinity: Curing the Virus*, but one of the most relevant for Total Inclusivity is 'Can all men develop progressive masculinity?'

> In theory, yes. In reality, no. For all men to adopt and perform progressive masculinity there would have to be a wholesale liberalisation of human values, not just away from violence, abuse, and rampant and avid economic competitiveness, but embracing a moral and ethical code which protects human society and individuals. This cannot be achieved independent of other factors, such as poverty, education, culture, corruption, drugs, crime, racism, and a deteriorating environment. But there are ways of encouraging males to adopt progressive masculinity.
>
> (Whitehead, 2021, p. 62)

What this means is that any organisation seeking to become a Totally Inclusive Community can only be led by men with progressive masculinity. If not, then there is little chance of the essential cultural shift taking place.

Why?

1   Because it will be too threatening to them personally and professionally
2   Because they will not recognise or accept the need for Total Inclusivity
3   Because they will recognise it challenges their sense of masculinity
4   Because it challenges how they see the world and their place in it
5   Because they will recognise it challenges their sense of power
6   Because they are incapable of adopting the style of leadership required
7   Because they lack the emotional intelligence demanded of TI Community leaders

There is more to be discussed on this topic of (gender) leadership, and in Chapter 10 I examine some of the issues in more depth, especially the questions that any aspiring TI Community leader, of whatever gender, must ask themselves.

But a key question is this – *'Am I fully committed to introducing TI, or am I paying lip-service to the ideal?'*

For men with traditional masculinity, the question will immediately test their resolve – they will have to personally commit to undergoing the necessary change in their attitudes, ideas, values and, indeed, male identity. For men with progressive masculinity, they won't need their resolve to be tested because they have already accepted that any organisation they lead must be TI.

In other words, male leaders with traditional masculinity are much farther behind on this journey of enlightenment than are male leaders with progressive masculinity. Can the traditional men be helped to move on? Yes, though one has to ask:

Who in the organisation is going to approach their male leader and suggest he submit to counselling and professional development to become a more emotionally intelligent and inclusive leader?

3 *Collapsed Masculinity*: This third global masculinity is the trickiest to define, largely because it does not actually exist as a distinct masculine identity. It is a rejection of conventional masculine values and, indeed, is

more akin to a type of male femininity. It could also be described as the nearest men have so far gotten to becoming androgynous.

At the same time, there is evidence that this masculinity is rising fastest in popularity among men, especially in Asia, causing the Chinese government, for example, to express real concern at the rise of a way of being male which is non-violent, expressly feminine and very likely celibate.

> In the Chinese context, 'meng' can be used to describe a range of things: from children's expressions to President Xi Jinping's new hairstyle. Notably, it is increasingly being used to describe loveliness in men. When a man is referred to as 'meng', there is a (positive) implication of femininity. The popularity of 'meng' in China, on the whole, represents a growing convergence among East Asian countries . . . The 'softness' of Pan-Asian soft masculinity also lies in its more sensitive and caring attitude toward women. The 'Herbivore Man' in Japan and South Korea, and 'Warm Man' in China, are all in line with this type of sensitive new guy.
>
> (Song, 2016)

> These herbivore men don't connect with others, they don't have their own families or have children and don't really contribute anything meaningful to society, either tangibly or intangibly. They are like parasites who often live with their parents. So you can imagine how it is going to affect society in the long run, socially and economically.
>
> (Tam, 2018)

So seriously does the Chinese government take this rise in collapsed masculinity among its younger male generation that it is now initiating a national programme of training and education to instil 'traditional masculine values' through schooling and other activities (Gao, 2021).

And certainly, more so than progressive masculinity, collapsed masculinity raises a host of questions for society and organisations. At time of writing, collapsed masculinity is more likely to be found in Japan, South Korea, Hong Kong and the megacities of China, Taiwan and Singapore so I am not making any claims that it is likely to be found in any significant number in the West. Though it does seem to be heading that way.

So how does collapsed masculinity impact Totally Inclusive Communities? Positively. This masculinity may be more traditionally feminine, passive and non-aggressive, and that simply means the men who express it are unlikely to be resistant to Total Inclusivity. Traditional masculinity does threaten men who exhibit collapsed masculinity – they risk, like gay men, being discriminated against, marginalised, abused – defined as the other. By way of evidence, the Chinese government is already initiating policies which serve to define these men as 'the other', the aim being to police and then eradicate their style of 'effeminate' masculinity.

The downside is that men with collapsed masculinity are less likely to put themselves forward as leaders. Admittedly, that is speculation, because to my knowledge no research has yet been undertaken on the capacity or willingness of men with collapsed masculinity to strive to lead organisations. But certainly, as is stated in Whitehead (2021), if the man with collapsed masculinity is a 'soloist' that is exhibiting social isolationist tendencies, then he won't even be working in an organisation, never mind leading one.

WOMEN AND TOXIC MASCULINE LEADERSHIP

As is detailed earlier, toxic leadership relates to a way of being a man which draws self-validation from emotional reticence/dysfunctionality and the aggressive exercise of authority/control/power over others. But women too can demonstrate toxic leadership. They too can be emotionally dysfunctional, homophobic, racist, bullying and aggressively orientated in their interactions with work colleagues, especially with those over whom they have authority.

There is absolutely no biological essence which imprints toxic behaviour on all men and progressive behaviour on all women. It is entirely a matter of socialisation, upbringing and education.

If you find this confusing or difficult to reconcile with your own identity, an easy way to understand it is as being like a virus. Masculinities and femininities circulate the social web like viruses and we can pick them up almost as easily, and unknowingly, as we can catch the flu. These viruses are not, however, all negative or damaging, but they do influence our behaviour and how we see ourselves and relate to the world. Social media, language, sexual orientation, fashion, life experiences, exposure to new ways of being/thinking, upbringing, relationships, education, all these and more conspire to create in us a sense of gender identity.

What we require from leaders of Totally Inclusive organisations is a gender identity which corresponds with progressive social values.

Yes, that's a very laudable aim but one complicated by the fact that different societies and communities define masculinity and femininity in diverse ways, though what we've seen over history is that male-dominated societies will define masculinity as aggressive and femininities as passive.

Now that humanity is starting to reject this binary, what emerges are multiple ways of being a man and a woman. Nowadays, there is much more choice as to how the individual decides to perform their gender identity.

So what is the problem? Well, the problem, or danger for women, lies in the fact that any masculinist organisation – defined as one which embraces the traditional gender binary in its core culture – will be full of masculinist viruses. Not surprisingly, then, a great number of women who enter such a male-dominated (masculinist) organisation and who seek to advance up the career ladder may well subconsciously/consciously decide that it is in their 'best interests' to emulate the dominant model of traditional masculine behaviour in order to appear convincing as leaders.

This is like picking up a virus – and it can have similar effects on the individual.

Women who try and perform traditional masculinity in their leadership role risk pushing the organisation more deeply into a masculinist culture. This is the anomaly which many of us recognise – an aggressive, divisive, toxic organisational culture, but headed by a woman.

But there is another danger here, and that is for the woman leader in terms of her well-being – she risks looking inauthentic and acting inauthentic. Indeed, there is plenty of research which shows how such women end up living a 'schizogenic' existence, torn between societal expectations of being traditionally feminine and the organisational expectations of being a masculinist-type leader (see Whitehead, 2016; also Mahdawi, 2021, discussion).

Which all takes us to a clear conclusion:

Having a particular type of genitalia does not guarantee a particular gender identity performance, nor does it ensure a particular leadership style. It is an indicator only.

Moving away from biologically deterministic approaches to Total Inclusivity, or indeed to life itself, demands we recognise and accept the multiplicity and complexity of gender performance. It is just too simpleminded to claim that all men behave in one way and all women the opposite. There are as many differences in the male category and the female category as there are between these groups.

So back to the core question: the best leader for Total Inclusivity?

The best leader is one who demonstrates progressive values not just in their language but in their actions.

Are you more likely to see this type of performance in women leaders than in men leaders?

Yes.

But don't allow that fact to stop you appointing men with progressive masculinity to leadership positions.

Although traditional male values still dominate global society, they are being pushed back by other forms of masculinity, and the most important type in terms of its ability to ensure Total Inclusive communities is progressive masculinity.

CHAPTER 8: REFLECTIONS, GUIDANCE AND COMMITMENTS

Reflection Exercise: What qualities do you associate with a good leader? How many good leaders have you worked for, and how many of these were women? How many of them men? What do you consider to be your primary leadership qualities? How do others see you as a leader?

Guidance for Implementation: Avoid thinking in gender-binary terms when you look at leaders and leadership styles. This chapter has shown how to avoid the binary-thinking trap and see more deeply into the dynamics and complexities of gender identity work. Use that knowledge to both test your own gendered leadership style and recognise how you can change to become more progressive as a leader.

Commitment: If you see gender binary values operating in your organisation, challenge them. Calmly make the point that women and men are not reduced to predictability based on their sex identity but have the capacity to be more creative and imaginative in their gender performance and gender identity. This serves to undermine any masculinist narrative operating within the organisation, either on the surface or below it.

NOTES

1 Jack Ma speaking at Gateway '17 Conference, Detroit, 21st June, 2017.
2 John Louth, Commander, Royal United Services Institute, UK, speaking in 2015.
3 Dany Cotton, London Fire Brigade's first female Commissioner, quoted in *The Guardian*, 5th March, 2017.

Nine

How safe do you feel right now? Assuming you are sitting at home, maybe a glass of wine or cup of coffee to hand, comfortable in your own private space, then it's likely you are feeling very secure and safe.

But what if you put down this book and walk outside – how safe do you feel then? Suddenly your physical safety margin has been reduced by a significant degree. Though it remains manageable – just remember to look right and left when crossing the road.

Let us further reduce that margin and heighten the risk: now it is 1 in the morning and you are out walking through your local park – alone. Maybe you would never do this, and for good reason. Because you know that danger lurks in those shadows. Sure, it may only be in your imagination, but that still feels real enough, in the dark, at 01.00 hours.

If you are a young, fit guy reading this, going through this imaginary risk assessment, then your first thought may be 'OK, I'm not worried about a midnight walk in the park because I can handle myself'. Fine. Are you also going to carry a knife, 'just in case'? And if you are, will that heighten or reduce the risk to your physical safety?

What if you are a female? How safe would you feel strolling in the park at 1 o'clock in the morning? Probably, not very.

Which is why you don't do it.

This is how you manage your safety every day of the week. You consciously minimise the risks; wearing a seat belt, not jay-walking; not taking five pills when the prescription states one; being careful about your online dating habits; taking a taxi home, not walking alone late at night.

This is what it means to be an adult – being constantly aware of what might happen. We call it being sensible, using one's common sense, 'self-policing' our behaviour.

Knowing that, why do we then willingly place our safety in the hands of someone else? Because that is precisely what we do when we go to work for an organisation.

We pass responsibility for our safety on to another person – our boss.

DOI: 10.4324/9781003244073-9

ARE YOU SAFE AT WORK?

At time of writing, COVID-19 has catapulted the very concept of 'health and safety' at work into an altogether higher, and much more confusing, realm. And perhaps it will stay there. Maybe humanity will never fully emerge from the threats contained in this global, constantly mutating virus. In which case, any discussion around safety, either in or out of the workplace, will be determined by where we are on the pandemic continuum, individually and as a global society. But this is not new. Humanity has come through even more horrific pandemics throughout its history, the most recent, prior to COVID-19, being the Spanish flu pandemic of 1918–1920. That killed more than 50 million of us.

What COVID and other threats to humanity tell us is that safety can be assessed any number of ways, but the most obvious one is physical. You may feel physically safe at work, but in 2018 US businesses still managed to pay out nearly US$60 billion in compensation to workers for non-fatal workplace injuries. That's more than a billion dollars a week (US Department of Labor, 2021).

Health and Safety at work is now big business. At time of writing, the average US health and safety manager salary is US$113,119 – twice the national average (Salary.com, 2021).

That health and safety manager will be familiar with one aspect of his job – the personal injury lawyer/attorney. There are websites focused exclusively on finding you a lawyer to make your case for compensation. According to one such website, average compensation is $52,900, and likelihood of payout (with an attorney)is 70% (Lawyers.com, 2016).

Given that health and safety is such big business, with lawyers and attorneys hovering around, eager to get you compensation, why is it that 1 in 5 US employees don't feel safe at work (Torres, 2017b)? In the UK that rises to a staggering 38%, and it is getting worse, not better. Indeed, if you work in London, for example, the percentage of employees feeling unsafe at work due to discrimination rises to 54% (ADP, 2019)!

There are occupational differences, with research exposing the levels of feeling unsafe which employees experience in various UK business sectors:

Arts and culture: 63%
Architecture, engineering and building: 52%
Travel and transport: 50%
Financial services: 49%
Education: 29%

These are just percentages. What do they mean in reality? Research published by Harvard and Stanford Business Schools in 2015 (Efythymiades, 2015) revealed that health problems associated with job-related anxiety account for more deaths in the US than Alzheimer's disease or diabetes. Expect the same to be true of the UK and, indeed, most industrialised countries.

How many bosses appreciate the seriousness of this problem?

Could the average CEO or COO, or indeed HR manager, recognise those figures?

How is it that 63% of employees in the arts and culture sector feel unsafe?

And as for education – what is happening in our schools to make a third of teachers feel unsafe?

What are we missing here?

What we are missing is how we define health and safety at work – and whose responsibility it is.

IDENTITY SAFETY

If I am motoring blissfully down my local superhighway and a speeding lorry smashes into my rear end, that is going to upset me. It may also render me hospitalised or worse. What it is not going to do is upset my sense of identity.

If you racially abuse me at work, that is not going to break my body, but the effect on my sense of self will be far greater and longer lasting than injuries sustained in a car accident.

When we were schoolchildren we'd chant "sticks and stones will break my bones but words will never hurt me". What a load of rubbish that is.

As is explored in Chapter 5, words matter.

The reason so many employees feel unsafe at work is because they are victims of violence.

At this point it is necessary to be clear as to what we mean by 'violence'.

- That which is or involves the use of force, physical or otherwise, by a violator or violators
- That which is intended to cause harm
- That which is experienced, by the violated, as damaging and/or violation
- The recognition of certain acts, activities or events as 'violent' by a third party, for example, a legal authority

As researchers into male violence have noted, more than one type of violence can be perpetuated against the individual:

> All these elements are themselves historically and culturally specific. What is not named as violence in one situation or time may become clear when it is named as violence elsewhere or subsequently. This, for example, is clear when what are at one time named as 'consensual' sexual-social relations are renamed as power relations, exploitation, abuse or harassment.
>
> (Hearn, 1995, p. 16)

What employees recognise, even if they cannot put it into these words, is that working in a hostile workplace means being subjected to violence – violence against one's sense of self, well-being, very identity.

The key word here is 'violation'. If I experience an act as a violation then that is what it is. And this violation can be existential and/or physical.

To get an insight into just how many organisations have a hostile environment for staff and how ubiquitous violation is, let us return to the comparatively 'safest' occupation, education.[1]

Canada: 750 cases of abuse reported in Canadian schools between 1997 and 2017 (Puzic, 2018)

France: Dozens of teachers dismissed for sexual abuse in primary and secondary schools; "thousands of children in French schools sexually abused by paedophile teachers" (Capon, 2015)

India: Coercive sex experienced by 6% of secondary school pupils in Goa alone (Patel and Andrew, 2001)

USA: A 2004 federal report estimated that in the state of California "422,000 public school students would be victims of sexual abuse before graduation" (US Department of Education, 2004)

Mexico: Claims that as many as 18 schools and childcare centres have adult employees who collaborate to sexually abuse pupils between the ages of three and seven (New York Post, 2021)

China: Uncoordinated mass stabbings, hammer and cleaver attacks on kindergarten and grade school children began in March 2010 and have continued every year since. Hundreds dead and injured[2]

UK: Over 14,000 victims claiming to have been abuse in schools and universities indicates a 'normalised rape culture' across all levels of UK education, including in prestigious private schools (Swanwick, 2021).

And the most dangerous classroom hazard? No, not an exploding science lab experiment but physical violence against teachers. The American Psychological Association reports that approximately 7% of teachers in the USA are threatened with injury every year. This doubles to 14% for female teachers (Chron, 2020).

We would all hope if not expect that our children and our teachers would be safe at school, but clearly that is not the case. And this despite the recent global implementation of extensive and much-needed child safeguarding measures.

Whatever the occupation, women employees are much more likely to work in a predatory environment and be subjected to abuse, harassment and violence than men. This results in women having to constantly police their behaviour, for example turning down after-hours drinking with male co-workers; pretending the sexist banter is acceptable; trying to be 'one of the lads' so as to be co-opted into the male-dominated culture; tolerating sexual comments and approaches from bosses (Torres, 2017a).

Credit Line: Cartoons drawn by Advanced Standard Group Co., Ltd.

But then, as actress Kiera Knightley stresses, none of this is rare for women; "every woman" has been sexually harassed in some way, a situation which Knightley finds "fucking depressing".

> Yes, I mean, everybody has. Literally, I don't know anyone who hasn't been in some way, whether it's being flashed at, or groped, or some guy saying they're going to slit your throat, or punching you in the face, or whatever it is, everybody has.[3]

MeToo didn't arise because women suddenly started to experience sexual harassment and violation in their professional lives, in their places of work. This phenomenon goes back through history. But what MeToo did is dramatically expose the casualness, the normalisation of male predatory behaviour, where any woman is at risk, no matter her fame, wealth, professional status or social power.

If a world-famous female film star can be abused by powerful men simply because she happens to connect with them or work with them, what chance, for example, does a Filipino housemaid have who works in the UAE?

Organisations around the world will have employees working in them who suffer regular sexual and racial harassment. Mostly the victims will be young and female and/or have a minority ethnicity. Why does this persist? We can argue that the organisation allows it to. It has failed to implement systems and procedures which protect the most vulnerable employees. But as I discuss in what follows, the problem goes deeper than the organisation itself.

But no matter the cause of the problem, the salient point is that no employee should have to suffer physical harm, threat or harassment just in order to keep their job. As Gabriel Union puts it:

> Sexual or physical violence, harassment, demeaning language, is not the price one should pay for seeking or maintaining employment. Period.[4]

Violation against a person is a lifetime experience. It doesn't just happen the one time. It happens every time the victim/survivor remembers the event. It will get replayed in their minds over and over again until it risks becoming an unmanageable depressive state forever lingering on their mental horizon. Long after the physical scars and bruises have healed, the mind still hurts.

No One Is Safe Without Total Inclusivity

When a person is raped or sexually harassed and abused, their very identity or sense of self is broken. It is more than a physical violation, it is a violation of who they are as a human being, an individual.

> You took away my worth, my privacy, my energy, my time, my safety, my intimacy, my confidence, my own voice, until now (anonymous).[5]

Violations can and do come in multiple, often unpredictable ways and situations. But all have one thing in common: they reduce the victim/survivor to a feeling of hopelessness, despair and nothingness.

Following are some very personal reflections as to how it feels to be racially abused, even if physical violence does not accompany the abuse:[6]

> "Like I am below humanity. [it feels] Like you're not real. Your words are never heard".
>
> "Crap. It makes me feel like I am not welcome. I feel like I cannot trust anyone if I can't trust the ones who were selected to protect".
>
> "I feel hated. I feel disgusted by who I am. I look in the mirror and pretend that I am a different color".
>
> "It is horrible. The color of your skin defines you for the rest of your life. It never ends, only when you die".
>
> "It feels awful, it's infuriating. It's disgusting that people think they are better than another person just because they have a different skin tone".

If you are a Black person reading this then these quotes won't surprise you. But what if you are a white person? Can you relate to these statements? If you've never been racially abused because of the way you look, your skin colour, have you the empathy to recognise the pain being experienced by those who have? Can you see how racism is a violation against a person's very sense of being, their core identity? This is why a so-called casual racist remark or multiple micro-aggressions, such as jokes about, for example, a person's hairstyle, skin colour or clothing, will accumulate to the point that they can destroy an individual's sense of self, undermine their confidence, reinforce their feeling of isolation, depression and sheer misery.

This is why safety at work starts not with the bosses but with ourselves. The individual employee can make a workplace hostile, or they can make it welcoming. That power is in all our hands.

WHO IS RESPONSIBLE?

If you sign a contract to work for an organisation then that organisation immediately assumes some level of responsibility for your health and safety. Of course, the level of responsibility changes according to the nature of the job; e.g. mining is going to trigger more H&S risks than selling insurance from home. Plus, employees are also responsible for maintaining their own health and safety. Which is why airline pilots can be prosecuted for turning up for work if testing shows they've consumed any alcohol during the previous eight hours.

Which organisational department oversees health and safety will depend largely on the type of industry it is in. But in most organisations health and safety will come under the remit of the human resource department. The standard HR statement regarding employee safety reads something like this (HR Gazette, 2019):

> It is up to HR to communicate, administer, and promote safety policies and make sure that everybody's on the same page and following the safety guidelines.
>
> Given that HR acts as an intermediary and facilitates communication between the employees and the organization's authority, this department is responsible for making sure that all the issues that employees face are heard by management.

It is HR's job to:

- take care that the values are respected and that the safety protection programme is taken seriously
- communicate the importance of occupational safety and health to management from both a legal and business perspective
- inform employees about their rights – if they notice unsafe work practices and procedures that are not in line with the adopted safety policies, they should be allowed to report these issues openly, as well as refuse to work without any repercussions, until these issues are solved
- ensure the investigation of an accident is properly conducted, as that will prevent similar accidents in the future.

And so it goes on, covering education and training, employee well-being, stress, mental health, staff inductions, staff exit interviews, even the introduction of rulings stating that employees don't send each other work emails at midnight. In other words, all the 'caring issues' inevitably get dumped on HR. Pity HR.

Is it realistic, indeed is it possible, that a single HR department can in itself change the minds, attitudes and actions of individual employees?

Of course not.

What we must face is that violence in all its forms is a social epidemic; expecting HR departments to solve the crisis in a single organisation is like expecting a town's police force to tackle global crime.

Which is why so many workplaces around the world are hostile environments, especially for women, LGBTQ+ staff and Black and minority ethnic employees – it is just too much for a single HR department to ever manage on its own.

What is being addressed here is not merely ensuring compliance with organisational rulings and policies and following up with appropriate investigations. It means recognising that it is essential we protect all identities within an organisation from being subject to or at risk from violation.

To imagine that a single (HR or personnel) department, no matter how efficient and dedicated, can in itself protect all employees from violation is to fail to understand Total Inclusivity – and violation.

UNDERSTANDING TI AS MORE THAN H&S

We live in societies in which violences are endemic. Therefore, to hope that such violences will not surface in organisations is wishful thinking. Similarly, to imagine that a single HR department can stop violent acts occurring in an organisation is nothing less than dangerous.

Take a single example; incidences of rape in the USA during 2018 (NSVRC, 2021).[7]

It is estimated that 734,630 people were raped (including threatened, attempted or completed rape) in the US in 2018.

And what about reporting these acts of rape against oneself?

Only 25% of these violations were reported to police.

And how about false reporting?

Data shows that false reporting for sexual assault crimes is low – between two percent and 10 percent.

Consequently, any organisational leadership, including HR, should assume the following:

1   That violences are occurring in the organisation much more frequently than they imagine to be the case.
2   That women are twice as likely to be victims of violation as men
3   That two-thirds of all violations, including rape and sexual harassment, will go unreported to senior management or HR
4   That anyone reporting violations is doing so reluctantly and that false reporting, while it does occur, is not the biggest problem facing organisations – it is occurrence and under-reporting
5   That this problem is not the single responsibility of the HR department

HR are simply the organisational judiciary – they are only part of the solution, not the whole or only solution.

POWER

Power, authority, status, control all combine to create hierarchies within organisations. But more than this, they create realms of protection for those at the top. The exercise of power is necessary in order to ensure the organisation proceeds along its declared strategy and vision. But this deployment of power is not always neutral and benign. As we have seen very vividly with the MeToo and Black Lives Matter movements, power can be performed as gender and racial violence against those who have less of it, and frequently it is.

As is stated earlier, every member of an organisation has a degree of power, the capacity to help create a protective and welcoming organisational climate or a hostile one. Yes, bosses have the most power and influence over their organisation's culture, and therefore they must recognise that how they behave will determine the culture to a large degree. But a big operation will have many bosses – from senior managers down to middle managers. Each and every single one of them must take responsibility for ensuring violations and violences do not occur and that, when they do, are properly dealt with. Ignoring such violations, or worse, contributing to them, will damage not just the victim but also the perpetrator and the organisation as a whole.

At time of writing two examples of how the toxic exercise of power led to a culture of violence and violations in the workplace went global.

Case Study No. 1: Hippo Knitting, a Taiwanese-owned company located in the tiny country of Lesotho, southern Africa. An investigation

No One Is Safe Without Total Inclusivity

by TIME magazine and the Fuller Project (Donovan and Nkune, 2021) exposed a culture of fear among the 1,000 garment workers, 90% of whom are women. The factory makes clothing predominantly for one brand: Fabletics, a popular US athletic-apparel line co-founded by actor Kate Hudson. Workers at the factory, who chose to remain anonymous, claimed that they had "lived in fear for many years". They were not safe at work. Though neither could they afford to lose their jobs.

- Women employees being subject to daily routine body searches which 'exposed their underwear and vulvas'
- Male supervisors pressuring women workers into sexual relationships
- Women workers humiliated and abused by management
- Women workers being 'forced to crawl on the floor by one supervisor as punishment'
- A woman worker having to urinate on herself because the same supervisor denied her permission to use the toilet
- Women workers being subjected to daily harassment from male supervisors
- Women workers regularly sexually assaulted and harassed

As two women workers put it: "We are tired, we need help, we work with bleeding heart. I hate my job, but I cannot leave because there is nowhere else to go".

Of course, it is not unreasonable to speculate that this grotesque culture at Hippo Knitting would have continued unnoticed if it were not for the fact the factory makes Kate Hudson's Fabletics sports gear. How many such factories are there around the world, especially in developing countries, were this sort of violence continues unabated for the simple reason no one hears about it? Too many to count.

The reaction from the Taiwanese owner, Grace Lin?

I am committed to addressing [the allegations] with the seriousness they deserve [and have] initiated a process of engaging an independent international auditor to establish the credibility and basis of these allegations.

The reaction from Kate Hudson?

A representative said that she had no knowledge of the reports before TIME and the Fuller Project reach out and that Fabletics management attested to Kate that they maintain the highest ethical and social standards in their factories and workplaces.

This story has all the usual ingredients which helped ensure it made its way onto the global media forums: TIME magazine investigation, glamorous film star, male sexual violence and women victims.

The second case study is rather different.

Case Study No. 2 Brewdog, a British independent brewer of craft beer. The company started in 2007 and is now a global operation with breweries in Berlin, Brisbane and Columbus, Ohio. It also operates 100 Brewdog bars across the world and is planning themed hotels. The company bosses may have been celebrating their global business success, but according to former staff it comes at a high price. In June 2021 staff posted an open letter on Twitter, signed by more than 60 former employees, in which they made a number of allegations (BBC News, 2021b).

- Staff too afraid to speak out about concerns
- A "culture of fear" and a "toxic attitude" to junior employees
- A violent, hostile work culture where toxic attitudes towards junior staff had "trickled down" through the business "until they were simply an intrinsic part of the company"
- Fear of repercussions for speaking out, challenging the hostile management style
- A 'cult of personality' around the company co-founders, James Watt and Martin Dickie
- The company's public image being totally at odds with its work culture

As one former employee put it: "Being treated as a human being was sadly not always a given for those working at Brewdog".

And the reaction from co-founder Mr Watt?

> We are committed to doing better, not just as a reaction to this, but always; and we are going to reach out to our entire team past and present to learn more. But most of all, we are sorry.

Duly chastened, the owners of Brewdog were immediately forced into a public apology and acceptance that they "didn't always get things right", clearly recognising that this sort of adverse global publicity can seriously undermine a brand image and, therefore, profitability.

When one drills down to the core of the problem both with Brewdog and Hippo Knitting what gets revealed are the following elements:

1 The unaccountable exercise of power over those who are vulnerable within the organisation.
2 The uncaring attitudes of the bosses feeds down through the organisational culture, eventually creating a highly violent and hostile workplace for all employees, especially those at the bottom of the hierarchy.
3 Because employees need jobs, this need too easily gets exploited by those who should never have been appointed leaders/managers in the first place. They not only lack empathy and compassion, they are bullies.
4 Performative, target-driven work conditions make a major contribution to this toxicity because they 'allow' managers to exert pressure over staff in the name of 'efficiency'.
5 Having physically distant, self-congratulatory, hands-off owners, wrapped up in their own unique reality bubble, ensures that the workplace oppressors go unpunished and the problems continue.

And so it continues, until, that is, the whole toxic mess gets posted on social media.

It is worth noting that both these companies had human resource departments, as do most sizeable business operations around the globe. What this tells us is that relying on HR to protect employees from violence and violation is a big mistake. HR staff can inadvertently get caught up in a hostile workplace environment and end up replicating it. HR too easily gets co-opted into the leadership reality, not the employee reality. The result is that the abuse and toxicity get rendered invisible and silenced because no one outside of the individual experiencing it is able or motivated to provide the necessary support to deal with it.

As a postscript to this story, at time of writing another independent brewery, Wormtown in Worcester, Massachusetts, USA, also found itself in the global spotlight for the wrong reasons, in this case "allegations of sexual harassment posted anonymously online" causing "all owners with exception of the co-founder, Ben Roesch, deciding to step back from any day-to-day or direct involvement in the operation of the brewery" (Petrishen, 2021).

What is it with these brewers? Is it something they're drinking?

WELL-BEING

If we don't feel physically or emotionally safe at work, can we ever achieve a sense of well-being at work?

It would seem unlikely.

And that recognition is important, not least because mental health well-being has emerged as one of the most powerful concepts over the past few years, generating discussion by big names in sport, politics, entertainment and business.

But what precisely is well-being?

Most dictionary definitions of well-being define it in these terms: 'the experience of health, happiness and prosperity'.

While Total Inclusivity recognises the usefulness of this definition, it doesn't work for organisations.

It is not the task of all organisations to make people happy, nor indeed to necessarily make them prosperous. As for personal health, certainly the organisation has a responsibility to ensure that it is not endangered or compromised, especially in the age of COVID-19. However, the individual is, in the final reckoning, largely responsible for their own state of health.

The Total Inclusivity definition of well-being (in organisations) is as follows:

Total Inclusivity means recognising, valuing, protecting and nurturing diverse identities, including those of race, gender, sexual orientation, class, disability, age, religion and language.

Yes, Total Inclusivity and well-being are one and the same thing. They share the same definition. There is no distinction between them either in principle or in practice. If an organisation is Totally Inclusive then it will have employees who are experiencing well-being in the organisation. It won't simply be rhetoric or confined to HR policies. It will be embedded in the work climate and culture and reinforced by the actions of every individual, from the company owner through senior management to the factory worker or delivery person.

So how much well-being is occurring in big and small companies today?

Businesses operate in a globally competitive environment, one made even more stressful and insecure through COVID-19, environmental issues and artificial intelligence. In which case one might argue that the likes of Brewdog and Hippo Knitting, not being massive global corporations, will be under tons of pressure to maximise 'efficiency'. This is not to excuse them but to distinguish them from, say, the likes of Amazon and Tesla Motors.

These two massive corporations have enough money and expertise to get well-being right for their many employees. So how are they doing in that regard?

Not very well, according to most studies.

To be sure, we are not aware of any current or former employees of Amazon and Tesla Motors claiming they are being forced to crawl along the floor like dogs or of women being sexually harassed on a daily basis. But nevertheless, staff at these two corporations do complain of highly stressful if not dysfunctional workplace cultures (Wong, 2017; Nalin, 2019; Indeed.com, 2021; see Chapter 10 for further discussion of Amazon.com work culture).

- Being expected to work 50, 60 or even 70 hours per week
- Constant video surveillance, productivity demands and bag searches before going home
- Pressure-cooker workplace climate for both blue-collar and white-collar employees
- Amazon employees being encouraged to anonymously report on each other through the company's Big-Brother-esque management software
- Employees put on notice that their jobs are on the line when they are distracted by personal crises such as cancer or death of a child
- The 'ruthless' and 'oppressive' treatment of employees by managers and the company
- Workers being treated 'like robots'
- Tesla factor workers revealing the "pain, injury and stress" of their jobs
- Tesla employees being dismissed after taking medical leave
- Employee concerns over safety being routinely ignored by Tesla managers
- Tesla actively hiding serious employee injuries and sending injured workers back to the production line
- 12-hour work shifts combined with intense performativity culture

Four global companies, two medium-sized and two extremely large. What do they appear to have in common, based on the evidence in now in the public domain?

An absence of employee well-being.

Does this toxicity arise from the attitudes and characters of the owners? Without doubt that must be a contributing factor. These types of bosses present themselves as 'fountains of all knowledge' and charismatic hero leaders. They are the company. Which may play well with shareholders but does little to protect the rights and welfare of employees, not least because it leads to congested decision making and a fear of upsetting those who really exercise control.

Leaders and owners have a duty of care to every one of their employees. This duty of care must supersede profitability, efficiency, productivity and the meeting of targets.

If you own a business that cannot survive without damaging human beings then that is not a business you are leading; it is a place of fear, loathing, discrimination, hostility and violence. The business may appear to be operating 'efficiently' from the outside, but if you step inside and experience the actual workplace climate for yourself, then you'll quickly realise the Dickensian if not lethal character of it.

If you cannot be in business without hurting people, then you shouldn't be in business.

If you cannot lead people without hurting them, then don't imagine you are a leader.

Creating a healthy workplace climate is not rocket science. All it takes is the emotional intelligence to realise what needs to be done and the will to do it. As I detail in the next chapter, if you are an owner, a boss, a manager or indeed a shareholder and you put profit before people then you are failing.

SUMMARY

Developed countries and multinational organisations around the world nowadays have access to the strongest laws, health and welfare systems, professional expertise in human relations and HR management, and knowledge of when individual wellness and well-being is being enhanced, protected, compromised or damaged. Following which, there can be no excuse for tolerating workplaces which are violent and deadly and which diminish the dignity and self-respect of human beings.

At risk here is not just the physical body of the employees but also their mental health. And the biggest risk to their mental health will be violations against their very sense of identity.

This is what Total Inclusivity demands must not happen. Total Inclusivity and the values it promotes and insists upon are the only safeguards against a toxic and hostile culture arising within the workplace.

But Total Inclusivity is not only the responsibility of the HR department, the boss/leader/owner, it is the responsibility of every member of the organisation.

Study any organisation with a toxic, dangerous, hostile work culture and certain factors immediately become apparent:

1 The bosses allow it to happen because they either behave that way themselves and/or they empower others to do so.
2 The toxicity creeps down through the organisational layers, infecting the whole organisation.
3 Fear and silence combine to create a workplace climate in which no one dares to speak truth to power.
4 The business is obsessed with profit but at the expense of people. Consequently, it has become a danger to everyone connected with it.
5 The materially successful business owners become complacent and self-congratulatory. In their hubris they end up believing their own marketing rhetoric and brand discourse.
6 Too much reliance has been placed on the capacity of the HR department to address, monitor and deal with 'employee issues'.
7 There is little or no accountability of senior managers and leaders by staff.
8 Women, junior employees, LGBTQ+ employees and Black, Asian and minority ethnic employees experience the greatest fear and risk to their body and identity in violent workplace environments.
9 Leaders have failed to set the standard for employee health, safety and well-being. They don't consider it part of their job. They too easily speak of profit and efficiency and too rarely of employee welfare.
10 There is no anonymous feedback loop from employees to bosses, and where there is one it is generally unused or ignored because staff are fearful of doing so.

Some of the least safe organisations will have in place the protocols and systems for safeguarding employees and all stakeholders. Indeed, these systems have mushroomed over the past decade, largely in response to a wave of online and real-time abuse, violence, discrimination and bullying in organisations. The necessity of such safeguarding is self-evident. However, safeguarding must go beyond police background checks on potential employees working in high-risk professions (e.g. teaching), measures taken against online bullying and sanctions imposed for racist, sexist and homophobic behaviour. The aim must be to create a community in which the very likelihood of someone being rendered unsafe is removed altogether – and that cannot happen if the organisation has not embraced Total Inclusivity. The Totally Inclusive organisation will still have the safeguarding systems in place, but more importantly, it will have created a work culture where those systems rarely if ever need to be triggered. As I say, there can be no safeguarding of all; indeed, no one is safe unless the organisation is Totally Inclusive.

CHAPTER 9: REFLECTIONS, GUIDANCE AND COMMITMENTS

Reflection Exercise: If you are a boss, then you'll find more questions on this and related topics posed in Chapter 11. If you are an employee, ask yourself what you've done to help make your workplace Totally Inclusive or not. And then reflect on what more you can do to counter any toxicity in your organisation.

Guidance for Implementation: Stop thinking of organisations as simply places to earn a living or have a job. They are much more important to society and the individual than that. Organisations are places we learn to be and become in life. We invest our identity in them, in which case we must ensure those identities are protected. When you look at successful global entrepreneurs, do you respect them for the wealth they've accumulated or for the common good they've generated?

Commitment: Commit to not remaining silent if you hear of, experience or know about violences or violations taking place in your organisation. Identify and confirm and then, if necessary, publicise. Though not before you've given your bosses the opportunity to deal with it within the organisation. Silence is driven by fear of consequence. If you feel that fear in your organisation then that alone suggests it is a long way from being Totally Inclusive.

No One Is Safe Without Total Inclusivity

NOTES

1 https://en.wikipedia.org/wiki/Sexual_abuse_in_primary_and_secondary_schools.
2 https://en.wikipedia.org/wiki/School_attacks_in_China.
3 Quoted in https://amp.theguardian.com/world/2021/jun/08/keira-knightley-says-every-woman-she-knows-has-been-harassed.
4 www.teenvogue.com/video/watch/powerful-quotes-from-the-metoo-movement.
5 www.yourtango.com/2017307474/inspirational-quotes-sexual-assault-victim-shaming.
6 www.theodysseyonline.com/how-does-it-feel-to-be-racially-discriminated-against.
7 The rape epidemic is not confined to the USA. In the year ending June 2021, England and Wales recorded the highest-ever number of rapes at 61,158, an increase of 8% over the previous year.

Inclusive Capitalism or Organisational Failure?

Ten

If you are a leader, manager, shareholder or someone even remotely interested in the continuing healthy state of your job, then you may well have found some of my arguments for what might otherwise be described as inclusive capitalism rather contradictory if not unlikely. And I can appreciate that. Indeed, is not the very term 'inclusive capitalism' the most obvious oxymoron?

Does it not seem that the world of organisations, both public and private, is, and has been for some decades, hell-bent on becoming exemplars of neo-liberalism? Certainly, that can be readily demonstrated without too much effort; managerialism; performativity; privatisation; the avid pursuit of profit at the expense of community; the avid pursuit of greater output at the expense of employee well-being; the avid pursuit of growth at the expense of the environment. The very concept of globalisation has been built on a particular economic system and organisational culture, and it is not one which favours diversity, equity, inclusion and justice.

However, perhaps all that is about to change. Not overnight, for sure, but the signposts are now starting to point in a rather different direction, one which is going to require organisations to embrace Total Inclusivity or at least a make a serious effort to do so. That or risk failure.

Worker's rights used to be a battle between bosses and unions. The bosses triumphed. But that was in the days before social media. Now every company, every boss, every leader is vulnerable to very public exposure of their behaviour, their language, their values, their organisational practices. Non-disclosure agreements won't be enough to save an individual's reputation, nor that of their company, once Facebook and Instagram messages start getting posted by disgusted clients and disgruntled current and ex-employees.

If the merits and innate value of Total Inclusivity aren't enough to convince owners and bosses to change their practices then maybe the risk of bankruptcy and a trashed reputation will.

DOI: 10.4324/9781003244073-10

THE COLLECTIVE UNCONSCIOUS IS SHIFTING

When Sigmund Freud and Carl Jung developed their theories of the (collective) unconscious a century ago, neither had reckoned with globalisation and the information society. Therefore, just what they'd make of the 21st century one can only speculate. But no doubt they'd be intrigued by one aspect of it – the way in which ideas and values instantly travel to the remotest parts of the world and duly take root in our subconsciousness, largely without us realising it.

An example is Total Inclusivity itself. As a term, 'Total Inclusivity' originates from a single person's imagination and experiences. However, as a concept and a range of possibilities, it is very much the product of the global collective unconscious.

In other words, the global collective unconscious is already shifting towards Total Inclusivity. This book is not presenting you with Total Inclusivity as something new and original, because the values, ideas and energy behind the concept are already out there in the public domain. All this book does is package and present it to you, the reader, along with the realities and the opportunities. This book is making real, articulating, that which you already feel, sense, know.

And what you feel, sense, know is quite simply this: you and your organisation must get on board for Total Inclusivity or risk being left behind. There is no going backwards, returning to the 1990s, 1980s, 1950s and certainly not any decade before that. There is now, globally, a powerful if not unstoppable movement for change towards a progressive agenda and set of values which fully embrace diversity, equity, inclusion and justice.

To be sure, there will be politicians together with groups in society who'll actively resist this. But a backlash is to be expected; a desire to return to something mythical and discriminatory, exclusive and divisive, feels safe if not natural for a lot of people. However, humanity is not heading in that direction.

It is increasingly apparent that there is a burgeoning desire across the globe for inclusive capitalism.

And just in case you have any lingering doubts as to the veracity of that statement, allow me to underscore it with some evidence.

THE EVIDENCE

1. Deliveroo

In March 2021, Deliveroo Holding PLC made its UK public debut on the London Stock Exchange. It promptly collapsed. Within minutes of the shares opening for sale they dropped by 31% – the worst performance in decades for a big UK listing.

Would-be investors abandoned this food-delivery start-up for a variety of reasons, but two in particular made headline news: (a) the style of leadership of the CEO, Will Shu, and the fact that he planned to retain control of the business for a further three years (Gopinath, 2021) and (b) the contentious issues around workers' rights and an increasing desire by investors to invest client's money responsibly. In short, ethical concerns developed into a big financial one (Davies and Makortoff, 2021).

> David Cumming, chief investment officer at Aviva Investors, said
> workers' rights were a key reason he had not invested in the business:
> "A lot of employers could make a massive difference to worker's lives
> if they guaranteed working hours or a living wage, and how companies
> behave is becoming more important".
>
> (ibid)

The fact that Deliveroo workers were protesting outside the London Stock Exchange and on strike across the UK on the first day of open trading merely underlined the ethical flaws in the Deliveroo business model (Butler and Jolly, 2021). To be sure, the crude capitalist model didn't deter all investors, and indeed, Goldman Sachs Bank purchased £75 million of shares in order to keep the share price propped up. But for a great many investors, and as David Cumming indicates, if companies are to prosper they now need to adopt an inclusive capitalist approach, which means, in effect, adopting the values of Total Inclusivity.

2. The Human Resource Officer

I raised the contradictory if not impossible role of HR departments in Chapter 9. But I am not alone in doing so. The trend over the past decades has been for HR leaders and departments to become increasingly enslaved by big data, using analytics to reduce labour costs, enforce compliance using standardised assessments and measures and encourage the adaptation of IT into every aspect of the workplace. All of which results in the marginalisation of the traditional areas of HR: recruitment, learning and professional development. In short, HR has been fully (if somewhat unwillingly) co-opted into the leadership reality at the expense of its role as a defender and support for employee rights and development. The global management consultants, McKinsey, recently did research on how chief human resource officers in some of Europe's biggest organisations feel about this shift.

> The vast majority of CHROs said they were eager to shift to a model we have come to call 'back to human'. The Covid-19 pandemic – which accelerated employee demands on HR to meet physical and mental health needs, as well as intensified moral concerns about a company's overall impact on society – lent urgency to their view that some core human element has been lost in all these technological advancements.
>
> (Khan et al., 2021)

No longer happy with their role as sidekicks for often discriminatory and unethical bosses, the CHROs overwhelmingly stated that there now needs to be a shift to people-centric policies (ibid).

The four areas where CHROs want to focus and percentage of respondents:

- Engage more directly and deeply with employees – 90%
- Let employees bring their whole person to work – 98%
- Pave the way to the 'new possible' – 85%
- Act as 'human capitalists' – 81%

The HR officer is the first line of defence against discriminatory practices and a violent workplace culture, so the fact that CHROs clearly recognise the trend towards inclusive capitalism and Total Inclusivity is to be welcomed and is an important indicator of the fast-changing collective (corporate) consciousness.

3. Corporate Backing for Racial Equity

You will know a lot about the murder of George Floyd in Minneapolis by a police officer in May 2020 and the subsequent global Black Lives Matter protests. But are you aware of just how much money has been poured into racial-equity initiatives by big business since then? Probably not. But you should, because it is yet another indicator of the changing zeitgeist. According to one study (Fitzhugh et al., 2020) more than 1,100 organisations committed a total of US$200 billion to racial-equity and racial justice initiatives in the year to May 2021.

> Much of these funds are being committed to providing affordable housing, lending in low- and middle-income and minority communities, and community development. Financial institutions were responsible

for most of the commitment, representing 90% of total commitments made in the past year . . . This is a critical moment. Corporate America is more focussed on the issue of racial justice than it has ever been. It is imperative to ensure that the unprecedented commitment of resources and focus toward racial equity is channelled effectively, proves impactful, delivers a high return on investment for society, and brings about real progress for individuals and communities.

(ibid)

This corporate backing for racial equity corresponds with an increasing number of major corporations, especially in the US, voluntarily disclosing more about the gender and racial makeup of their workforce. For many such companies, doing so will be a new experience. However, they are part of a growing trend towards 'fostering human capital' and recognising that 'investing in people' is the best way to 'unlock productivity' (Francis et al., 2021).

Who ever thought otherwise?

We live in a world driven by the need to pursue the accumulation of money in order not just to prosper but to survive. But this material impulse and the unethical and toxic behaviours it can engender need not be the whole story of humanity in the 21st century. The fact that big business is now starting to recognise the change in direction occurring in society and wants to be a visible and active part of that is a powerful indicator of the emergence of inclusive capitalism and the Total Inclusivity agenda.

4. Starbucks

The life of unconscious bias training (UBT) is turbulent to say the least. Even many progressive thinkers recognise that a dollop of UBT pitched to a group of staff for an hour or so isn't going to automatically improve self-awareness and racial attitudes. Nevertheless, when global corporations experience public anger and damaging publicity due to their employees' racist behaviour, UBT is to where they turn. An example is Starbucks. In April 2018, Starbucks CEO, Kevin Johnson, was forced into a public apology after two Black men were arrested after refusing requests to leave a Philadelphia store where they had not made a purchase. Somewhat bruised if not humbled by the social media outrage which followed this incident, Johnson was astute enough to realise he had to show penitence:

This reprehensible incident is a management issue and I am accountable to ensure we address the policy and the practice and the

training that led to this outcome ... Staff will be trained to better know
when police assistance is warranted and we will host a company-wide
meeting in coming days to discuss immediate next steps and underscore
our long standing commitment to treating one another with dignity ...
What happened was wrong and we'll fix it.

(SHRM, 2018)

Johnson was not alone in standing up and saying 'we got it wrong'. He
was publicly supported by Rosalind Brewer, Starbuck's COO. Brewer is
one of the few African-American executives of a multinational corporation. As she put it: "this incident was a teachable moment for all of us".

And just in case the Starbuck's leaders slipped back on their promise
to implement unconscious bias training, the Philadelphia mayor, Jim
Kenney, was there to bolster their resolve.

[I intend] to ask the city's Commission on Human Relations to examine
Starbuck's policies and procedures, including the extent of, or need for,
implicit bias training for its employees.

As we indicated in the introduction to this chapter, this age of instant-
opinion social media puts immense pressure on leaders to not just articulate where they stand regarding diversity, equity, inclusion and justice but
to prove it in their practices.

Failure to do that won't protect you no matter how far up the corporate food chain you sit. As the former KPMG UK boss, Bill Michael,
discovered to his cost in February 2021:

The UK chair of big four accounting firm KPMB has resigned after
allegedly telling staff to "stop moaning" about the Covid-19 pandemic
and that unconscious bias training was "complete crap".

(Goddard, 2021)

5. Ikea, France

Surveillance of some sort or another has become an integral part of the
human experience. However, if you are the boss and you imagine that
gives you carte blanche to spy on your employees, think again.

In June 2021, a French court ordered the home furnishings global
giant, Ikea, to pay US$1.3 million in fines and damages for a campaign
of spying on union representatives, employees and some unhappy French
customers. Two former Ikea France executives were convicted and fined

over the scheme and given suspended prison sentences. Other Ikea defendants were also given suspended sentences (Vaux-Montagny, 2021).

It didn't take long for a UK tabloid to put the whole sad and sorry episode into a neat and snappy headline: "Spy-kea!" (Hussey, 2021).

Let's hope Ikea can learn from this episode and quickly get back to doing what they do best – Scandinavian home furnishings – and stay away from the spy game, because clearly, someone at the top of Ikea has been reading too many John le Carré novels.

6. GB News

During the very week that Ikea was getting a slapping for spying on employees, it found itself in the news for a very different reason, this time on the side of the so-called woke brigade.

> A number of companies are pulling advertising from GB News just days after Britain's newest and most controversial TV channel launched with a self-professed mission to fight 'cancel culture'. Swedish giant Ikea and brewer Grolsch are among the brands that have either pulled or paused advertising on the channel, which they say does not align with their values.
>
> (Ziady, 2021)

Ikea's tweeted press release stated:

> We have safeguards in place to prevent our advertising appearing on platforms that are not in line with our humanistic values.

It is, of course, impossible to know the personal values of CEOs and COOs or, indeed, every employee of these companies, but what is possible to determine is the continuing polarisation of those who are for progressive values and those who are not. Eventually, every business, large and small, will need to publicly declare where it stands.

Whether they like it or not, can handle it or not, organisations are heading for Total Inclusivity. Those wishing to remain outside of Total Inclusivity will have to live with the (financial and media) consequences.

7. Independent and International Schools

In Chapter 2 I explained the importance and danger of bubbles, and how these bubbles contain our worldview, our certainties, our assumptions. We even invest our self-identity in the knowledges and myths contained in our individual bubbles. All the more painful, then, when they get burst. In mid-2020, following the dramatic and very vocal emergence of the global BLM movement, lots of organisations and their leaders had their bubbles burst, especially independent and international schools. Why these schools? Because they are elitist and exclusive by definition. If you create an organisation that presents itself as culturally and racially white/ Western, reinforced by the behaviours and rituals which go with such symbolism, and then staff them overwhelmingly with white teachers, don't be surprised if a tinge of institutional racism starts to emerge and take root over the decades of the school's existence. What BLM did was prick the bubble of complacency which enveloped some of the world's most expensive and elitist schools. These bubbles were burst, mostly, by ex-staff and ex-students, who, motivated by BLM, sent many thousands of letters to school leaders complaining of institutional and individual teacher racist behaviour and attitudes, often going back decades. One such school organisation was the English Schools Foundation in Hong Kong.

Hong Kong's biggest international school group ESF vows to look into student complaints of racism, inappropriate behaviour against teachers. Move sparked by letter from student accusing teachers of mocking Asian names and performing dubious uniform checks on female schoolmates. More than 1,100 signatures collected in petition calling for change.

(Ho-him, 2020a)

This all kicked off in June 2020. Within weeks, a number of parents had also spoken out against racism at ESF schools, and the signatures had risen to more than 2,000. As I say, even a decade ago such accusations would have likely remained in Hong Kong. Not today. This news instantly went global. In response, Belinda Greer, CEO of the English Schools Foundation, made the following statement in a letter to parents:

I wanted to give you my assurance that this is being treated extremely seriously – and at the highest possible level. While we pride ourselves on the values we hold as an organisation and place a huge emphasis on developing the character of the young people in our schools . . . perceptions are real and we cannot afford to dismiss them or be defensive in any way . . . the ESF group will never shy away from looking critically at ourselves.

(Ho-him, 2020b)

ESF was one of the biggest names in the elite independent and international school sectors to get a very public hammering on its lack of Total Inclusivity. But it wasn't alone. Other educational organisations who felt it necessary to quickly make a public statement supporting BLM and standing firmly opposed to 'racism, sexism, homophobia and abusive tendencies' included the international school teacher recruitment agency Search Associates (Search Associates, 2020); leading English independent schools such as Benenden all-girls School; (Tingle, 2020); Westminster School (Doward, 2020); Dulwich College (Hughes, 2021); and a number of elite girls' schools in New York City (Shapiro, 2020).

As one UK independent school headteacher commented to me at the time, "these letters of accusation and complaint from ex-students and staff have completely shocked and surprised me. I had no idea our school community had this problem and now I want to deal with it fully. It has been especially upsetting to realise our values, my values, were not being fully replicated throughout the school".

As I say, bubbles can be comforting. But for those in leadership positions, indeed anyone who prefers to see the world as it is, not through misty eyes, they are really dangerous.

8. A New CEO Playbook

If you imagined that being the boss was all about protecting and enhancing the bottom line, think again. Nowadays, CEOs and their teams need to be ready to weigh in on social issues and back that up by their own individual practices. Corporate giants such as Coca-Cola, Gillette, Delta Airlines are just a few of the global businesses now having to decide where they stand on social issues, and in these three cases, they've clearly come down on the progressive agenda.

> Big consumer brands like Coca-Cola and Delta Airlines for years have positioned themselves as forces for what they see as promoting the social good – an approach they displayed last summer after the death of George Floyd. Coca-Cola turned off its Times Square billboard for a day. Delta flew Mr Floyd's body to his family in Houston. The Atlanta-based companies were among the scores of big corporations around the country that pledged an array of money and initiatives towards racial justice amid the upheaval that Mr Floyd's death while in police custody unleashed.
>
> (George, 2021)

However, just how CEOs handle these treacherous cultural waters matters a lot. Get it wrong and you may find your company losing money, not making it. Which is what happened to Gillette following its 'toxic masculinity' ads campaign of 2019. So why was "Gillette's new ad campaign toxic" (Taylor, 2019)?

a   Consumers are sceptical of the motives of big business.
b   They don't relish being told how to behave by a profit-motivated company.
c   Avoid stereotyping all men (or women) and be creative in the messaging.
d   The use of the term 'toxic masculinity' in the ad was a "flat out mistake" (Hoft, 2019).

The risks of doing something that will upset part of your consumer base are significant. But the risks of doing nothing, saying nothing, not coming out and nailing your company's flag to the mast are even greater.

> [A company] coming out after protests shows an enormous weakness. That's the worst thing that could possibly happen, because you're [the CEO] looking at being reactive not proactive . . . It's a new world, and you have to have a new type of CEO. [in the past most CEOs just wanted to run a profitable business] If you look at the typical CEO's preparation, there's nothing in their background that prepares them for these types of activities.
>
> (George, 2021)

Inclusive capitalism can't simply be about the bottom line. It is much more entwined with issues of social justice, equity, diversity and inclusion. This is especially so for those companies and organisations which purport to add value to society, whether it be a school or a soft drink company.

One corporation that might consider itself too big to be concerned with inclusive capitalism because its already too big to fail is Amazon.

9. Amazon Heating Up

Taking a poke at the third-largest company in the world is a bit like aiming a shotgun at a barn door – you're bound to hit something. With a global workforce of 1.3 million and adding employees at the rate of

500,000 a year (Richter, 2021), Amazon doesn't just deliver the goods to its hundreds of millions of customers; it ensures the bacon gets delivered to a good many families. Just don't expect all those employees to be happy bunnies.

While Amazon can guarantee your parcel arriving on time pretty much regardless of where you live in the world, it finds employee satisfaction/retention an altogether more challenging task.

> Each year, hundreds of thousands of workers churn through a vast mechanism that hires, monitors, disciplines and fires. Amid the pandemic, the already strained system lurched . . . Even before the pandemic Amazon lost about 3 percent of its hourly associates each week, meaning that the turnover among its work force was roughly 150 percent a year.
>
> (New York Times Interactive, 2021)

Indeed, Amazon churns through so many employees a year that "numerous Amazon leaders in Seattle describe a nagging fear that the company will run out of Americans to hire" (Ovid, 2021).

One hundred fifty percent turnover in one year?! That is hardly an example of corporate efficiency, even if one's parcel does arrive on time. Maybe Amazon USA can ease up on the efficiency and focus more on the employee well-being? Seems a welcome trade-off.

That is the USA. What about Amazon operations in other parts of the world?

South Korea: "Mirroring conditions at Amazon in the US, at Coupang (SK) employees are literally being worked to death to keep up with delivery deadlines . . . [with] death, injury, inhuman conditions [resulting in workers being treated as] disposable objects" (Kim, 2021).

United Kingdom: "Ambulances called out 600 times to 14 Amazon warehouses in Britain between 2015 and 2018 [with] workers collapsing in unsafe, intense working conditions. Workers describe gruelling conditions, unrealistic productivity targets, bogus self-employment and a refusal to recognise or engage with unions unless forced" (Davies, 2020).

France: "Amazon workers walk out to protest working conditions" (BBC News, 2019b).

Canada: "People don't understand because they are getting their parcels everyday. They don't understand the slavery that goes into delivering your parcels" (Blackwell, 2020).

Germany: "Amazon workers strike on busy Prime Day over conditions and pay in Germany" (Denton, 2020).

With so many complaints, so much anger, such a lot of frustration at apparently inept and uncaring leadership, Amazon may have inadvertently started the latest global workers movement:

> Amazon workers from Italy to India are uniting to form a global movement that may have found Jeff Bezo's Achilles heel.
>
> (Leon, 2021)

So how has Bezos responded to what is a growing and increasingly public crisis for Amazon, at least in terms of his company's global image as a (non)caring employer?

> We need a better vision for how we create value for employees – a vision for their success. We have always wanted to be the Earth's most customer-centric company. Now, we are going to be the Earth's safest place to work.
>
> (quoted in Kantor et al., 2021)

We'll see. Meanwhile, Bezos and the other Amazon bosses, especially his successor, Andy Jassy, could reflect on a rather interesting shift in the attitudes of the global workforce:

> We've found that 70% of employees say their sense of purpose in life is defined by their work. And nearly half said that they're reconsidering the kind of work they do because of the pandemic. Millennials were three times more likely than others to say they were re-evaluating work.
>
> (Dhingra et al., 2021)

> In a March [2020] survey of 2,000 workers by Prudential Financial Inc., one quarter said they plan to soon look for a role with a different company. "People are seeing the world differently," said Steve Carrigan, a talent consultant who led human resources at LinkedIn during his earlier years. "It's going to take time for people to think through, 'How do I unattach where I'm at and reattach to something new?' We're going to see a massive shift in the next few years."
>
> (WSJ, 2021)

As Dhingra et al. (2021) point out: *help your employees find purpose — or watch them leave.*

If you imagine this resistance to being treated as a robot by bosses and a working life of repetitious, target-driven drudgery is exclusive to Western millennials or Amazon workers, think again. In Japan these workers declining to join in the performative rat race are called 'hikikomori' (Butet-Roch, 2018) while in China they're now referred to as 'lay-flatters' (Tan, 2021).

In August 2021, Amazon UK began offering new warehouse workers a £1,000 incentive joining bonus in a bid to get new staff. In October 2021, the Amazon sign-on bonus offered in some US locations became US$3,000. These are just some examples of big employers now struggling to recruit.

For the first time in a generation, it is workers, not bosses, who have the upper hand, and these workers (or non-workers) are only just beginning to discover and wield their power.

10. An Inclusive Performativity?

Mix Total Inclusivity with performativity and what do you get?

Answer: The Carlyle Group

You may not have heard of this American private-equity firm or its CEO, Kewsong Lee, but you should, because they are overturning the measurements traditionally applied to determine 'business success' and effective leadership — and they are doing it in the hothouse world of corporate financing.

An indicator of great leadership is not just recognising which curve to follow but ensuring you are just ahead of it. And that is exactly what Carlyle is demonstrating in what is, in effect, a big positive statement for Total Inclusivity:

> Last week [May 2021], the private-equity firm the Carlyle Group
> announced that it will link the compensation of its CEO, Kewsong Lee,
> to the firm's performance when it comes to hiring diverse candidates,
> fostering an inclusive culture, and diversifying its portfolio companies'
> boards. Carlyle employees' performance bonuses will also hinge on
> whether they meet individual diversity objectives. Women and people
> of color made up nearly two-thirds of the firm's US hires last year, and
> Carlyle reports that women manage more than half of its $260 billion
> in assets under management . . . Tackling gender and racial inequities

at firms and their portfolio companies – including those companies'
management teams – could change the face of business.

(McKinsey Quarterly, 2021)

Carlyle is also launching an incentive program that will reward
employees who have stood out in their contributions to progressing
diversity. Award recipients, who will be nominated by their peers and
chosen by group heads, will either receive a grant of restricted stock
units or cash.

(Butler, 2021)

Performativity – target-driven work culture and compensation – has long
been the antithesis of diversity, equity, inclusion and justice. Indeed, it
has long been the antithesis of a safe and healthy working environment.
But we should be happy to see it applied to the Totally Inclusive agenda.
Just so long as the people subjected to it, be they leaders or workers, are
supported, coached, guided and advised on implementation.

What won't work is if Total Inclusivity is simply turned into yet
another stick with which to beat already stressed employees. If Carlyle –
and other major companies such as Starbucks, Wells Fargo & Co. and
McDonald's that are now rolling out plans to tie executive compensation
to diversity targets – can really generate a Totally Inclusive work culture
in their mammoth operations then they will not only have safeguarded
their businesses and employees, they'll have helped introduce inclusive
capitalism.

And that will be more important and beneficial to the long-term future
of humanity than any number of burger bars, coffee shops or bank loans.

WHICH SIDE ARE YOU ON?

If a business, no matter how gigantic, is going to survive the 21st century,
one thing is for sure: it cannot afford to be on the wrong-side of history.
And with history speeding up before our very eyes, having a strong sense
about which direction humanity is heading is becoming an increasingly
important skill, especially for those with their hands on the organisational tiller.

This chapter provides just a few case study indicators, to which can be
added the following:

- A growing disconnect between what employees now want and what
  employers are offering

- Tens of millions of workers, especially in the USA, looking to leave their jobs because of dissatisfaction with their bosses and work culture
- Generation Z's antipathy towards working in organisations which lack interpersonal connection and authenticity
- The impact of climate change on the traditional capitalist model and work system
- Workers across the USA refusing to take on "backbreaking or mind-numbing low-wage jobs" (Reich, 2021)

If you are a leader then you may consider it safer to sit on the fence, stay quiet, pretend and hope all this social and cultural turmoil disappears and people return to life as it was in, say, the 1950s or even the 1990s. Perhaps you hope to be invisible.

It isn't going to happen.

Nothing stays the same; everything changes. And so do people. Humanity is changing right now – and fast. It is doing so very globally and very publicly. If you are not sure which direction to follow then that suggests inaction and fear. If you are a boss, a leader, a senior manager, someone with authority and power, you know that inaction is not an option – you also know that a fearful leader is no leader at all.

> By not understanding what their employees are running from, and what they might gravitate to, company leaders are putting their very businesses at risk.
>
> (De Smet et al., 2021)

If you haven't the will, confidence and self-belief to establish the ethical values necessary for your 21st-century organisation, if you cannot articulate your value system and in a way that motivates others to believe and trust in you and willingly give part of their lives, invest their identities in your organisation, then you cannot consider yourself a leader.

What you risk by being on the wrong side or by inaction is having to stand up like Jeff Bezos and the other bosses identified in this book, each of whom has reacted after the event; having to publicly acknowledge your failings as a leader, as an employer, and apologise accordingly.

That public apology, that humbling recognition that your organisation is discriminatory, cruel, violent, abusive, dangerous, harmful, predatory is going to stay with you all your life.

Credit Line: Cartoons drawn by Advanced Standard Group Co., Ltd.

When you are old and have energy only for the golf course, that memory will be as strong and secure in your mind as the money in your bank account. Only the money means nothing – it can only be spent, while the recognition that you were on the wrong side of history cannot be undone. No amount of wealth can compensate for the personal recognition that you got it wrong.

CHAPTER 10: REFLECTIONS, GUIDANCE AND COMMITMENTS

Reflection Exercise: How do you want to be remembered by those you worked with and those you led? When you are older and retired, which organisations and the leaders who employed you will you look back on fondly and which not? Why?

Guidance for Implementation: Imagine you are going for a job as a leader of a company. The job interview requires you to give a talk on ethics and leadership in organisations. What would you say? What would be your core message? Do you have a value standpoint? What is it?

Commitment: Inclusive capitalism is simply the pursuit of prosperity but not at the expense of people, communities, the environment, humanity's common good. Make a commitment to this way of living and working. Articulate it in your organisation. Be an Advocate for Total Inclusivity, because this is the key to inclusive capitalism.

Eleven

DOI: 10.4324/9781003244073-11

All leadership is a mask. Every boss is performing, engaging in impression management. There isn't one leader out there who does not suffer (at least occasionally) from stage fright: the fear that they'll forget their lines and be exposed as a sham, as fake, as hollow.

None of that should surprise us. Anyone who unfailingly believes in themselves regardless of the evidence, the circumstances or the opinions of others is at least a little bit in denial. As is stressed in this book, identity doesn't come fixed and permanent; it has to be constantly worked at. And for leaders, that identity work can be especially fraught.

The authority of leadership is held not in the mind of the leader but in the eyes of those they would seek to lead. If they stop believing then the leader is finished. And every leader instinctively knows this to be so – even if they can never admit it to themselves.

An official title will confer legitimacy, but it doesn't make people believe, and it certainly doesn't make them trust.

The most authoritative, compelling and persuasive leader has no desire to be leader. They can assume the role or not. They have no need to risk investing their self-identity in being boss.

The least authoritative leader is the one who needs to be boss because they need the title not just to legitimise their position but to legitimise who and what they desire to be.

This chapter is not designed for you to test out which type of leader you are or are likely to be, though that may well be an interesting secondary outcome of you reflecting on the questions it is going to put to you.

This chapter really only has one aim and that is for those who are or would be leaders to reflect on whether they can be effective leaders in the 21st century.

You may say to yourself, 'Okay, what you are really asking is can I lead an organisation to Total Inclusivity?'

No. The question is, 'Can you be an effective leader in the 21st century?'.

Disregard, for the moment, Total Inclusivity. Put that out of your mind completely.

Think only of what sort of leaders we need today and in the days to come.

Are you one of those?

LEADING INTO THE FUTURE

At time of writing global society is still reeling from the effects of the COVID-19 pandemic, with no clear sign of when or even if it will end. With more than 250 million confirmed cases and 5+ million deaths, the 21st century has gotten off to a bad start. Globalisation has been replaced by localisation and isolation, climate change is gathering apace, hate crimes are on the rise, billions are one paycheck or government handout away from financial catastrophe, and a great many people are slipping into QAnon-inspired delusion.

Dire as all that is, a century ago it was even worse. Having just seen the end of World War I, humanity was swept by Spanish Flu. A third of the global population became infected – 500 million. Fifty million died. Ten years later, the Great Depression arrived, to be shortly followed by Fascism in Italy, Germany and Japan. If you made it to the 1950s strong in mind and body, having not lost a loved one or close family relative through war, famine or pestilence, and had food on the table, you were one of the lucky ones.

The last 70 years have witnessed the most remarkable period in human history – unprecedented growth, prosperity, education, health care and technological marvels.

It is unrealistic to expect it to continue like that.

If you decide to be a leader you first must accept that you cannot be sure what you are leading towards. And then you must decide what difference you intend to make – not just to your life but to the lives of those who follow you into the unknown.

The rest of the book could now be turned over to simply outlining some of the known unknowns facing us all and to speculating on the unknown unknowns. But in the end, I am only guessing, or at best making an informed assessment. Unfortunately, leaders are expected to be more certain than that:

Is certainty not the essence of leadership? To believe in one's self
and, from that, to be able to articulate and publicly communicate an

appropriate and convincing organizational vision, is this not the very stuff
of the 'modern manager'? Certainly it would appear so.

(Whitehead, 2006, p. 51)

And therein lies the rub: to lead you have to present yourself as almost omnipresent, able to handle virtually any situation as and when it may arise, even though you can never prepare fully for every possible eventuality.

The reality is, most of the time you are barely on the curve, never mind ahead of it.

As I say, leadership is a mask, with impression management arguably the most important skill you'll need to survive.

THE QUESTIONS

Fifty questions. Don't rush at them and expect to have them all 'answered' in thirty minutes. Take your time. It may take you weeks to answer all these questions in a way which you are satisfied with. These are big questions to ask yourself. Some will be questions you've never ever considered before. Which is why I ask them – to trigger a response in you and get you to reflect, evaluate and if necessary change. And if you cannot answer some of these questions then that itself is an 'answer' you should reflect on. Why can't you answer them? What assumptions, habits, attitudes, beliefs are holding you back, blinkering you? What are you not seeing in yourself?

A tip: you might risk asking a nearest and dearest to answer these questions on your behalf to see how big a gap exists between their perceptions of you and your own. You might even risk asking a work colleague.

Whichever way you approach these questions, remember there are no right or wrong answers. And don't look for patterns – they are randomly presented en bloc so as to encourage you to reflect. They are not testing you as a leader so much as encouraging you to think, consider, self-evaluate. To ponder who you really are.

1 Why are you doing this? Life could be a whole lot simpler and less fraught if you simply stepped down, handed over to someone younger, more energetic, more confident, more determined than you. And there is always someone eager to do your job who believes they can do it better. You may not know them, but they are out there. Don't imagine you are indispensable. So what keeps you going? You must answer that before you can answer any other question.

2 Are you a boss or are you a leader? If you cannot distinguish between the two then you are a boss. Now reflect on what that says about you.

3 What do you want your dreams to be like when you are old and retired? Those dreams will be your life reflected back at you, night after night, for the remainder of your life. What you did, what you experienced, how you behaved won't ever leave you. And if you forget your past while you are awake, your mind will resurrect it in your dreams. There is no escaping the consequences of your actions.

4 Who are you modelling yourself on? Most likely it will be a parent. Most of us do. In which case, be careful. Remember your parents were heading into the unknown just like you are. Did they get it right or not? Do you see your parents as insecure, flawed human beings, or have you put them on a pedestal? In which case, how much of your life is spent trying to compensate for their weaknesses or meet their (unrealistic?) expectations of you?

5 Which do you trust more – data/numbers or your gut feeling? Both can be right, and both can be wrong. But only one of these two influencers connects with your heart. If you cannot trust your heart then why would anyone else trust it?

6 Who are you mentoring right now – formally or informally? If the answer is no one then what does that say about you, your style of leadership? If you are mentoring someone, why are you? For whose benefit is this, yours or theirs?

7 Do you relish taking risks? Of course you do. One of the attractions of leadership is to be able to assess the odds and beat them. But what, in truth, are you risking? Or indeed, who are you risking? Do you enjoy taking risks with the safety, well-being and security of others, or do you constantly put your own safety, well-being and security on the line? The skill is not in having the courage to take the risk but in having the intelligence to reduce it to a minimum.

8 What has been your legacy so far? You may only be young, with many decades ahead of you; nevertheless, already you will have generated some legacy, some history. How would you describe it? What is your story so far, at least from your perspective?

9 How would others write your story so far? What have you done to merit respect from those who know you?

10 What is your identity mix? We discussed this in Chapter 2. Have you now worked out the variables that intersect to make you who you are? Which of these identities stands out in your mind as most important in your work and career?

11 If you are a male leader, how has this particular identity influenced your work and career? And which type of masculinity do you perform at work?

12 If you are female leader, how have you negotiated the tensions between traditional femininity and traditional masculinity in your leadership role? In what ways are you a different gender at work to the one you are at home?

13 How did you get here? Who helped you? No one makes it on their own. Everyone gets a helping hand now and again. Who gave you a helping hand, and have you thanked them yet?

14 Do your workers trust you? Why not ask them?

15 Where do you feel most comfortable – in your office or on walkabout around your organisation? If you say on walkabout then you are very likely kidding yourself. Why is that?

16 How honest are you? And don't say totally. Only a misguided leader is totally honest all of the time. As leader you are expected to be able to keep secrets, maintain confidential information. The trick is recognising which secrets are being kept in order to enhance your position and which are being kept in order to enhance the organisation's.

17 Do you care about others? If you've read this far then it is almost certain that you do to some extent. While no book can generate emotional intelligence in a reader it can at least encourage the reader to reflect on their level of empathy, compassion, care for others. But what have you done recently to demonstrate that care to others, especially those who work with you?

18 Which of these two titles most appeals to you: organisational boss or community leader? What does that say about you, your style of leadership?

19 Look back on all the people you have promoted to senior management/leadership positions. Do they reflect your identity mix, your image or not? Why is that?

20 Have you become the boss you always hated or the leader you always admired and respected?

21 What is weakness in leadership and how do you sometimes express it? Indecision? Anger? Insecurity? Spitefulness? Do you imagine you've never expressed weakness in leadership, or are you in denial?

22 What does work–life balance mean to you in practice? Do you have it? Does your family think you have it? How important is it to you really?

23 How good an actor are you? For example, can you pretend to be angry with someone yet not feel angry at all? How much time do you spend each day concealing what is going on in your heart? What are the positives and negatives of this? Does it strengthen or weaken your character?

24 How often do you admit to being wrong – to subordinates? If never, reflect on what you are trying to hide.

25 What are you truly afraid of? Is it your physical health and well-being that bothers you or your identity well-being? In truth, there is only one answer to that question for all of us.

26 Do you think you live in a winner-take-all world? If not, what type of world are you living in?

27 When has trauma been good for you and in what way?

28 When was the last time you said sorry to someone who works for you? Do you never say sorry? Or are you saying sorry even when it isn't your fault? And when you say sorry, do you mean it?

29 Who do you trust? Can you list more than one or two names? If not, why not? What does that say about you?

30 Can you work productively with people who resist you? How do you harness resistance in a way which is productive and positive?

31 Do you feel the need to proselytise to those who work for you? Do you have an urge to create believers in your truth? Why is that?

32 What does the term 'communal good' mean to you? What contribution are you making towards it? Or are you making a negative contribution?

33 Do you forgive people who transgress against you? Can you let bad things go? Or do you hold on to them for a long, long time?

34 If you had to list the biggest single achievement of your working life so far, what would it be? What makes you especially proud of this achievement?

35 Do you see yourself as battling against society – you against the rest – or are you an embracer, an engager? Are you on the inside looking out or the outside looking in?

36 Who do you trust most in your organisation beyond yourself? Who do you instinctively go to when you have a problem, a query, a dilemma to resolve? Why them?

37 What have you learned about yourself during the COVID-19 pandemic, and how has this influenced your view of life and your job?

38 Do you recognise when your staff are burnt out? What action do you take to deal with that, to stop it happening?

39 What does your firm do to help create positive, enduring change in the world?

40 What do you most want to improve about yourself, your leadership style? Why? Can you do this on your own, or do you need guidance?

41 What did you most learn about yourself in your last job?

42 How would you define a 'superstar executive'? How does it match your identity?

43 What is it that you most fear your colleagues seeing in you?

44 What is your 'authentic self', and under what circumstances are you most likely to reveal it?

45 What side of you do you keep hidden at work?

46 What were your biggest failures? How did you benefit from them?

47 Does your leadership style encourage your workplace to be organic and creative or predictive and inhibited?

48 Can you see any value in lazy leadership?

49 How old are you in your head?

Credit Line: Cartoons drawn by Advanced Standard Group Co., Ltd.

50 When you are selling yourself, what do you imagine your brand image
     to be?

REFLECTIONS

See, no mention of Total Inclusivity. And the reason being no leader can
introduce Total Inclusivity unless they know who they are and are comfortable with that person. Unless they are wise and mature enough to
recognise the value of a community and the dangers inherent in inflexible organisational thinking. And if they are willing to put aside conservative conventional ideas surrounding leadership and embrace their inner
humanity, warts and all. If you are a leader committed to creating a work
culture dominated by spreadsheets, targets, appraisals, five-year plans,
hierarchies and all the other sterile components of performative, pseudo-
objective neo-liberalism then you are heading for failure – personal and
professional. That is not leadership by character; it is leadership by audit
and appraisal.

As a leader you don't know what is coming. But you still have to survive it. In which case you and your organisation can only survive it as a
community.

One of the most intriguing outcomes of COVID-19 and the dynamics
of the 21st century thus far is the way in which it is impacting how we
see the world and our role in it. As we discussed in Chapter 2, work,
professions, employment all matter to us not just materially but in terms
of how we assess our relevance in society. Are we contributing or not?
Right now, a lot of research suggests that more of us are looking for purpose in our lives, especially Generation Z and millennials (Dhingra and
Schaninger, 2021). Paid work can bring that purpose, though it is risky
investing in organisations. But so is getting married, and that act has traditionally brought purpose (if often temporarily) for countless millions
down the ages. However, marriage (and parenting?) may have gone out
of fashion, but our desire for a life of meaning remains as strong as ever.

The point is not what brings us purpose in our lives, because that will
change over time as we age and as society evolves.

The point is that we all need purpose. We all desire to be wanted,
valued, considered relevant.

Why should some of us be excluded from that most essential of quests
on the basis of race, gender, sexual orientation, disability, class, age, religion, or language? Why should some of us be denied opportunity, offered
only stereotypical opportunities or just ignored completely because we

don't happen to fit the 'brand' image of a company or boss? There is no moral justification, no ethical justification, and nor, in today's world, is there any business justification.

The Totally Inclusive Community requires a community leader. what it doesn't need is a boss. Sure, if employees want to call you 'boss' then fine. Just don't behave like one.

For a great many individuals, being leader is something they fell into by chance, or gravitated towards because others were not around to fill the vacancy or didn't wish to step up. It matters little how you got there but that you are there. Having taken on that role, assume it. Belong to it. Be it.

But to be a leader in an inclusive way, in a way which embraces Totally Inclusive values, you'll need to feel it in your heart. You will need to have a powerful desire to empower others to fashion a community of belonging. That is what you are leading. Get that right and everything else will follow; trust, belief, confidence and the ability to cope with the coming unknowns. Plus a lot of joy and satisfaction for everyone involved.

A FINAL QUESTION WHICH BOSSES/LEADERS MAY ASK OF TI

Before I end this chapter there is one final question which many bosses/leaders reading it may well ask, and it is not a question that has been addressed so far in the book, well not directly:

I know you may ask it because a leader of a major international organisation did so while I was writing the book:

> What about the underperforming employee? May they not read the
> book and imagine everyone gets a gold medal just for turning up stuff,
> snowflake stuff? Relatedly, the same black, queer employee may not 'fit'
> in even the most inclusive organisation – it may simply not be the 'right'
> organisation for them. Also, you may need to make it clear that 'Total
> Inclusivity' is not a platform for hobby-horses, polemics or unreasonable
> demands.

These are all understandable concerns any leader might have about the potential impact of Total Inclusivity upon their organisation.

My answer is that any organisation that has reached the stage of being a Totally Inclusive Community need not worry too much about employees abusing the perceived largesse of the management nor fret over whether employees consider their well-being violated if the coffee machine breaks down and they have to bring in their own flasks. Why? Because the values of TI will be embedded in the organisation in such a way as to protect against any potential abuses by any individual, be it the junior clerk or the CEO.

The community will be bigger than the individual but only by virtue of it having embraced all individuals and respected their identity mix.

Total Inclusivity does not mean creating organisational clones – demanding people subsume their individuality under the blanket rhetoric of the organisation. That is not a community; it is a production line. Total Inclusivity is not always and under all circumstances satisfying the demands of every single employee no matter how excessive and unreasonable. Nor is it about persisting with the employment of those who are demonstrably unsuited to the organisational culture and who cannot meet the expectations of their jobs.

It is about ensuring every single employee has their identity safeguarded and is duly protected from abuse, violence, discrimination and any practices which are violations against them. This is what it means to be a community – every single member of it contributes in a way which works for them and simultaneously works for the community; in return they are protected by that community though not to the extent that they can abuse that protection.

Yes, it does require understanding and flexibility on the part of leaders, and it demands a good level of emotional intelligence. Likewise, it requires employees to recognise that this community of which they are a paid beneficiary only gets to continue its existence as a Totally Inclusive Community if everyone works together and fulfils their contractual obligations willingly, committedly and in a spirit of unity.

Leaders will still have to lead; they will still have to take difficult if not unpleasant decisions in order to protect the whole organisation. And no, they cannot always please all the people all the time, and nor are they obligated to.

But they can be understanding. They can be reflective. They can ask themselves the questions posed in this chapter and, indeed, throughout the book. In the process expect them to become not just stronger and better leaders of others but inspiring leaders. Expect them to set standards which employees can recognise as worthy to follow. Not rules and standards imposed by authority, tradition, diktat or ego but standards and expectations rooted in humanistic values of diversity, equity, inclusivity and justice. That will require listening to all the voices of the community and making decisions based on Total Inclusivity values.

As stated in Chapter 1, with Total Inclusivity no one is excluded except those who choose to exclude themselves. The only person who cannot be excluded is you, the leader. Without your intelligent leadership inclusivity can never be total.

CHAPTER 11: REFLECTIONS, GUIDANCE AND COMMITMENTS

Reflection Exercise: The whole of this chapter is an exercise in reflection. If you've read this far then you're already a slightly changed person to the one who started it.

Guidance for Implementation: Address these questions in a spirit of adventure. Don't be hesitant, defensive or dismissive. Some of these questions contain deep truths for you, and to unearth them you'll need to dig deep into yourself. That takes courage. But then, so does going on an adventure, as does being a good leader.

Commitment: If you are lucky you'll have a long and productive life. Use it well. By well I mean not dedicated to material accumulation and personal status but for acquiring wisdom and knowledge. In the final reckoning, that is all that counts. Everything else is distraction. Commit to using your blessings to help others achieve theirs.

Twelve

Do you believe in your potential? If so (and I'd expect the answer to be yes) then do you also believe in the potential of others?

Of the two questions, the second is the most important, not just to Total Inclusivity but to the future of the human race. To your future.

None of us is an island; we are connected with each other, like it or not. No one can thrive on their own; indeed, no one can survive on their own. We are a global community; irrevocably interconnected despite our differences.

This idea of collective belonging is not new, but it links to an important concept which has taken root across global society over recent years: the 'new humanism'.[1]

> Being a humanist today means adapting the strength of an age-old message to the contours of the modern world . . . This work of 'self-fashioning' is a collective requirement, and here lies the importance of another critical aspect of the humanist message, which emphasizes the necessarily collective dimension of all accomplished living. Individuals become whole in society, as members of a community . . . Now more than ever before, our task is to work towards building this ideal community. . . . Being a humanist today means building bridges between North, South, East and West and strengthening the human community to take up our challenges together.
>
> (Bokova, 2010)

COVID-19 is a warning of what humanity faces as this century unfolds. It is a test of people's willingness to work together to resolve such crises. Climate change will most definitely bring even greater challenges. It already is doing so. What will be your role in addressing these problems? Do you believe only in yourself, your own potential, your own comfort, and demonstrate that by refusing to vaccinate, wear a face mask, make

DOI: 10.4324/9781003244073-12

no effort to reduce your use of plastic or your carbon footprint? Or are you a member of the global community and playing your part in trying to ensure its future?

If the latter, then you are already demonstrating new humanist values, and therefore it is a small step towards Total Inclusivity.

You cannot be a humanist and be a racist, misogynist, homophobe, discriminator. We all have a choice to make – to pull only for ourselves or to contribute to the greater good. If you've read to the end of this book then you already know what Total Inclusivity means and what it requires of you, of all of us.

Of all the points made in this book, perhaps the most important one is this:

We are all in this together. If we are learning one lesson from the 21st century it is that there is no escape from each other. You are who you are because of us all: ubuntu.

> When any person or community suffers, a piece of each of us suffers
> with them, whether we realise it or not. And though we are not meant
> to live in a state of suffering, we, as a people, are being conditioned to
> accept it.[2]

You might respond by saying, 'That's all well and good, but I have no power to change anything'.

Do you really imagine you have no power at all?

We all have one power, and that is the power to change ourselves. If you cannot change yourself then who and what is changing you? Because one thing is for sure, you are changing. Even reading this book has changed you in some small way.

Every action leads to a reaction, and every good action makes a positive contribution to the whole of humanity – and to the well-being of the individual. Every good thought is a direct counter to all those bad thoughts that bubble up within us all. It doesn't matter that humanity doesn't notice your good action, doesn't know your good thoughts. What is important is that you notice them and you repeat them. That is a something only you have power over.

And as for other humans, do you imagine you have no power to influence them?

If you are a parent your power and influence over your children is immeasurable.

If you are a lover/partner your power and influence over your soul-mate goes deeper than you can begin to imagine.

If you are a leader then you already know the extent and limits of your power.

if you are an employee worker, largely unnoticed by those above you, then your power to contribute to the well-being or negativity of the organisation is as great than you realise, greater than you know.

And even if you are none of the above, but simply spend your days messaging people on social media, do you seriously imagine your written comments cannot evoke emotional responses in others? That is another sort of power and one we can all wield to good or bad effect.

We can all be teachers, guides, mentors and coaches. It doesn't matter what your education level, life experiences or identity mix is – you have the power to make a positive contribution to someone, somewhere, at some time in your life. Do so regardless of their identity mix. That is Total Inclusivity in action.

We all connect. There is no such thing as individuality. Well, not in the sense of a person being completely and utterly outside society. You might like to imagine you are unique, different from everyone else. And indeed, at a psychological level that is true. But you didn't get here on your own. You are not the architect and sole director of your life. There are countless others who played a role, going back through time. Acknowledge as many of those unbidden influencers as you can. They've each contributed to the person you are today.

If humans have one unchangeable and relentless instinct it is to belong, to be socially connected, to contribute, to be part of something bigger than themselves. As COVID-19 has proved, humans are hardwired for connection, not isolation. Belonging is what makes us happy, makes us feel validated, gives us hope and inspires us to connect with others.

We all have a debt to each other because we all rely on each other to maintain our lives, our lifestyle, our well-being, our community of belonging.

This is why Total Inclusivity is not optional, because at one vitally important level it already exists: the total inclusivity of the social web.

This is not new. It didn't suddenly arrive with the 21st century. We have always been in this together. Much as we might like to create social distinctions around race, gender, sexual orientation, class, disability, age, religion and language, the reality is we all connect, and we always have done. It is just that with 7.7 billion of us together on this small and fragile planet, connecting becomes not just more important, it is also unavoidable.

Total Inclusivity is, then, simply recognising that inclusivity is elementary to the human condition. It is the engine of society, the essential character of community and the safeguard we all need.

And one of the most important elements in this social fabric is the organisation.

ORGANISATIONS AND COMMUNITIES

In a world of change, uncertainty and insecurity, organisations must become more than the vehicle for the wealth production of a few; they must become communities of belonging for all their members. They must cease being solely concerned with profit and increasingly concerned with the well-being of their employees, and that begins with recognising, valuing and safeguarding the identities of everyone.

Total Inclusivity is bigger and more important than profit, bigger and more important than any individual owner, shareholder or CEO. Total Inclusivity is more than an aspiration and greater than a rhetorical vision. It is a humanistic value system, feeding and nourishing the organisational climate, thereby enabling it to flourish in the 21st century. And if 21st-century organisations become Totally Inclusive, then so will wider society become Totally Inclusive.

As has been stressed throughout the book, organisations are not inflexible, predetermined and unchangeable entities. Organisations are processes; ongoing but in such a way as to invariably defy fixed five-year business plans, corporate strategies and the directives of those in charge. In other words, organisations, like the people who inhabit them, are contingent, fluid and heading for the unknown. The only way to survive the unknown is together; that is the central lesson from human history. And the only way to be together is as a community.

Belonging to a community is not only about the reinforcement of association with a workplace and a job, it is both an existential comfort and a survival mechanism. But the idea of an organisation as a 'family' or a community is nothing more than bland and cynical marketing rhetoric if it is not backed up by reality. And that reality must be embedded in the concept of Total Inclusivity. If you or your organisation are operating in a way which is divisive, separatist, discriminatory, marginalising of others, then there can be no community, and there can be no belonging to it.

This chapter, therefore, asks a simple question 'What next for you?' And there can only be one answer for anyone concerned with protecting not only their own identity and work association but also that of their colleagues – now and in the future.

That answer is to become an advocate for Total Inclusivity.

BECOMING A TOTAL INCLUSIVITY ADVOCATE

You have the power, you have the opportunity, and it is hoped this book has given you the motivation to become an Advocate for Total Inclusivity.

But what about the practicalities?

Here are some suggestions (adopt and adapt as you see fit):

Emphasise the Positive in You

1 Do good.
2 Reflect on your feelings and reactions to situations, events, people.
3 Be a positive voice.
4 Support others, and when the opportunities arise, mentor, coach, guide.
5 Be active; learn about TI and offer to help implement it in your organisation.
6 Become a TI auditor for your organisation.
7 Speak upwards – speak truth to power when you have to.
8 Listen downwards – don't ignore the voices of those below you in the system.
9 Know yourself before you claim to know and understand other selves.
10 Use your intelligence positively.
11 Know when to be silent and when to be loud.
12 Get allies in the organisation – build your community and expand it.
13 Take responsibility for your actions.
14 Recognise that everyone is anxious about what happens next.
15 Recognise your own privileges.
16 Recognise where those privileges come from.
17 Trust yourself to know the difference between right and wrong.
18 Accept that you have limited time, so use it well.
19 Keep your mind open to the realities of others.
20 Embrace the good in you and in humanity.

Avoid the Negative in You

1 Don't sit in judgement of others.
2 Don't put yourself on a pedestal of righteousness.
3 Don't imagine you have all the answers.
4 Don't be afraid – courage is needed at times.

5 Don't be harsh and vindictive towards those who resist – just be firm and resolute.
6 Don't give up.
7 Don't retreat other than in order to advance in a different direction.
8 Don't become corrupted by the illusions of power, control, authority.
9 Don't just preach Total Inclusivity, do it.
10 Don't imagine you will always get it right, and forgive yourself when you get it wrong.
11 Don't imagine your reality is the only one that counts.
12 Don't use Total Inclusivity as a stick to punish people with.
13 Don't forget that there once was a time when you knew very little and accept there is a lot more for you to learn.

This is your commitment to the total good. It requires emotional intelligence, confidence, courage and the awareness of your own strengths and weaknesses. It doesn't require you to be a leader – because everyone involved in Total Inclusivity is, by definition, a leader automatically.

We all lead and we all guide and we all follow.

We are the totally inclusive.

NOTES

1 The term 'new humanism' is utilised within the Total Inclusivity concept not as a theory of literacy criticism but to describe a humanist agenda for the 21st century and beyond.
2 Taken from a statement issued by the Duke and Duchess of York, 21st August, 2021, on the 'extremely fragile' state of the world amid the Taliban takeover of Afghanistan and the humanitarian crisis in Haiti.

Bibliography

ADP (2019) https://uk.adp.com/about-adp/press-centre/2019-06-20-london-workers-most-likely-to-feel-discriminated-against.aspx 20th June.

Agoda (2019) www.agoda.com/blog/pride-month-2019-gay-parades-lgbtq-marches?cid=-42 11th October.

American Psychological Association (2018) 'Guidelines for psychological practice with boys and men', https://www.apa.org/about/policy/boys-men-practice-guidelines.pdf August.

Aow, A., Hollins, S. and Whitehead, S. (2022) *Creating a totally inclusive school*. London: Routledge.

Barrett, F. J. (2002) 'Hegemonic masculinity: the US navy', in S. M. Whitehead and F. J. Barrett (eds) *The masculinities reader*. Cambridge: Polity.

BBC News (2019a) www.bbc.com/news/world-asia-47906070. Accessed 21st June, 2021.

BBC News (2019b) 'Amazon hit by Black Friday walkouts and protests in Europe', *BBC News* 29th November.

BBC News (2021a) 'Union creates hotline for disgruntled Amazon staff', *BBC News* 28th March.

BBC News (2021b) www.bbc.com/news/business-57428258 10th June.

Bishop, K. (2021) www.bbc.com/worklife/article/20211201-why-some-work-environments-breed-toxic-cultures. Accessed 10th December, 2021.

Blackwell, T. (2020) https://nationalpost.com/news/canada/working-conditions-are-hell-amazon-employees-not-surprised-its-warehouses-have-seen-hundreds-of-covid-cases 23rd December.

Bokova, I. (2010) 'A new humanism for the 21st century', *United Nations Educational, Scientific and Cultural Organization*, www.unesco.org. Accessed 17th August, 2021.

Bostock, B. (2020) www.businessinsider.com/coronavirus-women-leaders-handled-pandemic-better-than-men-study-2020-8 19th August.

Bourdieu, P. (1984) *Distinction: a social critique of the judgement of taste*. London: Routledge.

Brookings (2018) www.brookings.edu/blog/future-development/2018/09/27/a-global-tipping-point-half-the-world-is-now-middle-class-or-wealthier/ 27th September.

Buck, S. and Hardwick, B. (2021) www.fastcompany.com/90666944/a-sense-of-belonging-is-what-drives-wellbeing-and-its-disappearing 18th August.

Butet-Roch, L. (2018) www.nationalgeographic.com/photography/article/japan-hikikomori-isolation-society 14th February.

Butler, K. (2021) www.bloomberg.com/news/articles/2021-05-11/carlyle-to-tie-ceo-pay-worker-bonuses-to-diversity-goals?cid=other-eml-dni-mip-mck&hlkid=2204b4a8f 47042d398690abf40f573a1&hctky=12628122&hdpid=9f7816ec-a2f8-4bf9-bc6f-7267f7070985 11th May.

Butler, S. and Jolly, J. (2021) www.theguardian.com/business/2021/apr/07/deliveroo-workers-strike-as-shares-rise-on-first-day-of-open-trading 7th April.

Capon, F. (2015) www.newsweek.com/2015/04/10/national-scandal-break-france-over-decades-paedophile-cover-320218.html 4th August.

Cassidy, M. (2021) www.hrexchangenetwork.com/hr-talent-acquisition/articles/the-great-resignation-how-companies-can-cope-with-the-mass-exodus. Accessed 9th December, 2021.

Chron.com (2020) https://work.chron.com/hazards-being-teacher-9309.html 15th October.

Clegg, S., Kornberger, M. and Pitsis, T. (2005) *Managing and organizations*. Thousand Oaks: Sage.

Connell, R.W. (1996) *Masculinities*. Cambridge: Polity.

Davies, R. (2020) www.theguardian.com/technology/2020/oct/12/uk-must-compel-amazon-to-improve-worker-conditions-say-unions 12th October.

Davies, R. and Makortoff, K. (2021) www.theguardian.com/business/2021/apr/03/deliveroos-overheated-stock-market-flotation 3rd April.

De Beauvoir, S. (1953) *The second sex*. New York: Vintage.

Delgado, R. and Stefancic, J. (2012) *Critical race theory: an introduction*. New York: New York University Press.

Denton, J. (2020) www.marketwatch.com/story/amazon-workers-strike-on-busy-prime-day-over-conditions-and-pay-in-germany-11602609862 13th October.

De Smet, A., Dowling, B., Mugayar-Baldocchi, M. and Schaninger, B. (2021) '"Great attrition" or "great attraction"? The choice is yours', *McKinsey Quarterly* 8th September.

Detroit Historical Society (2021) https://detroithistorical.org/learn/encyclopedia-of-detroit/race-riot-1943.

Dhingra, N., Samo, A., Schaninger, B. and Schrimper, M. (2021) www.mckinsey.com/business-functions/organization/our-insights/help-your-employees-find-purpose-or-watch-them-leave?cid=other-eml-onp-mip-mck&hlkid=e05a3f62e7904bb6b 7342ca05203ad3e&hctky=12628122&hdpid=1139d6d3-0805-44d4-9410-9b4 21fa63e87 5th April.

Dhingra, N. and Schaninger, B. (2021) www.mckinsey.com/business-functions/organi zation/our-insights/the-search-for-purpose-at-work?cid=other-eml-alt-mip-mck&hdpid=835a6d4e-5cc9-46ce-b1f0-24fa0da9d908&hctky=12628122&hlkid= 21b1f902a020432ea09d625b1cabe0a3 3rd June.

Donovan, L. and Nkune, R. M. (2021) https://time.com/5959197/fabletics-factory-abuse-allegations/ 10th June.

Doward, J. (2020) www.theguardian.com/education/2020/jun/14/top-public-school-accused-of-toxic-culture-of-racism-among-pupils 14th June.

Eagleman, D. (2021) *Livewired: the inside story of the ever-changing brain*. Edinburgh: Cannongate Books.

EER (Employment Equality (Sexual Orientation) Regulations) (2003) https://www.legis
lation.gov.uk/uksi/2003/1661/contents/made

Efythymiades, A. (2015) www.personneltoday.com/hr/can-amazon-teach-us-workplace-
relations/ 19th October.

Elias, N. (2000) *The civilising process*. London: Blackwell.

Erasing 76 Crimes (2021) https://76crimes.com/76-countries-where-homosexuality-
is-illegal/ March.

Fitch, K. and Agrawal, S. (2015) https://news.gallup.com/businessjournal/183026/
female-bosses-engaging-male-bosses.aspx 7th May.

Fitzhugh, E., Julien, J. P., Noel, N. and Steward, S. (2020) www.mckinsey.com/featured-
insights/diversity-and-inclusion/its-time-for-a-new-approach-to-racial-equity?
cid=other-eml-dni-mip-mck&hlkid=12d53cedf85a4ddaa1cd4cf35a86114b&hctky=
12628122&hdpid=50c4cfc6-6e11-442c-85ea-5d26c7122102 2nd December.

Fitzsimons, T. (2019) www.nbcnews.com/feature/nbc-out/majority-americans-back-
lgbtq-protections-support-sliding-n987156 26th March.

Francis, T., Pacheco, I. and Gryta, T. (2021) www.wsj.com/articles/big-companies-
disclose-details-on-gender-race-in-workforces-11614594601?st=iia5mwsyp3dtccs
&reflink=article_email_share&cid=other-eml-onp-mip-mck&hlkid=2a866a5bd91
6487da37a5b7f3be6e431&hctky=12628122&hdpid=5071578f-1184-49ed-81a0-
deab5f707399 1st March.

Frank, R. B. (2020) *Tower of skulls*. New York: W. W. Norton & Company.

Gage, E. (2015) https://asia-research.net/women-in-south-east-asia-the-rise-of-soft-
power/ April.

Gao, H. (2021) www.nytimes.com/2021/12/31/opinion/china-masculinity.html. Accessed
2nd January, 2022.

Gardner, H. (2000) *Intelligence reframed: multiple intelligences for the 21st century*. New York: Basic
Books.

Garrow, V. (2016) *Presenteeism: a review of current thinking*. Brighton: Institute of Employment
Studies.

George, B. (2021) www.billgeorge.org/articles/with-georgia-voting-law-the-business-
of-business-becomes-politics/ 12th April.

Gerzema, J. (2013) www.microsoft.com/en-us/research/video/the-athena-doctrine-
how-women-and-the-men-who-think-like-them-will-rule-the-future/ 23rd April.

Gerzema, J. and D'Antonio, M. (2013) *The Athena doctrine: how women (and the men who think like
them) will rule the future*. New York: Jossey-Bass.

Gillet, R. (2016) www.businessinsider.com/google-is-the-best-company-to-work-for-in-
america-2016-4 29th April.

Goddard, E. (2021) www.independent.co.uk/news/uk/home-news/kpmg-uk-bill-
michael-unconscious-bias-b1801399.html 12th February.

Gopinath, S. (2021) www.bloomberg.com/news/articles/2021-03-31/deliveroo-ipo-
raises-2-1-billion-in-biggest-u-k-deal-this-year 31st March.

Gostaniank, A. and Ciechalski, S. (2021) www.nbcnews.com/news/us-news/georgia-
sheriff-s-official-under-fire-remarks-spa-shootings-anti-n1261359 18th March.

Graeber, D. and Wengrow, D. (2021) *The dawn of everything: a new history of humanity*. London:
Allen Lane.

Greatplacetowork (2019) 'Fortune 100 best companies to work for (R) 2019', www.greatplacetowork.com/best-workplaces/100-best/2019.

The Guardian (2017) www.theguardian.com/education/2017/aug/28/university-gender-gap-at-record-high-as-30000-more-women-accepted 28th August.

The Guardian (2021) www.theguardian.com/media/2021/mar/15/daily-telegraph-plans-link-journalists-pay-article-popularity 15th March.

Harari, Y. N. (2015) *Sapiens: a brief history of humankind.* London: Vintage (pp. 118–119).

Haynes, S. (2021) https://time.com/5947862/anti-asian-attacks-rising-worldwide/ 22nd March.

Hearn, J. (1995) *The violences of men.* Thousand Oaks: Sage.

Helgesen, S. (1995) *The female advantage: women's ways of leadership.* New York: Currency.

Helgesen, S. and Johnson, J. (2010) *The female vision: women's real power at work.* New York: Berrett-Koehler Publishers.

Hill Collins, P. and Bilge, S. (2020) *Intersectionality.* Cambridge: Polity (2nd edition).

Historyplex (2021) https://historyplex.com/ethnic-groups.

Hobbes, T. (2017) *Leviathan.* London: Penguin.

Hoft, J. (2019) www.thegatewaypundit.com/2019/08/get-woke-go-broke-gillette-back flips-after-12-billion-toxic-masculinity-disaster-hopes-to-lure-sexist-pigs-back-with-new-ad-campaign/ 22nd August.

Ho-him, C. (2020a) www.scmp.com/news/hong-kong/education/article/3090302/hong-kongs-biggest-international-school-group-esf-vows 24th June.

Ho-him, C. (2020b) https://sg.news.yahoo.com/ceo-hong-kong-english-schools-100229844.html 24th June.

HR Gazette (2019) https://hr-gazette.com/the-role-of-hr-in-workplace-safety/ 26th March.

Hughes, E. (2021) www.theoxfordblue.co.uk/2021/03/27/exclusive-oxford-students-testify-to-toxic-culture-at-dulwich-college/ 27th March.

Human Dignity Trust (2021) www.humandignitytrust.org/lgbt-the-law/map-of-criminalisation/ 15th July.

Hussey, T. (2021) www.express.co.uk/news/world/1450132/ikea-France-news-spying-staff-customers-personal-data-1-million-euro-fine-bosses-jailed-vn 15th June.

Indeed.com (2021) www.indeed.com/cmp/Tesla/reviews 18th July.

Ira, P. (2021) https://readcultured.com/5-seemingly-harmless-remarks-black-women-are-tired-of-hearing-f92713d441ea 21st February.

Jackson, P. A. and Cook, N. M. (eds) (2000) *Genders and sexualities in modern Thailand.* Bangkok: Silkworm Books.

Kantor, J., Weise, K. and Ashford, G. (2021) www.nytimes.com/interactive/2021/06/15/us/amazon-workers.html?campaign_id=158&emc=edit_ot_20210616&instance_id=33134&nl=on-tech-with-shira-ovide&regi_id=88254827&segment_id=60828&te=1&user_id=5017f78bcac86f42523f4538eaada735 15th June.

Kastelec, K. (2020) https://balkaninsight.com/2020/03/12/serbias-violent-homophobic-youngsters-are-victims-as-well/ 12th March.

Kennon, J. (2021) www.joshuakennon.com/the-six-common-biological-sexes-in-humans/. Accessed 17th July, 2019.

Kerfoot, D. and Whitehead, S. (1998) 'Boy's own stuff: masculinity and the management of further education', in *The Sociological Review,* 46(3), August.

Khan, T., Komm, A., Maor, D. and Pollner, F. (2021) www.mckinsey.com/business-functions/organization/our-insights/back-to-human-why-hr-leaders-want-to-focus-on-people-again?cid=other-eml-dre-mip-mck&hlkid=d5fde7b0304744aca64b2746 cd763bd0&hctky=12628122&hdpid=aaf4c4ca-1b10-4999-adfb-c5792a212f54 4th June.

Kim, M. (2021) www.scmp.com/magazines/post-magazine/long-reads/article/3137 503/death-injury-inhuman-conditions-korean-amazon 19th June.

Knights, D. and Willmott, H. (eds) (2007) *Introducing organizational behaviour and management.* London: Thomson.

Kreacic, A., Uribe, L. and Luong, S. (2022) www.brinknews.com/how-companies-can-rebuild-employee-loyalty/. Accessed 9th January, 2022.

Lawyers.com (2016) www.lawyers.com/legal-info/personal-injury/personal-injury-basics/personal-injury-how-much-can-i-expect-to-get.html 18th August.

Lee, P. (2021) *Leaders in succession.* Toronto: Tellwell.

Leon, L. F. (2021) https://inthesetimes.com/article/workers-world-unite-amazon-union-busting-organizing-labor-rights 15th April.

Liu, J. (2019) 'These are the best places to work in 2020, according to employee reviews', CNBC. www.cnbc.com/2019/12/11/glassdoor-the-10-best-companies-to-work-for-in-2020.html 11th December.

Madani, D. (2020) www.nbcnews.com/feature/nbc-out/j-k-rowling-accused-transpho bia-after-mocking-people-who-menstruate-n1227071 8th June.

Mahdawi, A. (2021) *Strong female lead: lessons from women in power.* London: Hodder Studio.

Malesic, J. (2022) www.theguardian.com/lifeandstyle/2022/jan/06/burnout-epidemic-work-lives-meaning?CMP=Share_iOSApp_Other. Accessed 7th January, 2022.

McKinsey Quarterly (2020) 'LGBTQ+ voices: learning from lived experiences', *McKinsey Quarterly* 25th June.

McKinsey Quarterly (2021) 'Intersection: committed capital', *McKinsey Quarterly* 20th May.

Mejia, Z. (2017) www.cnbc.com/2017/12/04/barack-obama-says-women-make-better-leaders-and-data-shows-hes-right.html 4th December.

Molina, S. (2021) www.thefoothillsfocus.com/city_news/asian-americans-frightened-frustrated-by-continued-hate-crimes/article_8c62d18a-91a4-11eb-9ef0-333a36e 53f67.html 2nd April.

Moor, A. (2019) https://bestlifeonline.com/guide-to-gender-pronouns/ 29th May.

Mwanza, K. (2019) https://moguldom.com/245117/indias-skin-lightening-industry-worth-almost-500m-and-60-percent-of-women-say-they-use-products/ 27th December.

Nalin, A. (2019) www.hotcars.com/things-tesla-employees-arent-allowed-to-do-at-work/ 21st April.

Nasdaq (2019) https://www.nasdaq.com/press-release/sp-global-releases-when-women-lead-firms-win-2019-10-16/ 16th October.

New York Post (2021) https://nypost.com/2021/06/01/mexico-report-suggests-child-sex-abuse-ring-at-some-schools/ 1st June.

New York Times Interactive (2021) www.nytimes.com/interactive/2021/06/15/us/amazon-workers.html?campaign_id=158&emc=edit_ot_20210616&instance_id=33134&nl=on-tech-with-shira-ovide&regi_id=88254827&segment_id=60828&te=1&user_id=5017f78bcac86f42523f4538eaada735 15th June.

Niemoller, M. (1946) https://en.wikipedia.org/wiki/First_they_came_. . . 21st August, 2021.

Nin, A. (1961) *Seduction of the Minotaur*. Chicago, Illinois: The Swallow Press.

NSVRC (2021) www.nsvrc.org/statistics 18th July.

Nyomi, N. (2021) 'Strengthening the impact of international education upon the pillars of access, diversity, equity, inclusion and justice', in *Educational Digest International*, XLVII, 25th June.

Osnos, E. (2021) *Wildland: the making of America's fury*. New York: Bloomsbury.

Ovid, S. (2021) 'Amazon is brilliant: why not at H.R?', *The New York Times on Tech* 16th June.

Patel, V. and Andrew, G. (2001) 'Gender, sexual abuse and risk behaviours in adolescents: a cross-sectional survey in schools in Goa', in *National Library of Medicine*, 14(5), pp. 263–267, September–October.

Payne, S. (2021) *Broken heartlands: a journey through labour's lost England*. London: Macmillan.

Petrishen, B. (2021) www.telegram.com/story/news/2021/05/28/wormtown-brewery-ownership-group-steps-back-after-sexual-harassment-claims/5244149001/ 28th May.

Pew Research (2019) www.pewresearch.org/social-trends/2019/01/17/generation-z-looks-a-lot-like-millennials-on-key-social-and-political-issues/.

Power, R. (2021) www.powerfulhistories.com/. Accessed 13th December, 2021.

Puzic, S. (2018) www.ctvnews.ca/canada/nearly-1-300-children-sexually-abused-by-school-staff-over-past-20-years-report-1.3973473 14th June.

Rehman, M. (2017) www.businessoffashion.com/articles/beauty/profiting-from-the-skin-lightening-trade 27th September.

Reich, R. (2021) 'Is America experiencing an unofficial general strike?', www.theguardian.com/commentisfree/2021/oct/13/american-workers-general-strike-robert-reich?CMP=Share_iOSApp_Other.

Richter, F. (2021) www.statista.com/chart/7581/amazons-global-workforce/ 5th July.

Salary.com (2021) www.salary.com/research/salary/benchmark/health-and-safety-manager-salary 1st July.

Sarup, M. (1993) *An introductory guide to post-structuralism and postmodernism*. London: Harvester Wheatsheaf (2nd edition).

Search Associates (2020) www.searchassociates.com/news-events/diversity-equity-and-inclusion/ 26th August.

Shapiro, E. (2020) www.nytimes.com/2020/06/17/nyregion/nyc-private-girls-schools-chapin-brearley-spence-racism.html 19th June.

SHRM (2018) www.shrm.org/ResourcesAndTools/hr-topics/behavioral-competencies/global-and-cultural-effectiveness/Pages/Starbucks-CEO-Calls-for-Unconscious-Bias-Training.aspx 16th April.

Smigiera, M. (2021) www.statista.com/statistics/255591/forecast-on-the-worldwide-middle-class-population-by-region/ 20th March.

Song, G. (2016) www.eastasiaforum.org/2016/07/26/changing-masculinities-in-east-asian-pop-culture/ 26th July.

Stevens, R. (2021) https://medium.com/illumination-curated/5-of-the-most-hurtful-racial-microagressions-i-have-heard-in-my-life-268f9dcb525b 25th March.

Superscholar (2021) https://superscholar.org/the-gender-gap-in-higher-education/.

Swanwick, N. (2021) www.simpsonmillar.co.uk/media/school-abuse-has-rape-culture-become-normalised/ 13th April.

Tam, L. (2018) www.scmp.com/lifestyle/families/article/2147743/how-herbivores-hermits-and-stay-home-men-are-leaving-generation 27th May.

Tan, C. K. (2021) https://asia.nikkei.com/Economy/China-watches-lay-flatters-as-risk-to-economy-5-things-to-know 19th June.

Tatum, B. D. (2017) *Why are all the Black kids sitting together in the cafeteria?* New York: Basic Books.

Taylor, C. (2021) www.forbes.com/sites/charlesrtaylor/2019/01/15/why-gillettes-new-ad-campaign-is-toxic/?sh=16d9c5e75bc9 15th January.

TechRepublic (2018) www.techrepublic.com/article/top-5-things-to-know-about-working-with-millennials/.

TechRepublic (2020) www.techrepublic.com/article/what-do-millennials-want-and-expect-to-get-from-work/.

Thomas, L. (2020) www.news-medical.net/news/20200717/COVID-19-outcomes-better-in-countries-with-female-leaders.aspx 17th July.

Times Higher Education (2016) www.timeshighereducation.com/news/men-in-higher-education-the-numbers-dont-look-good-guys/2011807.article September.

Tingle, R. (2020) www.dailymail.co.uk/news/article-8879249/Parents-headmistress-40-000-year-Kent-girls-boarding-school-racism-row.html 26th October.

Torres, M. (2017a) www.theladders.com/career-advice/men-women-after-work-happy-hour 5th July.

Torres, M. (2017b) www.theladders.com/career-advice/safe-at-work-hostile-environment 15th August.

Tucker, I. (2021) www.theguardian.com/science/2021/mar/21/sherry-turkle-the-pandemic-has-shown-us-that-people-need-relationships 21st March.

UN News (2021) 'Endemic violence against women "cannot be stopped with a vaccine" – WHO chief', *UN News* 9th March.

UNESCO (2009) *Global education digest.* Quebec, Canada: UNESCO.

United States Department of Education (2004) *Educator sexual misconduct: a synthesis of existing literature.* Washington: PPSS.

United States Department of Labor (2021) www.osha.gov/businesscase.

Vaux-Montagny, N. (2021) https://abcnews.go.com/International/wireStory/ikea-france-execs-face-verdicts-alleged-worker-spying-78283278 15th June.

Whitehead, S. M. (2002) *Men and masculinities: key themes and new directions.* Cambridge: Polity.

Whitehead, S. M. (2006) 'Contingent masculinities: disruptions to 'man'agerialist identity', in S. M. Whitehead (ed) *Men and masculinities: critical concepts in sociology (vol. II, materialising masculinity).* London: Routledge.

Whitehead, S. M. (2016) 'Masculinities in management: hidden, invisible, and persistent', in S. Kumra, R. Simpson and R. J. Burke (eds) *The Oxford handbook of gender in organizations.* Oxford: Oxford University Press.

Whitehead, S. M. (2017) *Asian women on the rise.* 5th Asian Academic Society International Conference, Khon Kaen University, Thailand 26th–27th July.

Whitehead, S. M. (2021) *Toxic masculinity: curing the virus: making men smarter, healthier, safer.* London: AG Books.

Whitehead, S. M. and Barrett, F. J. (eds) (2002) *The masculinities reader*. Cambridge: Polity.

Whitehead, S. M. and Dent, M. (eds) (2002) *Managing professional identities: knowledge, performativity and the "new" professional*. London: Routledge.

Whitehead, S. M. and O'Connor, P. (2022) *Creating a totally inclusive university*. London: Routledge.

Whitehead, S. M., Talahite, A. and Moodley, R. (2014) *Gender and identity: key themes and new directions*. Oxford: Oxford University Press.

Wong, J. C. (2017) www.theguardian.com/technology/2017/may/18/tesla-workers-factory-conditions-elon-musk 18th May.

WSJ (2021) www.wsj.com/articles/heres-why-record-numbers-of-americans-are-quitting-their-jobs-11623963188 17th June.

Zenger, J. and Folkman, J. (2019) https://hbr.org/2019/06/research-women-score-higher-than-men-in-most-leadership-skills 26th June.

Ziady, H. (2021) https://edition.cnn.com/2021/06/16/media/gb-news-advertising-boycott/index.html 17th June.

Printed in the United States
by Baker & Taylor Publisher Services

Printed in the United States
by Baker & Taylor Publisher Services